SHOESTRING SHOPPING GUIDE FOR 2001

FACTORY OUTLETS AND WAREHOUSE SALES IN ONTARIO

As featured in the weekly columns
by Cathie Mostowyk
in The Toronto Star and GTA Today

A Personal Message from
Cathie Mostowyk
(Author of The Shoestring Shopping Guide©)

The Shoestring Mission:
The mission of the Shoestring Shopping Guide is not to tell you where to buy things 'cheap', but to search the ever-expanding marketplace for quality name-brand products available through warehouse and factory outlets and clearance and dispersal sales. We personally visit each location to verify that the savings are real. The information in the columns, which originally appeared in the Toronto Star, has been updated, however it is always wise to call the store or event organizer to confirm details, including dates and times. Thousands of shoppers have told us that without Shoestring, they never would have been aware that such outstanding value-shopping opportunities exist.

Our web site may be accessed at www.toronto.com/shoestring. Please visit our weekly columns and home page for a weekly update on 'insider shopping'. We value your feedback and welcome your experiences, ideas and constructive criticism. You may e-mail us at shoestringshopping@home.com or send a fax to: 416-236-4781.

Linda Sherman is now working with us as Director of Sales. To advertise in the Shoestring Shopping Guide, please contact her at 416-232-0254 or e-mail at <lsherman@idirect.ca>.

Sharon Allan Retires:
For over ten years, Sharon Allan and I have been directing thousands of readers to the best quality and value available in Ontario for their shopping dollars. This year Sharon has moved on to other interests. Without her partnership, creativity and tireless energy through the years, the Shoestring Shopping Guide would not have become the success it has. We thank you Sharon and wish you every success in the years ahead.

Copyright © 2000
All rights reserved

No part of this publication may be reproduced, stored in a retrieval system, or transmitted in any form by any means, photocopying, electronic, mechanical, recording or otherwise, without the prior written permission of the copyright holder.

This publication is designed to provide the most accurate and authoritative information possible in regard to the subject matter covered. However, given the nature of this information, the authors/publishers disclaim any inaccurate statements contained in the publication. Advertisers assume full responsibility for all content of advertisements and any claims made against the publisher because of such contents.

Compiled by
CATHIE MOSTOWYK

Design, Layout & Production by Cybercom Inc., Toronto, Ont. Canada
(416) 385-7973
Printed in Canada   ISBN 0-969 8862-9-2

table of contents

FOR THE FAMILY
- FAMILY WEAR 5
- MEN'S WEAR 22
- CHILDREN'S FASHIONS & BABY NEEDS 26
- WOMEN'S FASHIONS 33
- FOOTWEAR 46
- BRIDAL FASHIONS & ACCESSORIES 57
- JEWELLERY & ACCESSORIES 59
- SPORTSWEAR & GEAR 63
- PERSONAL & HEALTHCARE PRODUCTS 71
- FOOD FAIR 78

FOR THE HOME
- HOME FURNISHINGS & APPLIANCES 95
- HOME DECORATING & HOUSEWARES 105
- FABRICS & LINENS 124

LEISURE TIME
- ARTS, CRAFTS & BOOKS 133
- TOYS, PARTY NOVELTIES AND PACKAGING 139
- FLORIST, GIFT BASKETS 147

BUSINESS
- OFFICE SUPPLIES 151
- COMPUTERS & ELECTRONICS 153

MISCELLANEOUS
- RESALE GOODS 158
- A LITTLE BIT OF EVERYTHING 172
- MALLS 178
- DUTY FREE 184

WAREHOUSE SALE CALENDAR 185

INDEX 188

T.B.A. TO BE ANNOUNCED - DATES NOT AVAILABLE AT PRESS TIME

THIS SYMBOL INDICATES WAREHOUSE SALES

GREY BOXES AROUND TEXT LISTINGS ARE VERY SPECIAL.
THEY REPRESENT OUR ADVERTISERS WITH CORRESPONDING PAGE NIMBERS TO THEIR ADVERTISEMENTS.

for your family

- Family Wear
- Men's Wear
- Children's Fashions & Baby Needs
- Women's Fashions
- Footwear
- Bridal Fashions & Accessories
- Jewellery & Accessories
- Sportwear & Gear
- Personal & Healthcare Products
- Food Fair

for your family

Family Wear

ATHLETIC SPORTS SHOW - EXERCISE AND BODYWEAR
Manufacturing on the premises using domestic labour & fabrics, they are able to pass considerable savings on to the consumer. Great stock of athletic/aerobics gear, and outer/swimwear. They also stock fleece in children's, women's & men's sizes. Savings of 40% or more. Visa & MasterCard are accepted.

Location: 2350 Cawthra Rd. (Q.E.W. to Cawthra Rd.), Mississauga.
Hours: M. to F. 9 - 6, Sat. 9 - 6, Sun. 12 - 5
Open 9-8 during Christmas season.
Telephone: (905) 272-0813

BLOW OUTS - DESIGNER'S CLEARANCE OUTLET
A trip to Thornbury wouldn't be complete without a stop to check out this shop of brand name clothing for the whole family. Semi-annual sales, end of summer and just after Christmas. Call for details.

Location: 40 Bruce St. S. (south off Hwy. 26 at the lights - Bruce St. becomes Marsh St. in Clarksburg), Thornbury.
Hours: M. to Sat. 10 - 5:30, Sun. 12 - 4
Telephone: (519) 599-5315

BARDEAUS FAMILY FASHIONS AND SPORTING GOODS CENTRE
We dont know of any other place where you can rent a tux, buy fishing gear, gut and wood frame snowshoes, better brand name clothing, jewellery, books, darts, souvenirs and a hundred and one other items in a store owned by one family for over eighty years and no its not Eaton's. Semi annual clearances happen Feb./Mar. and Aug./Sept. with interesting ambiance and competitive everyday prices year round.

Location: 88 Sykes St., N., Meaford
Hours: Monday to Saturday 9-6, closed Sunday.

Family Wear

CAMP CONNECTION GENERAL STORE
Not your average general store, but rather a one stop shop for the family with everything you can imagine that includes a wide range of fashion items, basic clothing and accessories, and of course camp supplies.....if you are sending one of your children off to school you may want to buy iron-on labels with your child's name which they can do on site for you in about a minute. All at guaranteed low prices.

Location: Lawrence Plaza, 526 Lawrence Ave. W. (northwest corner of Bathurst St. and Lawrence Ave.), Toronto
Hours: M to Fri 10:00 a.m. - 9:00 p.m.,
Sat 10:00 a.m. - 6:00 p.m., Sunday noon - 5:00 p.m.
Telephone: 416-789-1944

CAULFEILD OUTLET STORE
Those of you heading north to cottage country can enjoy a break from driving, by stopping to save at the Barrie location. Men's and ladie's shirts, shorts, pants, sweaters, jackets and more are offered at outlet store prices. As well, check out their great selection of Joe Boxer Men & Girlfriend while you're there. There are also seconds and overruns in sleepwear. The Barrie location clears out excess fabric by the yard & has a limited selection of household items. Savings of up to 80%.

Location: 1400 Whitehorse Rd. (Allen Rd. north past Sheppard Ave. to Steeprock Dr.), Downsview.
Hours: M. to F. 10 - 5, Sat. 10 - 5
Telephone: (416) 636-5900

Location: 60 Bell Farm Rd. (exit Duckworth Ave. off Hwy. 400), Barrie.
Hours: M. to F. 9:30 - 5, Sat. 10 - 4
Telephone: (705) 737-0743

See advertisement on page A2

CHOCKY'S
For over 40 years, Chocky's has stood as Toronto's best bet for name brand clothing at wholesale prices. Calvin Klein, Elita, Jockey, Penmans, Gym Master, Hanes & Non Fiction - are just some of the great buys. Whether it is Christmas, Back to School or Summer Camp, it's a true shopping paradise.

Location: 2584 Yonge Street (Chocky's on Yonge - north of Eglinton), Toronto.
Hours: 7 days a week, call for hours
Telephone: (416) 483-8227

Location: 327 Spadina Ave. (1-1/2 blocks north of Dundas St.), Toronto.
Hours: 7 days a week, call for hours
Telephone: (416) 977-1831

CLARKSBURGERS - recycled clothing and 'things'
Sharon's mom gets credit for this find with its top quality designer labels at wonderful prices. Hannelore, the owner, is so particular that many items look brand new. Some vintage clothing and other things as well as lots for women and men and a small selection of children's wear.
Location: **201 Marsh St., (south of the Beaver River bridge on east side-south of Thornbury), Clarksburg.**
Hours: W. to Sun. 11-5.
Telephone: (519) 599-6811.

CLUB MONACO - OUTLET STORES
As an on-going clearance store this is certainly a favourite with our teens for its well known and well loved clothing label. Find great savings on Club Monaco fashion essentials and casual basics for men and women, boys and girls.
Location: **Colossus Centre 7575 Weston Rd.(at Hwy. 7) Woodbridge.**
Hours: M. to F. 10 - 9, Sat. 9 - 6, Sun. 11 - 6
Telephone: (905)265-0733
Location: **East Woodbridge Centre 200 Windflower Cr.(at Hwy. 7 & Weston Rd.) Woodbridge.**
Hours: M. to F. 10 - 9, Sat. 9 - 6, Sun. 11 - 6
Telephone: (905) 851-0927
Location: **Heartland Centre (just south of Hwy. 401, take Hwy. 10 south to Britannia Rd. and go west), Mississauga.**
Hours: M. to F. 10 - 9, Sat. 9 - 6, Sun. 11 - 6
Telephone: (905) 890-6744
Location: **Woodside Centre 3105 Hwy. 7 East(at Woodbine Ave.) Markham.**
Hours: M. to F. 10 - 9, Sat. 9 - 6, Sun. 11 - 6
Telephone: (905) 940-0097   See advertisement on page 8

D & G TOGS INC.
Four times a year they open up to the public with savings on sportswear for the whole family. Golf shirts, T-shirts, sweats & more, priced well below retail prices. Warehouse Sales: Nov./Dec., March, May/June, September.
Location: **418 Gibraltar Dr. (S. of Derry Rd., E. of Hwy. 10), Mississauga.**
Telephone: (905) 564-8390

Family Wear

CLUB MONACO
OutletStore

They've got style.
They've got amazing value.
And they're really, really big.

Great prices on Club Monaco for Men and Women; Boys and Girls.

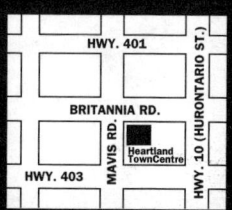

Heartland Town Centre
5930 Rodeo Dr. (at Mavis & Britannia Rd.)
Mississauga
905.890.6744

Mon. – Fri. 10am – 9pm
Sat. 9am – 6pm
Sun. 11am – 6pm

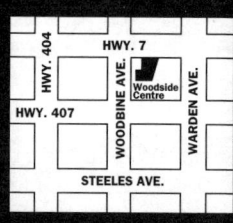

Woodside Centre
3105 Hwy. 7 East (at Woodbine Avenue)
Markham
905.940.0097

Mon. – Fri. 10am – 9pm
Sat. 9am – 6pm
Sun. 11am – 6pm

Colossus Centre
7575 Weston Rd.
Woodbridge
905.265.0733

Mon. – Fri. 10am – 9pm
Sat. 9am – 6pm
Sun. 11am – 6pm

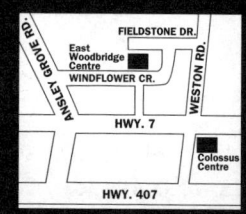

East Woodbridge Centre
200 Windflower Cr.
Woodbridge
905.851.0927

Mon. – Fri. 10am – 9pm
Sat. 9am – 6pm
Sun. 11am – 6pm

CLUB MONACO
OutletStore

clubmonaco.com

DANIER LEATHER - FACTORY OUTLET
These outlet store locations are always stocked with marvelous leather fashions at discounted prices, but in January the prices are lower still. Right now they have particularly good prices on ladie's outerwear, but you'll find lots of stock in both men's and ladies casual wear and jackets. With four locations now to choose from, you're probably closer than you think!

Location: 3175 Highway 7 at Woodbine, (just east of Woodbine Ave.), Markham.
Hours: M. to F. 10 - 9, Sat 9:30 - 6, Sun 11- 5
Telephone: (905) 940-4660

Location: 365 Weston Rd. (between Rogers Rd. & St. Clair Ave. W.), Toronto.
Hours: M. to Sat. 10 - 6, Sun. 12 - 5
Telephone: (416) 762-6631

Location: 90 Kingston Rd., Durham Centre(north of Hwy 401) Ajax.
Hours: M. to F. 10 - 9, Sat. 10 - 6, Sun. 12 - 5
Telephone: (905) 426-5181

Location: Heartland Mall, 5950 Rodeo Dr., Mississauga.
Hours: M. to F. 10 - 9, Sat. 9:30 - 6, Sun. 12 - 5
Telephone: (905) 501-1333

EDDIE BAUER
If you're thinking new clothes for fall, this outlet store is well stocked with fall clothing, as well as some spring and summer clearance merchandise. Their pricing policy is very simple - everything is 50% of the original ticketed price. You really can't beat that for quality Eddie Bauer clothing - Wheelchair accessible

Location: 201 Aviva Park Drive (first lights north of Steeles Ave. off Weston Road), Vaughan.
Hours: M. to F. 10 - 7, Sat. 10 - 6, Sun. 12 - 5
Telephone: (905) 850-7016

ENDS - CLEARANCE OUTLETS
There's a constantly changing assortment of ladie's & men's clothing. Discontinued & end-of-lines, liquidations & samples from all over the world in bins & on tables, giving it all a party atmosphere. It not difficult to find designer wear at ridiculously low prices, buried among casual & outerwear selections.

Location: 140 Avenue Rd., (at Davenport Rd.), Toronto.
Telephone: (416) 968-7272

Location: 1930 Queen St. E., (east of Woodbine Ave.), Toronto.
Telephone: (416) 699-2271

Location: 417 Bloor St. W., (west of Spadina Ave.), Toronto.
Telephone: (416) 960-1961

Family Wear

Family Wear

THE FACTORY STORE
Muskoka's Fashion Factory Outlet offers tee shirts and an extensive line of fleece wear available in child, youth and adult sizes in cotton and poly cotton. Their gallery of over 1000 heat applied designs includes Wildlife, Native and Inuit art, pets, humour, sports and an extensive fashion line. Check out their great plaid shorts and pants available for youth and adults made there in Muskoka.

Location: 41 Manitoba Street, Bracebridge.
Hours: M. to Sat. 9 - 6, Sun. 12 - 4 (Summer hours daily from 9 - 9)
Telephone: (705) 645-1332
Location: 66 King William St., Huntsville.
Hours: Open 7 days a week year round.
Telephone: 1-800-353-3413

GARY GURMUKH SALES LTD.
This always promises to be an excellent sale for those shopping for licensed merchandise from the NHL, MLB, NBA and others as well as Canadian souvenir merchandise. Items included shirts, mugs, hats etc. that have mainly been discontinued, are ends of lines, or samples. Cash or VISA only. December Warehouse Sale. New location.

Location: 179 Bartley Drive, Toronto
Telephone: (416) 298-1610

HARPUR'S CLOTHING COMPANY LTD. - FACTORY OUTLET
Casual quality sportswear such as sweatshirts, pajamas, T-shirts and baseball caps are on sale, with excellent prices on 'almost-perfects' and discontinued lines. The stock comes and goes and you may have to ring the doorbell, but this outlet is well worth a visit.

Location: Warehouse: 2780 Dufferin St. (south of Lawrence Ave.), Toronto.
Hours: M. to F. 9 - 5
Telephone: (416) 781-2181

HI-TEC FACTORY DIRECT
On the way to cottage country why not make a quick detour for better buys on footwear for the great outdoors. They also have some unreal deals on basic shorts and tee shirts originally produced for Parks Canada.

Location: 1988 Commerce Park Dr., Building C (south-east side of Hwy. 400 and Innisfil Beach Rd.- exit #85), Innisfil.
Hours: Seven days a week 10 - 5
Telephone: (705) 431-1160

HILL STREET BLUES

Hill Street Blues carries just about all of the current branded men's and women's jeans, tops and bottoms, all priced at "buy one get the second for 50%". The brands are well known names like Hilfiger, Polo, Replay, Silver, Levis, Calvin Klein, Manager, Diesel, Buffalo, Big Star and more. If you buy only one pair of jeans, they'll even give you a raincheck for the second pair at 50% off for a future purchase. There are a couple of exceptions - Levis, Big Star and Replay are not included in the special pricing, as they are already well priced (Levis are sold at one low price of $49.99).

Location: Richmond Hill Plaza, 10520 Yonge Street (approximately one mile north of Major Mackenzie Drive), Richmond Hill.
Hours: M. to F. 9:30 - 9, Sat. 9:30 - 6, Sun. 11 - 5
Telephone: (905) 737-3936

INTERNATIONAL - WAREHOUSE SUPERSTORES

These clean, well displayed stores offer designer quality and styling in mostly men's and some ladie's fashions, without designer label prices. Inventory is seasonal, with exceptional buys on off-season merchandise. Their locations are numerous so call (416) 785-1771 for a location nearest you.

Location: 111 Orfus Rd., North York.
Hours: M. to F. 9 - 9, Sat. 9 - 6, Sun. 10 - 5
Telephone: (416) 785-1771

JACK AND PETER'S PLACE

This discount outlet has been in business in the same location for over 30 years, and continues to offer well known names in clothing at discount prices. Lots of sweaters, suits, and blouses in stock as well as great deals on sportwear for the younger crowd. Always great deals.

Location: 161 Spadina Avenue, Toronto
Hours: M. to Sat. 8:30 - 5:30
Telephone: 416-971-5207

JUST DEALS

A manufacturer that continually needs to be cleared of samples, overruns. The place is small and but prices are from $1.00 up.

Location: 4490 Chesswood Drive, Unit 6, (between Dufferin and Keele Sts. south of Finch Ave.), Downsview.
Hours: M. to F. 9 - 5:30, Sat. 10:30 - 1:30
Telephone: (416) 638-3862

---

*Time may be a great healer,
but it's also a lousy beautician..*

Family Wear

KAD-OH! - CLOTHING OUTLET
As a retail/wholesale operation they have quite a mix of product with some brand names in casual and dress clothing for the family. Rack after rack is crammed with merchandise at great prices.

Location: **20 Champlain Blvd. Unit 103, (just east of the Allen Expressway and south off of Wilson Ave.), Toronto.**
Hours: M. to F. 10 - 7, Sat. 10 - 6
Telephone: (416) 636-4303

KETTLE CREEK OUTLET STORE
Clothing from previous seasons at 50 - 80% off. Lots of men's and women's denim jeans and cotton twill pants from $19.99, men's shirts and polos from $14.99 - $29.00, and women's sweater sets, skirts dresses and more at substantially reduced prices. For other locations please call their head office at (416) 256-1145.

Location: **100 Wingold Avenue (one block west of Dufferin Street, one block south of Tycos Drive), Toronto.**
Hours: M. to Sat. 10 - 7, Thu. 10 - 9
Telephone: (416) 256-4832

Location: **Dixie Outlet Mall, Mississauga.**
Hours: M. to F. 10 - 9, Sat. 9:30 - 6, Sun. 12 - 6
Telephone: (905) 271-0369

Location: **Warden Power Centre. (Warden and St. Clair) 725 Warden Avenue, Scarborough.**
Hours: M. to F. 10 - 9, Sat. 9:30 - 6, Sun. 12 - 5
Telephone: (416) 751-3880

LABELS
LABELS is the newest retailing initiative from Dylex and offers 25 - 65% off designer and brand name fashions for both family and home. We arrived at the opening of the store in Oakville, and were impressed by the amount of inventory and variety. They mainly carry clothing for the family, with some home decor items. We found the best buys in the lingerie and sock section, and loaded up with basics for our teenagers. A friend found a fabulous pair of suede jeans for $89 and was thrilled, but the menswear yielded no bargains - however, stock changes regularly so it's worth checking back. All locations are wheelchair accessible.

Location: **2501 Hyde Park Blvd. (Hwy 403 and Dundas Street), Oakville.**
Telephone: (905) 829-8255

Location: **30 Great Lakes Drive (Trinity Commons at Hwy 410 and Bovaird Drive),Brampton.**
Telephone: (905) 789-7548
Hours for Oakville and Brampton are: Monday to Friday 9:30 - 9, Saturday 9-6, Sunday 11-5

Location: 1025 Wellington Road (Toys 'R Us Plaza), London.
Telephone: (519) 668-6059
Hours for London are Monday to Saturday 9:30 - 9, Sunday 11-5

LE FIRME
Bursting at the seams with men's and women's designer fashions. The owners go direct to Italy and buy from Versace, Dolce, Gabbana, Ferre and Prada Sport. They also carry beautiful Christian Dior and J.P. Tods Bags.
Location: 95 East Beaver Creek, Unit 3, north off Hwy. 7 just east of Leslie St.), Richmond Hill.
Hours: M. to Sat. 11 - 6
Telephone: (905) 707-8727   See advertisement on page A18

LEN'S MILL STORE
This popular warehouse offers brand-name clothing for the entire family at discount prices & a wide selection of yarns, fabrics & craft supplies.
Location: 215 Queen St. W., Cambridge.
Hours: M. to W. 10 - 5, Thu. & F. 10 - 9, Sat. 10 - 5, Sun. 12:30 - 4:30
Telephone: (519) 658-8182
Location: Brantford.
Telephone: (519) 752-5072
Location: Guelph.
Telephone: (519) 836-2412
Location: Hamilton.
Telephone: (905) 560-5367
Location: Hawkesville.
Hours: closed Sundays
Telephone: (519) 699-6140
Location: London.
Telephone: (519) 686-3502
Location: Port Dover.
Telephone: (519) 583-0800
Location: Waterloo.
Telephone: (519) 743-4672

T.B.A. TO BE ANNOUNCED - DATES NOT AVAILABLE AT PRESS TIME

THIS SYMBOL INDICATES WAREHOUSE SALES

Family Wear

LEVI'S OUTLET
Great saving, great selection that's what keeps savvy shoppers coming back to the Levi's Outlet. Levi's 501s, Red Tab, silver Tabs, tops and bottoms for men, women and children, can all be found at savings of 30, 40, 50% or more off regular retail prices. You'll find a huge selection of first quality, ends of lines and irregulars. New merchandise arrives regularly, so there's always something new.

Location: **Mississauga -Central Parkway Mall**
Telephone: (905) 270-7362
Location: **Waterloo - St. Jacobs Factory Outlet Mall**
Telephone: (519) 886-0675
Location: **Cookstown -**
Cookstown Manufacturer's Outlet Mall
Telephone: (705) 458-0544
Location: **Niagara Falls - Canada One Factory Outlets**
Telephone: (905) 354-4049
All locations open 7 days a week.
See advertisement on page A5

MALABAR
Are little toes heading to a dance class? Point them in this direction & you'll find dance shoes, dance/exercise wear, accessories, theatrical makeup & more.

Location: **14 McCaul St. (just N. of Queen St. W.), Toronto.**
Hours: M. to F. 9:30 - 6, Sat. 10 - 5
Telephone: (416) 598-2581

MARKY'S WAREHOUSE OUTLET - OFF-PRICE STORE
It's fun, casual and there are lots of basics in a wide range of first-quality clothing for kids and adults at this outlet store. In the underwear department, you'll find Calvin Klein, Jockey, Mexx for ladie's, and several other well-known brands.

Location: **7171 Yonge St. (at Doncaster Ave., just north of Steeles Ave.), Thornhill.**
Hours: M. to F. 10 - 9, Sat. 10 - 6, Sun. 11 - 5
Telephone: (905) 731-4433

There is always death and taxes; however,
death doesn't get worse
every year..

MILLWORKS FACTORY STORE
Manufacturing in Canada since before Confederation, Carhartt uses denim of industrial strength to make work clothes, and the toughest outdoor wear you can buy that's as rugged as the people who wear them.

Location: 20 Bermondsey Rd., (just north of O'Connor Dr.), Toronto.
Hours: M. to F. 10 - 9, Sat. 10 - 6
Telephone: (416) 285-6992

McGREGOR SOCKS FACTORY OUTLETS
These outlets offer brand name socks and hosiery at up to 50% off - and have a pricing structure in place that lets you save more the more you buy. Brands include Calvin Klein, Levi's, GUESS, Dockers and popular McGregor brands like Weekender, Premium and Happyfoot. Great deals on irregular and discontinued items. Bring some friends and take advantage of bulk discounts. "Their prices will knock your socks off!"

Locations: 30 Spadina Avenue, Toronto
Hours: Monday to Saturday 10-5
Telephone: (416) 593-5353, ext. 344

Locations: 70 The East Mall at the Queensway
Hours: Tuesday to Saturday 10-5
Telephone: (416) 252-3716, ext. 450

Locations: 1360 Birchmount Road (just north of Lawrence Ave.), Scarborough
Hours: Tuesday to Friday 10-6, Saturday 10-5
Telephone: (416)-751-5511, ext. 5511

See advertisement on page A25

MUSKOKA LAKES WAREHOUSE SALE
Now that the weather has turned chilly, it's time for a new fleece or maybe a sweater. This sale offers Non-Fiction samples, sweats, sweaters and fleece as well as shirts, scarves and bags New this year will be a selection of linens that include sheets, duvet covers, towels, blankets and more. No GST or PST, and prices are up to 50% off suggested retail. Please note that all sales are final, and no cheques.

Location: 2735 Matheson Blvd. East, Unit 6 (north of Eglinton Ave. East, west of Renforth Road. The entrance is on Explorer Drive), Mississauga.
Hours: Wed to Fri 12-8, Sat 10-5
Telephone: (905) 629-2829

Family Wear

Family Wear

NEW YORK CLOTHING COMPANY
Just opened and featuring DKNY for both women and men, the stock is primarily jeans and active wear - all perfect for casual dressing. Quality is excellent, lots of selection and discounts start at 30% of Canadian retail. Wheelchair accessible.

Location: **Cookstown Manufacturer's Outlet Mall, (south east corner of Hwy. 400 and Hwy. 89), Cookstown,**
Telephone: (705) 458-4190
Hours: Regular mall hours are M. to F. 10-9 Sat., Sun. and holidays 9-6.

NORAMA DESIGN INC.
A great opportunity to pick up savings on jackets, sweats, hats and more from this company that specializes in corporate silk screen and embroidery design. Sweats start at $5, track suits from $25 and mitts for a looney! Warehouse sales several times a year.

Location: **475 Fenmar Drive, (north of Finch Ave., between Islington Ave. and Weston Road), North York.**
Telephone: (416) 744-6994

NORTHERN REFLECTIONS AND GETAWAY
Just one more reason to make the trip to Dixie Outlet Mall. This outlet for the chain of retail stores clears seconds and samples through this location. We purchased a warm, plaid flannel lined child's coat for just $20. There were stacks of plaid, cotton sweaters requiring a fast session with a sewing needle for just $10, and there were many other opportunities for bargain hunters searching for savings on family wear.

Location: **Dixie Outlet Mall (Dixie Rd and Q.E.W.), Mississauga.**
Hours: M. to F. 10 - 9, Sat. 9:30 - 6, Sun. 12 - 6
Telephone: (905) 278-9487

NOVITA FASHIONS
Original designer pieces for men & women are constantly cleared from this spacious outlet. Samples, clearances & off-season items from designers such as Versace, Moschino & Trussardi. Most are sample sizes; 6 - 12 for ladies, 36 - 42 for men.

Location: **1668 Avenue Rd., Toronto.**
Hours: M. to Sat. 10 - 6
Telephone: (416) 781-0673

> Conscience is what hurts when everything else feels so good.

ON THE FRINGE
Hot from The Motorcycle Show, and certainly known among the Harley Davidson crowd, is this tiny location with its wide assortment of leather garments. Their children's wear with little leather bomber jackets and vests is adorable, but they carry much more for men and women both in accessories as well as jackets, vests and even three piece suits. Because they actually do the manufacturing, prices are very reasonable for the quality, service is personal - most items are custom either by design or in fit and yes, they certainly do alterations.

Location: 3333 Lakeshore Blvd. W. (between Browns Line and Kipling on south side), Etobicoke.
Hours: M. & T. 10 - 6, W. to F. 10 - 7, Sat. 10 - 3 Call ahead first.
Telephone: (416) 255-1976

THE PANTYHOSE SHOP - BELLISSIMO
It's nice to know where to warm those toes and to get good socks and hose at lower than average prices all year long. There is a nice selection of top name brands in men's socks as well as pantyhose, tights, socks and undergarments for women. They carry Warners, Papillon, Vogue, Elita and other high end labels.

Location: 136 Winges Rd., Unit 16 (south side of Hwy. 7 between Weston Rd. & Whitmore Dr. look for pantyhose on yellow banner), Woodbridge.
Hours: M. to Sat. 9 - 6
Telephone: (905) 851-9929

PARNETT TEXTILES
As manufacturers and importers, they have an assortment of clothing - ladies tops, sweaters, tee shirts, men's golf shirts, biking shorts etc. - that continually need to be cleared of samples, overruns and the odd second. The place is tiny and prices average between $3 and $15.

Location: 4490 Chesswood Drive, Unit 6, (between Dufferin and Keele Sts. south of Finch Ave.), Downsview.
Hours: M. to F. 9 - 5
Telephone: (416) 638-3862

ROOTS CANADA LTD. - CLEARANCE CENTRES
Instead of yearly warehouse sales, Roots has opened a year-round clearance centre. Ends of lines, off-season and factory seconds are being sold at rock-bottom prices. An annual sale in February features 35 - 70% off all merchandise in the outlet store. Always popular sweats, shoes, jackets and bags are available in adult and kid sizes. No cheques.

Location: 101 Northview Blvd., (Hwy 7 & 400) Woodbridge.
Hours: M. to F. 10 - 9, Sat. 10 - 6, Sun. 11 - 5
Telephone: (905) 264-0478

Family Wear

Location: 5950 Rodeo Dr. Heartland Centre, Mississauga
Hours: M. to F. 9:30 - 9, Sat. 9:30 - 6, Sun. 11 - 5
Telephone: (905) 948-1700
Location: 1168 Caledonia Rd., North York.
Hours: M. to F. 10 - 9, Sat. 9:30 - 6, Sun. 12 - 5
Telephone: (905) 501-1200
Location: Woodside Centre, 3175 Highway 7, Markham.
Hours: M. to F. 9:30 - 9, Sat. 9:30 - 6, Sun. 11 - 5
Telephone: (905) 948-1700

SAMPLE SHOP
This small shop offers a terrific variety of fur lined coats in various styles with fabrics that range from wool and poplin to micro-fibre.. Prices range from $195 - $395 and include GST. There are mink and wool/cashmere blend coats, as well.
Location: 1093 Queen St. W. (at Dovercourt), Toronto.
Hours: M. to Sat. 10 - 4, Sun. 11 - 4
Telephone: (416) 534-3533

SHARC SALES - WAREHOUSE CLEARANCE 💰
Clothing for the whole family. Samples, overruns, discontinued styles and bankruptcy clearances. Kids jeans range from $10 to $25; tops are $7 to $20. Warehouse sale May to June.
Location: 2 Essex Ave., Unit 4 (Bayview Ave. and Hwy. 7 area), Thornhill.
Hours: Call for hours.
Telephone: (905) 882-9840

SPARE PARTS CLOTHING OUTLET
Location: 59 Samor Road, Toronto
Hours: Thu. - F. 11 - 7, Sat 11 - 6, Sun 11 - 5
Telephone: (416) 781-2171

ST. MARCO IMPORTING
Normally this company imports products from Italy for resale to retailers, but it is now selling direct to the public out of its warehouse. Inventory is very traditionally Italian and includes infants baptismal wear, socks and clothing. As well, there is a large selection of undergarments in cotton and wool for the entire family. High quality, if not glamorous.
Location: 331 Trowers Rd., units 1 and 2 (south of Highway 7 and west of Weston Rd. Park in the back.), Woodbridge.
Hours: M. to F. 9 - 5, Sat. 10 - 5
Telephone: (905) 850-0149

THE STOCKROOM

It's just one of those lucky finds for those who love tees and sweats. Brand name, first quality Hanes and Fruit of the Loom are all at great prices, and the clearances on logo'd items are excellent. Our teens especially like the 15 oz. hooded sweatshirt for $14.10 and tee shirts starting at $2.50. The sister company that shares the building, turns the product into promotional wear by doing screenprinting and embroidery. Cash only.

Location: 115 Tycos Drive, Toronto.
Hours: M. to Thu. 8:30 - 4, F. 8:30 - 5, closed weekends.
Telephone: (416) 785-5230

SUSSMAN'S - MEN'S AND LADIE'S WEAR

We were amazed to find this 'little store that grew' in the tiny town of Arthur. Now one of the largest independent retailers, their three locations on the main street total 40,000 square feet of quality, better brand men's and ladie's clothing. After ninety years in business they offer not only great selection, a full range of sizing and pricing, on the spot alterations and excellent service but always less than full retail pricing. Last season's ladies fashions are 50% and then another twenty percent off regular retail, newly arrived spring fashions are at least 10% off and at the outlet location past seasons stock is 70% off.

Location: Junction Hwy. 6 and Hwy. 9,(main store is on the southeast corner, casual wear on the northwest corner and outlet store 1 block south on west side), Arthur.
Hours: M. to Thu. 9 - 6, F. 9 - 9, Sat. 9 - 6, Sun. 11 - 5; Outlet opens one hour later and closes one hour earlier.
Telephone: (519) 848-2660

TIGER BRAND KNITTING - FACTORY OUTLET

7000 sq. ft. of true factory outlet shopping with 100% cotton casual wear for the entire family. Tiger Brand makes each garment from the knitting stage of the fabric to sewing the finished product. The store is well decorated & the staff is helpful. Lots to choose from, most goods are first quality, but look for treasures in the seconds bin.

Location: 96 Grand Ave. S (across from Southworks Mall) Cambridge.
Hours: M. to W. 9:30 - 6, Thu. & F. 9:30 - 8, Sat. 9 - 6, Sun. 11 - 5
Telephone: (519) 624-7844

Family Wear

T.B.A. TO BE ANNOUNCED - DATES NOT AVAILABLE AT PRESS TIME

THIS SYMBOL INDICATES WAREHOUSE SALES

Family Wear

TOM'S PLACE
Located in the heart of Kensington Market, Tom's Place is the premier location for the best selection of designer's quality men's and women's wear at below retail prices. With a selection of over 8,000 top brand name suits, this location has become the destination of the shopper with discriminating taste. Both men and women will be pleased with now expanded selection of business and casual clothing for every season or event. Featured in "The New York Times" and "America Airlines' magazine, Tom's Place is a one stop shopping experience for visitors to Toronto where on request, your purchases can be finely finished the same day. So, remember, for the best clothing at the best prices, the best place to shop is Tom's Place. website— www.toms-place.com

Location: 190 Baldwin St.(between College St. & Dundas St., west off Spadina Ave. in the heart of Kensington Market) Toronto
Hours: M. to W. 10-6, Thurs. & Fri. 10-7, Sat. 9-6, Sun. 12-5
Telephone: (416) 596-0257

See advertisement on page A26

UB WORLD FASHION OUTLET
And now an outlet full of fashions for teens and young adults of both sexes with racks of clothing from around the world, loaded with colour and following the latest trends.

Location: 55 Orfus Rd., (west off Dufferin St., north of Lawrence Ave.), North York.
Hours: Sat. to W. 10 - 6, Thu. & F. 10 - 8 Hours may change later.
Telephone: (416) 256-4777

UNIVERSITY CLASS - FACTORY OUTLET
Even if you don't have a student in your home, who can resist a sweatshirt with custom embroidering emblazoned with "HARVARD" or "UNIVERSITY OF TORONTO", or maybe even your company name? This small, family owned business carries a wide range of high quality sweatshirts, jackets, hats, t-shirts and more.....just about anything that can be embroidered. Prices are generally 30% less than you'd expect to pay on campus, or at the university bookstore. Ask about their new line of corporate wear as well.

Location: 234 Hood Rd. (north of Steeles Ave., east of Warden Ave.), Markham.
Hours: M. to W. & Sat. 10 - 6, Thu. & F. 10 - 8, Sun. 12 - 5
Telephone: (905) 479-9929

T.B.A. TO BE ANNOUNCED - DATES NOT AVAILABLE AT PRESS TIME

💰 THIS SYMBOL INDICATES WAREHOUSE SALES

URBAN BEHAVIOUR
As one of the smaller fashion chains for trendy young men and women, Urban Behaviour has several retail stores and they now have an outlet at Heartland as well as 65 Orfus Road. Like every one else in the clothing biz, merchandise is beginning to change over to the next season - when we were at the Heartland location a number of stores were light on selection - expect more merchandise to be arriving daily.
Location: Heartland Centre, (facing Britannia Rd., Between Mavis Rd. And Rodeo Dr.), Mississauga,
Telephone: (905) 568-4121.
Hours: M. to F. 11-9, Sat. 10-6, Sun. 11-6.

THE WAREHOUSE- CLOTHING CLEARANCE CENTRE
Look for great deals on brand name clothing that is mainly for men and women with some for children. We found excellent buys on Bugle Boy wear, great deals on winter stock as well as lots of samples, socks and other better quality clothing items Brand names such as North 44 & Britches are sold as well as numerous other popular labels we are not allowed to mention! Call Ben to find out more!
Location: 574 Gordon Baker Rd. (south of Steeles Ave. E, west off of Victoria Park Ave.), Scarborough.
Hours: M. to Sat. 11 - 6, Sun. 12 - 3:30
Telephone: (416) 497-2659

WEEKEND WARRIOR - MANUFACTURER'S CLEARANCE OUTLET
Fashions for the whole family with mainly casual designs and right now primarily spring/summer styles, this manufacturer clears out their own labels as well as others at discounted pricing. Items include lots for ladies - skirts, dresses, as well as more casual wear; buys on golf shirts, sweat suits and more for men and summer short outfits, fleece wear and other pieces for children. Cash and Interac only.
Location: 210 Milner Ave., Units 5 & 6 (just off Markham Rd., north of the 401 Hwy.), Scarborough.
Hours: Thu. & F. 12 - 8, Sat. 10 - 6, Sun. 10 - 5
Telephone: (416) 297-1973

WINNERS - OFF-PRICE FAMILY WEAR
If you haven't visited a Winners store, you don't know how easy it is to take advantage of discounts of 20 to 60% on clothing for the whole family. With a dozen stores in the Golden Triangle, they are very conveniently located. Call 1-800-646-WINN to find a store nearest you.
Location: Burlington, Calgary, Cambridge, Edmonton, Hamilton, London, Markham, Richmond Hill, Ottawa, Sarnia, Windsor, & Winnipeg.
Telephone: 1-800-646-9466

Family Wear

for your family

Men's Wear

ARROW SHIRTS - FACTORY CLEARANCE STORES
You'll find a great selection of men's and some women's clothing and accessories at clearance prices.
Location: 112 Benton St., Kitchener.
Hours: M. to F. 8:30 - 5, Sat. 9 - 6, Sun. 12 - 4
Telephone: (519) 743-8211
Location: 41 Brockley Dr., Hamilton.
Hours: M. to F. 10 - 6, Sat. 9:30 - 6, Sun. 12 - 4
Telephone: (905) 578-0055
Location: Dixie Outlet Mall, 1250 South Service Rd., Mississauga.
Hours: M. to F. 10 - 9, Sat. 9:30 - 6, Sun. 12 - 4
Telephone: (905) 891-3982

FORSYTHE FACTORY STORES
Look for a full range of men's and some ladies clothing being cleared at discount prices.
Location: Cookstown Manufacturer's Outlet Mall, Unit 9B, Cookstown.
Hours: M. to F. 10 - 9, Sat. & Sun. 9 - 6, holidays 9 - 6
Telephone: (705) 458-0436

FREEMAN FORMALWEAR - WAREHOUSE SALE
Tuxedos previously used in their rental stock are being sold for $99. Formal shirts are $9.99. Also a large selection of used accessories at low prices. Sale on while inventory lasts. Warehouse sale in October, call for details
Location: 111 Bermondsey Rd., north entrance, (east of the Don Valley Parkway, south of Eglinton Ave.) Toronto.
Hours: M. to F. 9 - 9, Sat. 9 - 5, Sun. 12 - 5
Telephone: (416) 288-1919

GREG NORMAN OUTLET
Most guys can only dream of golfing like the 'Shark' but now they can dress the part and save at the same time. Usually 20 percent and more off retail and a whole collection to select from. Wheelchair accessible.

Location: **Cookstown Manufacturer's Outlet Mall, (south east corner of Hwy. 400 and Hwy. 89), Cookstown**
Hours: Mall hours are Monday to Friday 10-9, Saturday, Sunday and holidays 9-6
Telephone: (705) 458-7097

HARRY ROSEN MENSWEAR OUTLET STORE
Nothing beats the selection and value at the only location in Canada. Offering exclusive to Harry Rosen imported designer and classic menswear collections. Suits, sportscoats, shirts, ties, coats, and sportswear as well as the finest shoe collection anywhere. From the Harry Stores across Canada at substantial savings of 30% to 70%. Many items have been best sellers and when you find them at the Outlet Store you will know why. Shop early, there is always a line up on the week-ends.

Location: **Heartland Centre (1 mile west on Brittania Rd. from Hurontario St. & 401)**
Hours: M. to F. 10-9, Sat. 9:30-6, Sun. 11-5
Telephone: (905) 890-3100

HATHAWAY FACTORY STORE
We found a large selection of men's dress and sport shirts, as well as miscellaneous items such as ties, boxer shorts and knit shirts. Selection includes both first-quality and seconds. Cotton-blend shirts are approximately $22.95, 100% cotton shirts are $24.95 and seconds go for as little as $13.95.

Location: **707 St. Lawrence St. (east on Hwy. 401 to the Edward St./Prescott exit, south on Edward, right on Wood St., follow Wood St. to St. Lawrence St. and turn right), Prescott.**
Hours: M. to F. 9:30 - 4:30, Sat. 9 - 4
Telephone: (613) 925-1530

JACK FRASER - MENSWEAR OUTLET STORE
Newly opened this year, this outlet carries a large inventory of current season's first quality suits, ties, shirts and casual wear at great prices. Tailoring is done on site for a small fee. All suits are 50% off regular retail.

Location: **44 Apex Road (west off Dufferin Street, north of Lawrence Ave.), Toronto.**
Hours: M. to Sat. 9:30 - 6, Sun. 12 - 5
Telephone: (416) 780-2150

Men's Wear

Men's Wear

MILLENIUM 💰
The space may get crowded with buyers but with savings of 50 to 70% off retail prices on samples, and ends of lines of quality men's and ladie's wear, it should be worth checking out. No credit cards. April and November Warehouse Sales.
Location: **624 King St. W., Suite 100, Toronto.**
Hours: M. to F. 9 - 6
Telephone: (416) 703-3988

MOORES MENSWEAR
Clearance centres: We are often asked why there aren't more menswear clearance centres, so just for you, Moores has two locations. Savings of up to 70% on a variety of discontinued and end-of-line menswear including suits, sport jackets, ties, shirts etc. make this a spot to check out for the man in your life.
Location: **129 Carlingview Dr. (take the Carlingview exit off Highway 401; the store is just south of the Novotel Hotel), Etobicoke.**
Hours: M. & T. 9:30 - 6, W. to F. 9:30 - 9, Sat. 9:30 - 5, Sun. 10:30 - 5
Telephone: (416) 675-1900
Location: **3711 Lawrence Ave. E. (east of Markham Rd.), Scarborough.**
Hours: M. to Tues. 9:30 – 6, W. to F. 9:30 - 9, Sat. 9 - 6, Sun. 11 - 5
Telephone: (416) 675-1900

RENNIE - THE SHIRT STORE - FACTORY OUTLETS
This Canadian manufacturer of quality shirts for men has three locations, open daily with better deals on shirts (including tall sizes), as well as sweaters, hosiery, boxer shorts and ties. They are Canada's largest private label shirt manufacturer.
Location: **430 Elizabeth St., Guelph.**
Hours: M. to Sat. 9 - 5, Sun. 12 - 5
Telephone: (519) 824-9440

RIDOLFI SHIRTMAKER INC. - FACTORY SHOWROOM
Chairman of the Board material, these beautifully made men's shirts are available at the small showroom at 50 - 70% off retail price. They will also custom make shirts.
Location: **2901 Steeles Ave. W. #19 (southeast corner at Keele St.), Downsview.**
Hours: M. to F. 9 - 5, Sat. 10 - 3
Telephone: (416) 667-0028

ROYAL SHIRT COMPANY LTD
Not only do they manufacture high quality casual and dress shirts for better quality menswear stores across Canada, but they will also custom make a shirt. Visit their second floor outlet location, and you will find thousands of shirts in hundreds of imported fabrics and styles at wholesale or less, well marked and displayed. Visa or cash only. Warehouse sales usually 2 weeks before Father's Day & Christmas.

Location: **40 Addesso Drive (just east of Hwy. 400 and north of Steeles Ave.), Concord.**
Hours: Call for specific dates and times.
Telephone: (905) 738-4676

THE SUIT EXCHANGE
This outlet carries a slightly different flavour of menswear, with a much more European look. Imports include Valentino, Fendi, Kenneth Cole, Alfred Sung, Pronto Uomo and more. This outlet has less traditional, more trendy looks with lots of inventory at up to 50% off retail pricing.

Location: **55 Orfus Road (west off Dufferin Street, north of Lawrence Ave.), Toronto.**
Hours: M. to F. 11 - 9, Sat. 10 - 6, Sun. 11 - 6
Telephone: (416) 782-4900

TIMBERLAND - OUTLET STORE
Brand new, not only at this location but in the outlet sector, this store is nicely merchandised, the help is friendly and its chock full of bargains - basically for men with both clothing and their famous footwear - some selection in footwear for women and children too. The product is excellent quality with most of the savings in the neighbourhood of 30% off regular retail and range up to 50%.

Location: **Heartland Centre, (just east off Mavis Rd. between Britannia Rd. W and Matheson Blvd.), Mississauga.**
Hours: M. to F. 9:30 - 9, Sat. 9:30 - 6, Sun. 11-5.
Telephone: (905) 507-0004

Men's Wear

> I always wanted to be a procrastinator, never got around to it.

for your family

Children's Fashions & Baby Needs

BABY PLUS AND BUNKS 'N' BEDS
Babies in Barrie have it made with these two stores at one location. You'll find good pricing and selection on baby and juvenile furniture, plus a varied inventory of baby items from garments to safety supplies to strollers and more.

Location: 14 Cedar Pointe Dr., building 4A (Hwy. 90 exit, first street west of Hwy. 400), Barrie.
Hours: M. T. & Sat. 9 - 6, W. to F. 9 - 9, Sun. 11 - 5
Telephone: (705) 734-9356

BEAUTY INDUSTRIES - MILL OUTLET
If you have a young child or require a gift for one, this is the spot that manufactures and sells quality clothing in sizes newborn to 14. There is also a department with seconds at great savings. Cash and Visa accepted. Call to be included on mailing list.

Location: 270 Sherman Ave. N. (north off Barton St. E., just past the train tracks), Hamilton.
Hours: M. to Sat. 10 - 5
Telephone: (905) 549-1357

CRAWFORD AND CO. - BOYS' CLOTHING
This store specializes in boy's designer fashions at 30 to 50% off. Great selection and great service. Husky sizes carried.

Location: Lawrence Plaza (Lawrence Ave. and Bathurst St.), Toronto.
Hours: M., F. & Sat. 10 - 6, T. to Thu. 10 - 9, Sun. 12 - 5
Telephone: (416) 782-8137

---

*Never be afraid to try something new.
Remember, amateurs built the
ark..Professionals built the Titanic..*

DAN HOWARD'S MATERNITY - FACTORY OUTLETS
This store is a marvelous spot for maternity clothes. Fall and winter merchandise is being cleared now and is exceptionally well-priced.

Location: 257 Dundas St. E., (between Cawthra Rd. & Hwy. 10), Mississauga.
Hours: M. & Thu. 10 - 9, T., W., F. & Sat. 10 - 6, Sun. 12 - 5
Telephone: (905) 848-6776

Location: 300 Steeles Ave. W. (in Toys 'R' Us Plaza), Thornhill.
Hours: M. & Thu. 10 - 9, T., W., F. & Sat. 10 - 6, Sun. 12 - 5
Telephone: (905) 731-6177

DEAR-BORN BABY EXPRESS
This shop continues to offer great value for all your baby needs at very competitive prices. Right now, it has a large selection of winter clearance items at savings of up to 70%, as well as custom crib linen at 50% off. It is an authorized dealer for Perego, Moriguean, Lepine, Evenflo, Graco and many more. Ask about the photography service while you're there.

Location: 72 Doncaster Ave. (one light north of Steeles Ave.), Thornhill.
Hours: M. to W. & Sat. 10 - 6, Thu. & F. 10 - 9, Sun. 12 - 5
Telephone: (905) 881-3334

DIAPER FACTORY OUTLET
Discounted prices on brand-name first quality disposable diapers in bulk packaging. Good prices on bulk wipes and refills also. Stock up for your baby needs.

Location: 1150 Sheppard Ave. W. (two blocks west of Allen Expressway), North York.
Hours: M. to W. 10 - 6, Thu. & F. 10 - 8, Sat. 10 - 6, Sun. 12 - 5
Telephone: (416) 222-2288

Children's Fashions & Baby Needs

Life is an endless struggle full of frustrations and challenges, but eventually you find a hair stylist you like..

Children's Fashions & Baby Needs

DIAPERS ETC. - FACTORY OUTLET
As you might suspect, this shop offers savings in bulk on diapers by the case. Prices start at $ 21.99 for 120 medium-sized diapers. The price goes up as the size increases. You can also find mega bottles of baby shampoo, with extra savings on baby oil, lotion, powder and Vaseline. A current in-store special is tubs of 160 thick baby wipes for $2.99 - and if you're purchasing diapers at the same time, the price gets even better.

Location: **106 Saunders Road, Barrie.**
Hours: M. to F. 10 - 7, Sat. 10 - 6, Sun. 10 - 5
Telephone: (705) 721-9555

Location: **44 Zorra St. (south off the Queensway, east of Kipling Ave.), Etobicoke.**
Hours: M. to F. 10 - 8, Sat. 10 - 6, Sun. 10 - 5
Telephone: (416) 503-0313

Location: **7 Stafford Drive, Brampton.**
Hours: M. to F. 10 - 8, Sat. 10 - 6, Sun. 10 - 5
Telephone: (905) 450-1955

Location: **90 Northline Road, Scarborough.**
Hours: M. to F. 10 - 8, Sat. 10 - 6, Sun. 10 - 5
Telephone: (416) 752-0222

DISCOUNT CHILDREN'S
Walk up one flight and save a whole lot on children's sizes newborn to age 16 (lots for the first and less for the latter). A good selection of great brand names like Milton Funwear, Kooshies, Beaver Canoe, Barbie, Looney Tunes and Gusti are offered year round at always less than retail.

Location: **130 Orfus Rd. (north east corner at Caledonia Rd.)**
Hours: M to W 9-6; Thurs and Fri 9-7,
Sat 10-6, and Sun 11-5.
Telephone: (416) 251-9096

FAIRLAND
10,000+sq. ft. of children's clothing, from infant to hard to fit husky sizes for boys and girls. Discounts of up to 30% off manufacturer's retail prices. Familiar names include Buffalo jeans, OshKosh, Pickles, Krickets, Manhattan & more.

Location: **241 Augusta Ave. (Kensington Market area), Toronto.**
Hours: M. to Sat. 9 - 7, Sun. 12 - 5
Telephone: (416) 593-9750

T.B.A. TO BE ANNOUNCED - DATES NOT AVAILABLE AT PRESS TIME

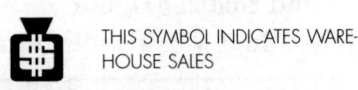

THIS SYMBOL INDICATES WAREHOUSE SALES

IANA CHILDREN"S CLOTHING OUTLET
Just up the street from tMagnotta Winery is this small outlet store packed with lovely high-end, high quality children's wear. Sizes from newborn to 14 (more of the smaller sizes) with a European style and flavour. Summer and spring merchandise is 30-40% off, and previous season's merchandise is 50% off. All sales final.

Location: 571 Chrislea Road, Unit 4 upstairs (Langstaff and Weston Road area), Woodbridge
Hours: Tuesday to Saturday 10-5
Telephone: (905) 856-2530

INTERNATIONAL KIDS - IMPORTERS OUTLETS
These fashion forward outlets are chock full of the latest colours, styles and fabrics for kids.
Location: 107 Orfus Rd, North York.
Hours: Call for individual stores hours.
Telephone: (416) 256-7779
Location: 1119 Kennedy Rd., Scarborough.
Telephone: (416) 752-8369
Location: 1235 Finch Ave. W., Downsview.
Telephone: (416) 630-0026
Location: 255 Queen St. E., Brampton.
Telephone: (905) 455-5928
Location: 518 Lawrence Ave. W., Toronto.
Telephone: (416) 785-3319
Location: Dixie Outlet Mall, Mississauga.
Telephone: (905) 274-2374
Location: Erin Mills Town Centre, Mississauga.
Location: Hillcrest Mall, Richmond Hill.
Telephone: (905) 508-4525
Location: Oshawa Shopping Centre, Oshawa.
Telephone: (905) 579-0707

JACK RABBITS CLOTHING COMPANY
Evolving out of their home-party based business, this Canadian manufacturer of quality children's clothing is now sold through five on-going outlets. Sizes range from 12 months to pre-teen with savings of 20 - 60% off regular pricing now available year round.
Location: 132 St. George St., Brantford.
Hours: M. to F. 10 - 5:30, Sat. 10 - 5
Telephone: (519) 751-4791
Location: Cookstown Manufacturers Outlet Mall, RR#1, 3311 Hwy. 89, Cookstown.
Hours: Regular Mall Hours.
Telephone: (705) 458-2512

Location: 1105 Wellington Road, London
Hours: Regular Mall Hours.
Telephone: (519) 622-6111
Location: Southworks Outlet Mall, 64 Grand Avenue S., Cambridge.
Hours: Regular Mall Hours
Telephone: (519) 686-9462
Location: St. Jacobs Factory Outlet Mall, 25 Benjamin Rd., Unit 4, Waterloo.
Hours: Regular Mall Hours.
Telephone: (519) 885-2894

KID'S COSY COTTONS - FACTORY OUTLET

As the name indicates, this Canadian company sells bright, comfy, cotton children's clothes. Not only do they have a catalogue and regular retail stores but they clear out last season stock and over-runs through this location and their special summer sale runs until the end of July.

Location: 2620 Lancaster Rd. (opposite the Tommy and Lefebvre Sale), Ottawa.
Hours: M. to F. 10 - 4
Telephone: (613) 523-2679

PETITE PALETTE

Another great sale of children's and women's wear from this line that's usually available via home parties. Delightful designs at savings of 60% off the regular retail price. T.B.A. Warehouse Sale.

Location: 548 King St. W. (top floor above Ace Bakery), Toronto.
Telephone: 1-800-668-4548 or (416) 504-8440

PLUMLOCO CLOTHING COMPANY

This company has a line-up of great deals on previously owned clothing in excellent condition- sort of like your father's closet only huge! Well organized, nicely presented and friendly to teens on a budget as well. The other half of the store carries their own lines of new clothing under the label of Calienta so those who may not shop recycled will enjoy scouting out the new!

Location: 114 Mississauga St. E., Orillia.
Hours: M. to Thu. 10 - 6, F. 10 - 9, Sat 10 - 6, Sun 10 - 5.
Telephone: (705) 325-1419
Location: 373 George St. N., Peterborough.
Hours: M. to Thu. 9:30 - 6, F. 9:30 - 9, Sat 9:30 - 6, Sun 10 - 5.
Telephone: (705) 742-4840.
Location: 65 Hurontario St., Collingwood.
Hours: M. to Thu. 10 - 6, F. 10 - 9, Sat 10 - 6, Sun 10 - 5.
Telephone: (705) 445-9091

SNUGABYE FACTORY OUTLET
New mothers will recognize this name in quality baby clothing. This outlet now brings you disposable diapers as well. Sizing starts at medium, with 120 diapers/case for $23.99. Pull-ups for older kids are $16.99/case for 40. As always, there is a good selection of infants and toddlers sleepwear, underwear and bedding at prices 40 to 70% off retail prices.

Location: 188 Bentworth Ave., (corner of Caledonia Rd. and Bentworth Ave.), Toronto.
Hours: M. to Sat. 10 - 5
Telephone: (416) 783-0300

See advertisement on page A16

SNUG AS A BUG
During the Fall Sale and the upcoming Christmas Sale stock will be packed to the rafters with items all at amazing reduced prices. Refreshments for adults and kids and the chance to win an exciting prize every day of the sale. A special colouring table for the kids and discounts and deals for adults.

Location: 91 Brandon Ave., Toronto
Sale Hours: Wed: 10-7; Thurs/Fri. 10-6; Sat: 10-5
Tel: 1-800-387-4324

SPOTLITE CASUAL WEAR
Spotlite is a warehouse outlet carrying approximately 6,000 to 8,000 pieces of children's Canadian made fashion clothing under the labels Gumboots, Timmy Tom Tom, and Frannie Flowers. The savings on first quality, in season merchandise is between 35 - 45% off suggested retail price. Sizes range from 6 months to size 14.

Location: 95 West Beaver Creek, Unit 15, Richmond Hill.
Hours: M. to Sat. 10 - 5, Sun. 12 - 5
Telephone: (905) 882-1113

See advertisement on page A22

TEDDY BEAR DIAPER SERVICE - FACTORY OUTLET
The company offers a cloth diaper service, but has a small outlet offering bargains on related items, such as pool pants, maternity/ nursing products. Cash or Visa accepted.

Location: 246 Brockport Dr., Unit 27 (west of Hwy. 27 and north off Belfield Rd.), Etobicoke.
Hours: M. to F. 9 - 4:30
Telephone: (416) 798-2328

Children's Fashions & Baby Needs

> Politicians and diapers have one thing in common. They should both be hanged regularly and for the same reason.

Children's Fashions & Baby Needs

WEEBODIES FACTORY STORE

As you might expect, this factory store carries clothing for small people - great quality, comfortable cotton and fleece clothing that both kids and moms love. Sizes range from newborn to age 10. With 30 - 70% off during this sale, it just may be time for some new funky clothing for the kids.

Location: 481 North Service Road West, Suite A31 (exit at Dorval Road; between Dorval Road and 4th Line Road, Oakville.

Hours: Tues. to Sat. 10 - 5
Telephone: (905) 827-7004

> An optimist thinks that this is the best possible world. A pessimist fears that this is true..

T.B.A. TO BE ANNOUNCED - DATES NOT AVAILABLE AT PRESS TIME

THIS SYMBOL INDICATES WAREHOUSE SALES

for your family

Women's Fashions

ANNA THE FASHION OUTLET 💰
Anna sells nicely tailored career wear at about 40 per cent off the regular retail and if you need to mix sizes or would like an extra skirt or pair of pants made - no problem! Check for sale in the middle of January.

Location: **2399 Cawthra Rd., Unit 24-25, (east side, north of the Queensway), Mississauga.**
Hours   M. to F. 9-5:30, later on Wed to 7 and Saturdays 10-3:30.
Telephone: (905) 896-0807.

AU COTON - LIQUIDATION CENTRES
Au Coton offers great savings in 100% cotton casual wear for women.
Location: **Dixie Value Mall, 1250 South Service Rd., Mississagua.**
Location: **Warden Power Centre, 725 Warden Ave., Scarborough.**

BARB'S FASHION OUTLET 💰
Barb has two wonderful clothing shops in the surrounding towns and clears the balance of stock out of this location in Stayner. Save up to 80% on great ladies' wear names such as Susan Bristol. Be prepared to buy off-season. Some children's wear. January and July clearance sales. Call for dates.
Location: **257 Main Street East, Stayner.**
Hours: M. to Sat. 9:30 - 5:30, F. 9:30 - 9, Sun. 12 - 4
Summer hours: Sun. 12 - 4; open Sundays in December - 12 - 4
Telephone: (705) 428-3977

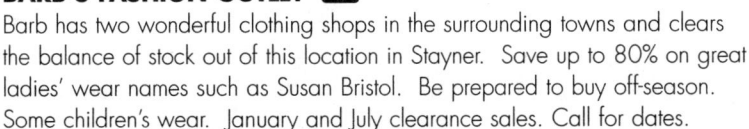

Q. What kind of coffee was served on the Titanic?
A. Sanka.

BLUE BAYOU FACTORY OUTLET
Readers may recognize the name from their regular mall locations. Situated in front of their distribution centre, this outlet features their own Canadian made, pre-washed ladies casual wear with great pricing, good quality and a nice selection. Call for Warehouse sale dates and details.

Location: 88 Doncaster Ave., (east off Yonge St., north of Steeles Ave.), Thornhill.
Hours: M. to W. & Sat. 9:30 - 6, Thu. & F. 9:30 - 9, Sun. 12 - 5
Telephone: (905) 771-9159

BLUE SURF OF CANADA - SWIMSUIT FACTORY OUTLET
Whether you're into aqua aerobics or off to the beach you may want to check out this Canadian manufacturer of ladies swimwear. With a large selection of suits, including plus sizes, they offer up to 40% off retail on current seasons and 50 to 60% off on past seasons.

Location: 804 Ritson Rd. South (exit south on Ritson Rd. from Hwy. 401, between Bloor and Wentworth St. on west side), Oshawa.
Hours: M. to F. 11 - 5, Sat.12 - 3
Telephone: (905) 728-7359

BRAEMAR/BRAEMAR PETITES - CLEARANCE STORES
These off-price clearance stores receive ongoing shipments of merchandise from the Toronto area Braemar & Braemar Petite stores. You'll find a wide selection of savings on fall & winter stock, as well as spring & summer goods at up to 70% off. All sales are final. Major credit cards accepted.

Location: Markville Shopping Centre, 5000 Hwy. 7, Markham.
Hours: M. to F. 10 - 9, Sat. 9:30 - 6, Sun. 12 - 5
Telephone: (905) 477-9930

BROOKER'S
Brooker's has moved to larger premises. Lots of first-quality designer labels in a complete size range. T.B.A. Warehouse Sale.
Location: 33 Glen Cameron Road, #4 Thornhill.
Telephone: (905) 889-1356

CHERRY'S DESIGNER OUTLET
Selling glamour at a bargain is something this outlet has become famous for. True couture goods are sold for far less than original prices. Many items have been brought in from Joy Cherry's store, or are brought in from New York. If you have a dressy event to attend, drop in here first! January Warehouse Sale.
Location: 398 Steeles Ave. W., Thornhill.
Hours: Wed. to Sat. 10 - 6, Thurs. 10-7, Sat. 10-6
Telephone: (905) 709-3606

THE CASUAL WAY CLEARANCE SALE

If Santa gives you any $$$ this year, you just might want to spend it at this well known retailer of women's casual clothes. Their clearance sale starts on December 26, and most merchandise will be priced at approximately one third off regular prices......and every two weeks afterwards, prices will continue to drop until all winter merchandise is gone. They carry a wide selection of brand names that include Liz Claiborne, Jax, Jones New York, DKNY and more. Nothing is a final sale - full refund within 10 days.

Location: 2541 Yonge Street, Toronto
Hours: Monday to Friday 10-9:30, Saturday 9:30 - 6, Sunday 12-5
Telephone: (416) 481-1074

THE COAT CLUB

Choose from one of the largest selections of men's and women's coats and jackets all under one roof. Look for name brand labels such as Hilary Radley, Jones New York, Utex and more as well as Coat Club's own line of coats and jackets at unbeatable prices ! You'll find more than just great coats when you visit – scarves, gloves, and hats to compliment any coat and even women's sweaters, tops and casual pants on sale every day. Coat Club is your store for more than just great coats !

Location: Heartland Centre, Rodeo Dr. (Mavis Rd. & Brittania Rd.), Mississauga.
Hours: M. to F. 10 - 9, Sat. 10 - 6, Sun. 11 - 5
Telephone: (905) 502-1010

Location: 72 Steeles Ave. W. (at Yonge St.), Thornhill
Hours: M. to F. 10 - 9, Sat. 10 - 6, Sun. 11 - 5
Telephone: (905) 886-5252

Location: Dixie Outlet Mall, Mississauga
Hours: M. to F. 10 - 9, Sat. 9:30 - 6, Sun. noon - 6
Telephone: (905) 271-8180

Location: 57 Northern Blvd., NE corner Hwy 7 (Hwy 400 at Power Centre), Woodbridge
Hours: M. to F. 10 - 9, Sat. 10 - 6, Sun. 11 – 5
Telephone: (905) 264-8989

Location: Durham Centre, 40 Kingston Rd., (Harwood exit off Hwy 401), Ajax.
Hours: M. to F. 10 - 9, Sat. 10 - 6, Sun. 11 – 5
Telephone: (905) 426-3555

Location: Trinity Commons (Hwy 410 and Bovaird Drive) Brampton.
Hours: M. to F. 10-9, Sat. 10-6, Sun. 11-5
Telephone: (905) 790-9998

Plus locations in Ottawa, Calgary and Windsor.

See advertisement on inside back cover

Women's Fashions

COTTON GINNY – POWER CENTRES OUTLETS
Cotton Ginny Power Centres and Outlets offer exceptional value on comfortable clothing – without sacrificing style. Come and see us at various ends of the city for great selection at unbeatable prices. Up to 80 % off on selected merchandise daily.

Location: **Brockington Plaza, 1725 Kingston Rd., Pickering.**
Hours: M. to F. 10 - 9, Sat. 9:30 - 6, Sun. 12 - 5
Telephone: (905) 686-3035

Location: **Lawrence Plaza, 528 Lawrence Ave. W. (at Bathurst), North York.**
Hours: M. to F. 10 - 9, Sat. 9:30 - 6, Sun. 12 - 5
Telephone: (416) 784-1389

Location: **Meadowland Power Centre. 14 Matindale Cres. Ancaster..**
Hours: M. to F. 9:30 - 9, Sat. 9:30 - 5:30, Sun. 12 - 5
Telephone: (905) 648-9868

Location: **Warden Power Centre, 725 Warden Ave., Scarborough.**
Hours: M. to F. 10 - 9, Sat. 9:30 - 6, Sun. 12 - 5
Telephone: (416) 751-5058

Coming soon Trinity Common (Hwy 410 & Bovaird Dr.) Brampton.

EMMANUEL BITINI FASHION OUTLET
Career women will delight in the 10,000 square feet of better brand name, quality ladies wear that is always at better than retail prices. The inventory includes some dressier clothing as well as a large collection for junior sizing.

Location: **49 Orfus Rd., (west off Dufferin St., south of Hwy. 401), Toronto.**
Hours: M. to Sat. 10-6, Sun. 12-5:30.
Telephone: (416) 782-3211.

FEMINE LA FLARE INC. - IMPORTER'S OUTLET
Ladies, if you love Victorian cotton sleep wear then you should check out this tiny location that is big on selection and bargains. Also includes a limited supply of other types of women's fashions.

Location: **6130 Tomken Rd., (west side, between Derry Rd. and Hwy. 401), Mississauga,**
Hours: M. to F. 9 - 5.
Telephone: (905) 564-1042.

> I don't mind going nowhere as long as it's an interesting path..

F.I.N.D.S.
For the past 10 years, this store has offered designer labels for less. Now F.I.N.D.S. has expanded & includes its own ladies clothing line styled after great designer wear; ideal for the corporate woman at half the cost.
Location: 120 Adelaide St. W., Unit C5 (Richmond/Adelaide Centre), Toronto.
Hours: M. to F. 10 - 6
Telephone: (416) 601-1676

FREDA'S
We love shopping here, and with the newly expanded retail space, there's even more selection and choice. Freda designs beautiful garments that include women's suits, evening wear and casual wear. Currently their fall/winter collection is priced at up to 50% off, with additional warehouse inventory being cleared at 50 - 80% off. Isn't it time to boost those winter blahs with a new outfit? Sizes available 4-20. Website www.freidas.com
Location: 86 Bathurst Street (soutwest corner of King Street and Bathurst St.), Toronto.
Hours: M. to F.9-6, Thursdays until 8, Sat. 9:30-6
Telephone: 416-703-0304
See advertisement on page A10

HOLT RENFREW'S - LAST CALL
As new merchandise hits the regular retail shelves at Holt Renfrew stores, this dispersal outlet fills up with great buys on off-season clothing. They also carry men's clothing. New arrivals weekly.
Location: 370 Steeles Ave. W. (between Yonge and Bathurst St. on the north side, look for Harvey's), Thornhill.
Hours: M. to F. 10 - 9, Sat. 10 - 6, Sun. 12 - 5
Telephone: (905) 886-7444

IMAGES THAT SUIT
If you love fashion, and your wardrobe needs a boost, drop into this designer warehouse sale that delivers fashion at 50% off their entire spring and summer line. This company has built its business on consulting and providing personalized service, with brand-name labels in women's wear such as Della Spiga, Olsen, Conrad C., Jones New York, Evan Picone and many more! They clear off-season stock at savings of 50 to 80% off the regular retail price. January and July Warehouse Sales.
Location: 260 Richmond St. W. Suite 201 (2 blocks W of University Ave.), Toronto.
Telephone: (416) 593-5287
Location: 6511A Mississauga Rd., Mississauga.
Telephone: (905) 814-7933
See advertisement on page A12

Women's Fashions

Women's Fashions

J. MICHAEL FASHION OUTLET STORE
This store offers savings of 30 to 80% off original prices on ladies fashions. Expect to find a wide variety from inventory supplied by regular J. Michaels stores. Also, fashion shows are held monthly; check the store for dates.
Location: **5985 Rodeo Rd., Heartland Town Centre (corner of Britannia and Mavis Rds.), Mississauga.**
Hours: M. to F. 10 - 9, Sat. 9:30 - 6, Sun. 12 - 5
Telephone: (905) 507-8675

JAYSET - MANUFACTURER'S CLEARANCE STORES
Canada's largest ladies wear manufacturer (for the record and only in the book - this is Peter Nygard), has several mall locations featuring famous brand name stock. This is a favorite outlet for seconds, over-production and discontinued clothing at greatly discounted prices.
Location: **499 Main St., Shoppers World (NW corner of Steeles Ave. and Hwy. 10), Brampton.**
Hours: M. to F. 10 - 9, Sat. 9:30 - 6, Sun. 12 - 5
Telephone: (905) 450-5465
Location: **700 Lawrence Avenue West. Lawrence Square, (NW corner of Lawrence Ave. & Allen Expressway), Toronto.**
Hours: M. to F. 10 - 9, Sat. 10 - 6, Sun. 12 - 5
Telephone: (416) 782-5853
Location: **725 Warden Avenue. Warden Power Centre, Scarborough.**
Hours: M. to F. 10 - 9, Sat. 9:30 - 6, Sun. 12 - 5
Telephone: (416) 752-5168
Location: **Bramalea City Centre, Bramalea..**
Telephone: (905) 790-1455
Location: **Bridlewood Mall, 2900 Warden Ave., Scarborough.**
Hours: M. to F. 10 - 9, Sat. 9:30 - 6, Sun. 12 - 5
Telephone: (416) 491-1720
Location: **Dixie Outlet Mall, southwest corner of Dixie Rd. and Q.E.W., Mississauga.**
Hours: M. to F. 10 - 9, Sat. 9:30 - 6, Sun. 12 - 5
Telephone: (905) 278-9489
Location: **Malvern Town Centre, 31 Tapscott Rd., Scarborough.**
Hours: M. to F. 10 -9, Sat. 9:30 - 6, Sun. 12 - 5
Telephone: (416) 293-7556
Other locations: Bowmanville, Ottawa, London and Kitchener

JONES FACTORY FINALE
Great selection of career and casual clothing to meet all your lifestyle needs at 40-60% off Manufacturers suggested retail prices – EVERYDAY. Jones New York, Jones New York Sport, Jones & Co., Rental Rowan, Evan-Picone and much more. Sizes include regular 4-16, petite 2P-14P, and woman's 14W-24W – seven locations. Great fashions and service which is rarely found in discount stores.

Location: **388 Applewood Cres. (west off Jane St., just south of Langstaff Rd.), Vaughan,**
Hours: M. to S. 9:30-6 and Sun. 12-5.
Telephone: (905) 760-6068

Location: **1201 Division St., (Hwy. 401, exit 617 to Division St. south), Kingston.**
Hours: M. to W. and Sat. 10-6, Thurs. and F. 10-8, Sun. 12-5.
Telephone: (613) 545-7878

Location: **Windsor Crossing Premium Outlet Mall at 1555 Sandwich Parkway, LaSalle**
Hours: M. to F. 10-9, Sat. 9-6 (Jan.-May), 9-9 (June-Dec.), Sun. 10-6.
Telephone: (519) 250-4888

Location: **Southworks Outlet Mall at 64 Grand Ave. S., Cambridge,**
Hours: M.-W. 9:30-6, T.-F. 9:30-8, Sat. 9-6, Sun. 10-6;
Telephone: (519) 740-3777

Location: **JAG Factory Outlet at 80 St. Regis Cres. N. (east off Keele St., between Sheppard and Finch Ave.), Downsview**
Hours: Tues. to F. 10-6, Sat. 10-5, Sun. 12-5
Telephone: (416) 635-7212

Location: **The Cookstown Manufacturer's Outlet Mall 705-458-2122**

LA FORÊT
This outlet carries high-end women's clothing at greatly reduced prices. They buy directly from New York and Paris. A two piece jacket and skirt suit which sells regularly for $399 can be picked up here for $289.

Location: **53 Orfus Rd. (off Dufferin St., south of Hwy. 401), North York.**
Hours: M. to Sat. 10 - 6, Sun. 12 - 5
Telephone: (416) 783-6814

Women's Fashions

What was the best thing before sliced bread?

Women's Fashions

LADIES DESIGNER FASHIONS 💰
Willy has current name brand ladies clothing at 30-80 % off retail with new stock arriving daily. She carries sizes for 2 to 20. Fall and spring sale. Call for information.
Location: Pinery Plaza, Hwy. 26 (west of Collingwood and Blue Mountain Rd.), Collingwood.
Hours: M. to Sat. 10 - 6, Sun. 10 - 5
Telephone: (705) 446-0875

LANCE LORENTS
Another elegant addition to your wardrobe might include a beautiful Italian sweater, now being cleared from inventory at this importer. Look for cardigans, crews, swing coats, suits and more imported from France and Italy.
Location: 500 Glencairn Avenue (northwest corner of Bathurst Street and Glencairn Avenue), Toronto.
Hours: M. to F. 10 - 6, Sat. 10 - 4
Telephone: (416) 782-7864
See advertisement on page A16

LE CHATEAU - FASHION OUTLET
This outlet carries a wide range of the newest and hottest fashions for teenagers and the in-crowd. Lots of stock, with items ranging from 30 to 70% off original prices. If your teenager loves the look of Le Chateau fashions, she'll love these bargains. Items may be slightly flawed, are overruns, or out of season, but prices are excellent.
Location: 47 Orfus Rd., Toronto.
Hours: M. to W. 10 - 6, Thu. & F. 10 - 9, Sat. 9:30 - 6, Sun. 12 - 6
Telephone: (416) 787-4214

LE FIRME
Bursting at the seams with men's and women's designer fashions. The owners go direct to Italy and buy from Versace, Dolce , Gabbana, Ferre and Prada Sport. They also carry beautiful Christian Dior and J.P. Tods Bags.
Location: 95 East Beaver Creek, Unit 3, north off Hwy. 7 just east of Leslie St.), Richmond Hill.
Hours: M. to Sat. 11 - 6
Telephone: (905) 707-8727
See advertisement on page A18

LEVY'S DISCOUNT DESIGNER ORIGINALS - LADIES, MEN'S & CHILDRENS FASHIONS
Smart consumers regularly shop here for first-quality, in-season designer outfits with at least 40 to 50% off retail prices.
Location: 541 St. Clair Ave. W., Toronto.
Hours: M. & T. 10 - 6:30, W., Thu. & F. 10 - 8, Sat. 10 - 6, Sun. 12 - 5
Telephone: (416) 653-9999

THE LINGERIE HOUSE
Brand names in lingerie such as Nancy Ganz, Calvin Klein, Olga, Warner's and Triumph are sold every day at 15 to 25% below retail prices. Most merchandise is current and seasonal. They also carry maternity needs, sleepwear and workout wear.
Location: 2098 Queen St. E. (Beaches), Toronto.
Hours: Call for store hours.
Telephone: (416) 699-1804
Location: 2223 Bloor St. W. (at Runnymede), Toronto.
Hours: Call for store hours.
Telephone: (416) 766-5742
Location: 406 Spadina Rd. (north of St. Clair), Toronto.
Hours: M. to F. 10 - 7, Sat. 10 - 6
Telephone: (416) 482-9476

LIZ CLAIBORNE/DKNY JEANS
Not only is this a wonderful opportunity for ladies to stock up on great deals on these top designers but they have a great selection of men's dress shirts, polo's, pants and other apparel. Warehouse sale - call for details.
Location: 5700 Keeton Cres. (off Matheson North of Eglinton), Mississauga,
Hours: Call for store hours.
Telephone: 905-712-4130

LIZZY-B UNIFORM SALES
Stock up on various uniforms, especially those worn in the health services industtry. Over 25 colours to choose from. All regular inventory is heavily discounted to clear.
Location: 185 Limestone Cres., North York.
Hours: M. to F. 9 - 5
Telephone: (416) 739-6662 or Toll Free 1-800-268-8668

LORNE'S FASHIONS - FACTORY OUTLET
You'll find coats, suits, separates & accessories for men & women in a wide variety of fabrics, styles & colours. Many pieces are manufactured under Lorne's private label, but he also manufactures for many of the best clothiers in the country. Custom tailoring is available. Lorne's is conveniently located in the popular Spadina Ave. garment district.
Location: 101 Spadina Ave. (Between Queen St. & King St.), Toronto.
Hours: M. to Sat. 9 - 6, Sun. 10 - 6
Telephone: (416) 596-1058

LYNN FASHIONS - FACTORY CLEARANCE 💲

This outlet is open year-round and stocks in-season brand name ladies clothes at deep discount prices. Sizes 4-20 from very casual to formal. Summer and winter deep discount sales.

Location: **116 Orfus Rd., North York.**
Hours: M. - Thu. 10 - 6, F. 10 - 9, Sat. 9:30 - 6, Sun. 12 - 5
Telephone: (416) 784-3052

MARILYN'S

Well known for her designer clothing at discount prices, this sale brings even more savings. Her shop is loaded with assorted designer dresses, pants, skirts and blouses, with some priced as low as $20! Lots of knowledgeable sales staff to help you put together a new look.

Location: **130 Spadina Ave., Toronto.**
Hours: M. to F. 10 - 6, Sat. 10 - 5
Telephone: (416) 504-6777

NORMA PETERSON

Casually elegant cotton knits with sizes that range from super petite to size 24, with prices of at least 50% off. This ongoing outlet sells ends of lines, overstocks and samples of ladies clothing.

Location: **82 Doncaster Ave. Thornhill.**
Hours: M. to W. 10 - 6, Thu. & F. 10 - 8, Sat. 10 - 6, Sun. 12 - 5
Telephone: (905) 882-8221

PARKHURST - WAREHOUSE SALE 💲

Lots of ladies and men's sweaters and accessories will be cleared from inventory, so this just could be the right opportunity to stock up for yourself or for gifts. Wheelchair accessible.

Hours: Call for hours
Telephone: (416) 421-3773 or 1-800-268-0456
Location: **22 Research Road, in the east end of the building (two blocks south of Eglinton Avenue, east at Brentcliffe, Toronto. Park and enter at rear of building.**
New Location: Southworks Outlet Mall, 64 Grand Ave. S. Cambridge.

T.B.A. TO BE ANNOUNCED - DATES NOT AVAILABLE AT PRESS TIME

💲 THIS SYMBOL INDICATES WAREHOUSE SALES

PHANTOM INDUSTRIES - FACTORY OUTLET STORES 💰
This well known manufacturer of hosiery and body wear has many locations. Check out the fabulous selection of pantyhose, irregulars and first quality (no runs), swimsuits, Gilda Marx body wear, socks and tights all at approximately 60% below retail prices - a real find if you like stocking up on the basics! Occasionally this manufacturer clears out inventory directly out of their distribution and head office location. Always a great sale, look for savings on swimsuits, hosiery, sportswear and aerobicswear. All sales final. Cash, VISA and Interac. Twice yearly warehouse sales occur the first Sunday in November and the last Sunday in April. Call their head office for details.

Head Office 207 West. Rd. (north of St. Clair Ave. W.) Toronto.
Telephone: (416) 762-7177.
Location: Black Creek Super Value Centre, 605 Rogers Rd., Toronto.
Telephone: (416) 652-6256
Location: Dixie Outlet Mall, 1250 South Service Rd., Mississauga.
Telephone: (905) 278-2147
Location: Durham Centre, 40 Kingston Rd. E., Ajax.
Telephone: (905) 426-5735
Location: Lawrence Plaza, 492 Lawrence Ave. W., Toronto.
Telephone: (416) 785-432
Location: Thornhill Square, Bayview Ave. and John St., Thornhill.
Telephone: (905) 889-2135
Location: Warden Woods Mall, 725 Warden Ave., Scarborough.
Telephone: (416) 750-9241   See advertisement on page A19

PICADILLY FASHIONS - LADIESWEAR FACTORY OUTLET
The 1,500 square foot outlet clears out seconds and samples of fashions that are casual to elegant, in interlocks and slinky fabrics. The factory is bright, tidy and full of deals, including plus sizes.

Location: 2825 Dufferin St. (east side, south of Lawrence Ave.), Toronto.
Hours: M. to F. 10:30 - 5, Sat. 10 - 3
Telephone: (416) 783-1869

RAN'S MATERNITY WAREHOUSE SALE 💰
Drop in to their sales which feature seasonal merchandise ranging from 30 - 70% off. November Warehouse Sale.

Location: 20 Maud St., Suite 401 (west of Spadina between Richmond and Adelaide St.), Toronto.
Hours: M. to F. 9:30 - 6 (call for weekend hours)
Telephone: (416) 703-1744

ROCOCO DESIGNERS OUTLET
Shop for ladies in-season designer fashions all year round. Models Nancy & Anita have two similar stores in Quebec that have been a resounding success. Here you'll find one-of-a-kind show pieces, samples & excess stock from designers in Canada, the U.S. and Germany.

Location: 12994 Keele St. (just south of King Side Rd.), King City.
Hours: T. to F. 10 - 6, Sat. 10 - 5, Sun. 12 - 5
Telephone: (905) 833-4284

ROMANTIC NIGHT BY LILIANNE - FACTORY OUTLET
An exclusive line of Canadian-made peignoirs, nightshirts, teddies & camisoles in polyester, silk and cotton at 30 to 70% off regular prices. Call for year end sales.

Location: 4544 Dufferin St., Unit 13 (just south of Finch Ave.), Downsview.
Hours: M. to F. 9 - 5 with special hours for Christmas and Valentine's day.
Telephone: (416) 665-6181

SUPER SELLERS
Okay guys - we know that buying lingerie isn't always easy, but it's always appreciated! So drop in to see Danny, and buy brand names that are always discounted by at least 25%. Lots of variety that includes pantyhose, tights, lingerie and activewear from Calvin Klein, DIM, Warners, Vogue and others. Major credit cards accepted.

Location: 488 Yonge St. (1-1/2 blocks north of College St.), Toronto.
Hours: M. to F. 10 - 7:30, Sat. 10 - 6:30
Telephone: (416) 925-5031

TALBOTS WAREHOUSE SALE
This annual sale is a great opportunity to purchase women's spring/fall sports wear, casual wear, dresses and accessories at prices that are 60-80% off retail in both petite and misses sizes. We bought some wonderful outfits there last year, and of course we'll be back again this year! Wheelchair accessible - no cheques.

Location: International Centre, 6900 Airport Road, Toronto.
Hours: Call for hours
Telephone: (905)660-0500

TONI+WAREHOUSE
Designer fashions for women sizes 14-22 abound at this excellent warehouse sale. Toni+ debuted Ralph Lauren in plus sizes last fall with the end of season merchandise being cleared at 50 per cent off retail. Other great names include Anne Klein, Ellen Tracy, Jones and Nygard with fall/winter fashions discounted 60 to 90 per cent off regular retail.

Call for warehouse sale dates and hours.
Location: 1140 Sheppard Ave. W., Unit 16, (west of Allen Expressway and beside Idomo on north side)
Telephone: (416) 633-9331.

See advertisement on page A27

WARNER'S - FACTORY OUTLET STORE
With brand names such as Calvin Klein, Warner's and Olga, this outlet is a must for anyone looking for new bras and briefs. All sales are final, no refunds or exchanges.

Location: Dixie Outlet Mall, 1250 South Service Rd., (off the QEW between Dixie and Cawthra Rds.), Mississauga.
Hours: Mall hours - M. to F. 10 - 9, Sat. 9:30 - 6, Sun. 12 - 5
Telephone: (905) 891-2885
Location: Warden Power Centre, 725 Warden Ave., Scarborough.
Telephone: (416) 285-4389
Location: Cookstown Mfrs. Outlet Mall, (400 & 89 Hwy) Cookstown.
Location: St. Jacobs Factory Outlet Mall (Hwy 401 take Hwy 8 West to Kitchener-Waterloo, then Hwy 86 to Waterloo to Road 15, left to Farmers' Market Road)

ZACKS – FASHION OUTLET
The latest Women's fashions with savings up to 70% off every day. Four locations across Southern Ontario to serve you.
Location: Guelph Centre, upper level, 55 Wydham St., Guelph.
Telephone: (519) 824-0420
Location: Towne Centre, 200 Broadway St., Tillsonburg.
Telephone: (519) 842-7182
Location: 2501 Steeles Ave. West, Toronto.
Telephone: (416) 736-1638
Location: 31 King St. North, Waterloo.
Telephone: (519) 886-4980
Call for Hours

Zacks
FASHION OUTLET

The latest women's fashions with savings up to 70% off everyday, in regular, petite and plus sizes.

Four Locations across Southern Ontario to serve you:

GUELPH:
Upper level
Guelph Centre
55 Wydham St.
N1H 2T8
(519) 824-0420

WATERLOO:
31 King St. N.
N2J 2W6
(519) 886-4980

TORONTO:
2501 Steeles Ave. W.
M3J 2P1
(416) 736-1638

TILLSONBURG:
Tillsonburg Town Centre
200 Broadway St.
N4G 5A7
(519) 842-7482

Hours vary by location. Please call for details.

Women's Fashions

for your family

Footwear

ALDO - CLEARANCE OUTLET
With hundreds of stores across Canada, this popular footwear chain carries not only their own famous brand name but several others as well. The following four locations are their clearance stores for the greater Toronto area.

Location: **332 Yonge St. (northwest corner at Dundas St.), Toronto.**
Hours: M. to F. 10 - 9, Sat. 10 - 6, Sun. 12 - 5
Telephone: (416) 596-1390

Location: **663 Yonge St. (at Charles St.), Toronto.**
Hours: M. to F. 10 - 9, Sat. 10 - 6, Sun. 12 - 5
Telephone: (416) 323-3385

Location: **Dixie Outlet Mall (Dixie Rd. and Q.E.W.), Mississauga.**
Hours: M. to F. 10 - 9, Sat. 9:30 - 6, Sun. 12 - 6
Telephone: (905) 891-0773

Location: **Shoppers World, 499 Main St. S. (northwest corner at Hwy. 10 and Steeles Ave.), Brampton.**
Hours: M. to F. 10 - 9, Sat. 9:30 - 6, Sun. 12 - 5
Telephone: (905) 874-9476

BATA SHOE OUTLET/ ATHLETES WORLD OUTLET
Both shops carry the well known Bata brand of footwear and athletic wear with samples, factory seconds, discontinued styles, ends of lines and some firsts.

Location: **197 Front St E., Toronto.**
Hours: M. to F. 10 - 8, Sat. 10 - 6, Sun. 11-5
Telephone: (416) 203-6103

Location: **Dixie Outlet Mall, (Dixie Rd. and Q.E.W.), Mississauga.**
Hours: M. to F. 10 - 9, Sat. 9:30 - 6, Sun. 12-6
Telephone: (905) 271-6814; Athletes World (905) 271-9218

Other Location: *Trenton.*

BEST SHOE
Another well-known name in retailing, Cal Corp has three off-price clearance stores. Off season shoes from their 9-West, Calderone and Pino Carina lines are regularly sold through this clearance outlet. No cheques.

Location: 3225 Hwy. 7 E. (1 block east of Woodbine Ave.), Markham.
Hours: M. to F. 10 - 9, Sat. 10 - 6, Sun. 11 - 5
Telephone: (905) 947-9993

Location: Heartland Town Centre (Britannia & Mavis), Mississauga.
Hours: M. to F. 10 - 9, Sat. 11 - 6, Sun. 12 - 5
Telephone: (905) 507-1022

Location: Collossus Centre
Telephone: (905) 856-0126

BOCCI SHOES - OUTLET STORE
When Bocci's regular retail outlets are down to their last three or four pairs of shoes, they're sent to Bocci's warehouse. Chances of finding some current styles are good. The footwear is organized by size and savings are up to 70%. Bocci carries only men's and women's shoes - none for children.

Location: 1126 Finch Ave. W., Downsview.
Hours: M. to F. 10 - 6, Sat. 10 - 5, Sun. 12 - 5
Telephone: (416) 736-1732

BONNIE STUART SHOES - OUTLET STORE
This outlet offers imperfect and discontinued national brand children's footwear. Visa accepted.

Location: 141 Whitney Place, Kitchener.
Hours: Thu. 4 - 8, Sat. 9 - 3
Telephone: (519) 578-8880

CANLY SHOES
Excellent prices at three locations offering men's and women's quality footwear and accessories.

Location: 180 Steeles Ave. W., Thornhill.
Hours: M. to F. 10 - 9, Sat. 10 - 6, Sun. 12 - 5
Telephone: (905) 886-2363/4379

Location: 4517 Chesswood Dr. (between Dufferin and Keele St.), Downsview.
Hours: M. to F. 10 - 9, Sat. 10 - 6, Sun. 12 - 5
Telephone: (416) 630-5802

Location: Lawrence Plaza (Lawrence Ave. and Bathurst St.), Toronto.
Hours: M. to F. 10 - 9, Sat. 10 - 6, Sun. 11 - 5
Telephone: (416) 783-9931

Footwear

DACK'S SHOES
Dack's Shoes, Canada's premier retailer of quality men's foorwear since 1834, offers substantial savings on factory seconds and discontinued lines. Shoes regularly retailing from $120 $335 have been reduced to $29.95 to $234.95. Come visit one of the original outlet stores, in operation since 1965.

Location: 595 Trethewey Dr.
(S. of Lawrence Ave., E. of Jane St.)
Hours: M. to Sat. 9-6
Telephone: 416-241-5216.

Jump to it!

Great Savings on Men's Footwear!

Enjoy savings of up to 70% off regular retail prices on an excellent selection of Dack's Classic dress shoes, casuals and famous brand name men's footwear.

• End-of-lines • Samples • Odd Sizes • Factory Seconds

Dack's FACTORY OUTLET

595 Trethewey Drive • **Tel. (416) 241-5170**

MON.-SAT. 9 AM - 6 PM • **VISA, MasterCARD, AMERICAN EXPRESS, INTERAC**

Q. What's the difference between roast beef and pea soup?
A. Anyone can roast beef.

FACTORY SHOE
In the shoe business since 1956, this outlet features better buys on a wide assortment of footwear for the whole family, as well as quite a selection of safety shoes and boots.
Location: 1151 Upper James Street, (Upper James at Lincoln Alexander Parkway), Hamilton.
Hours: M. to F. 9 - 9, Sat. 9 - 6, Sun. 11 - 5
Telephone: (905) 318-9799
Location: 2640 South Sheridan Way (Q.E.W. at Winston Churchill Blvd.), Mississauga.
Hours: M. to F. 9 - 9, Sat. 9 - 6, Sun. 11 - 5
Telephone: (905) 855-7817
Location: 686 Victoria St. N. (next to Expressway) Kitchener.
Hours: M. to F. 9 - 9, Sat. 9 - 6, Sun. 11 - 5
Telephone: (519) 743-2021
Location: Corner of Wharncliffe & Southdale, London.
Hours: M. to F. 9 - 9, Sat. 9 - 6, Sun. 11 - 5
Telephone: (519) 685-6199

FOOTWEAR FACTORY OUTLET
In its 3rd year of operation, this outlet has proven that quality products at discount prices are what consumers look for. With names like Wolverine, Point Zero, Puma, Avia & Caterpillar, they offer a large selection of over 1200 pairs of footwear & a growing assortment of casual/athletic apparel. Open 7 days/week (excluding holidays) - check out this awesome store.
Location: 29 Plains Rd. W., Burlington.
Hours: M. to Thu. 10 - 6, F. 10 - 5, Sat. 10 - 6, Sun. 12 - 5
Telephone: (905) 681-3338
Location: 5075 N. Service Rd., Burlington, Ont.
Hours: M. - F. 10 - 6
Telephone: (905) 823-7415

GERTEX FACTORY OUTLET
Socks, socks, and more socks - for the whole family and with savings to boot! Shopping will find novelty socks for babies and children, deals on budget pantyhose, tights and bags of sports socks are all at less than retail at this factory outlet.
Location: 9 Denisley Ave. (E. off Keele St., 3 streets S. of Lawrence Ave.)
Hours: M. to F. 8:30-5
Telephone: 416-241-2345

GORDON CONTRACT

Speaking of shoes, here's an unusual outlet. This store provides Toronto's Police, Fire, Ambulance and Public Works employees with their regulation footwear - and now you too can buy. Of course, styles are limited. Other footwear is available as well.

Location: 552 Queen Street West (east of Bathurst Street), Toronto
Hours: M. to F. 10 - 5, Sat. 10 - 4
Telephone: 416-504-5503

Location: 20 Bermondsey Road (west of Victoria Park Ave., south of Eglinton Avenue E.), Toronto.
Hours: M. to F. 9-5, Sat. 10 - 4
Telephone: 416-757-6214.

INGEBORG'S SHOES - WAREHOUSE OUTLET

Ingeborg's offers European shoes and handbags at clearance prices, and specializes in wide fittings.

Location: 1681 Finfar Ct., Mississauga.
Hours: M. to Sat. 9 - 5, Sun. 11 - 4
Telephone: (905) 823-7415

JOE SINGER SHOES LTD. - DISCOUNTED LADIE'S FOOTWEAR

High-end, high-style, high-quality, - All types of shoes. They also carry a wide selection of shoes, boots & purses, at least 30% off new stock & more off last season's footwear. Size 5-12 in all widths.

Location: 10165 Yonge St., Richmond Hill.
Hours: M. to Sat. 10 - 6, Sun. 12-5
Telephone: (905) 884-0360

Location: 2852 Danforth Ave., Toronto.
Hours: M. to W. 10 - 6, Th. to Fri. 10 - 8; Sat. 9:30 - 6, Sun. 12-5
Telephone: (416) 693-6045

Location: 53 Orfus Road, La Foret Plaza, Toronto.
Hours: M. to S. 10 - 6, Sun. 12-5
Telephone: (416) 782-1281

Location: 903 Bloor St. W., Toronto.
Hours: M. to F. 10 - 7, Sat. 9:30 - 6, Closed Sun.
Telephone: (416) 533-3559

KAUFMAN FOOTWEAR - FACTORY OUTLET

Kaufman Footwear has been manufacturing quality footwear for over 90 years. A huge selection of Sorel boots and hikers, Black Diamond rubber and workboots and Foamtread slippers are available in factory seconds, over-runs and discontinued lines. Something for the whole family!

Location: 6 Shirley Ave., (Conestoga Parkway, north of Hwy. 401, exit at Wellington St. E.), Kitchener.
Hours: Hours are seasonal, please call for details.
Telephone: (519) 749-3207

LITTLE SHOE PALACE
Get off on the right foot with all major brand names in children's footwear like Nike, Reebok, Stride-Rite, Keds, Minibel, Babybotte, Sorel & Mannique Moda.
Location: 3189 Bathurst St. (S. of Hwy. 401), Toronto.
Hours: M. to W. & F. 10 - 6, Thu. 10 - 7:30, Sun. 10 - 5 (Closed Saturdays)
Telephone: (416) 785-5290
Location: 67 Doncaster Ave. (E. off Yonge. St. S. of Hwy. 7), Thornhill.
Hours: M. to W. & F. 10 - 6, Thu. 10 - 7:30, Sun. 10 - 5 (Closed Saturdays)
Telephone: (905) 731-8520

McGREGOR SOCKS FACTORY OUTLETS
These outlets offer brand name socks and hosiery at up to 50% off - and have a pricing structure in place that lets you save more the more you buy. Brands include Calvin Klein, Levi's, GUESS, Dockers and popular McGregor brands like Weekender, Premium and Happyfoot. Great deals on irregular and discontinued items. Bring some friends and take advantage of bulk discounts. "Their prices will knock your socks off!"
Locations: 30 Spadina Avenue, Toronto
Hours: M to Saturday 10-5
Telephone: (416) 593-5353, ext. 344
Locations: 70 The East Mall at the Queensway
Hours: Tuesday to Saturday 10-5
Telephone: (416) 252-3716, ext. 450
Locations: 1360 Birchmount Road (just north of Lawrence Ave.), Scarborough
Hours: Tuesday to Friday 10-6, Saturday 10-5
Telephone: (416)-751-5511, ext. 5511
See advertisement on page A25

THE NEXT STEP - CLEARANCE STORE
This is the only outlet for a chain of 25 stores all of which carries great names such as 9-West, Liz Claiborne, Wolverine, Sperry Topsider, Rockport and dozens of others at excellent pricing.
Location: Dixie Outlet Mall, 1250 South Service Rd., (south west corner of Dixie Rd. and Q.E.W.), Mississauga.
Hours: M. to F. 10 - 9, Sat. 9:30 - 6, Sun. noon - 6.
Telephone: (905) 891-3458.

T.B.A. TO BE ANNOUNCED - DATES NOT AVAILABLE AT PRESS TIME

THIS SYMBOL INDICATES WAREHOUSE SALES

Footwear

PAYLESS SHOESOURCE

If any of you have shopped at Payless stores in the States, you'll recognize this name as one which offers quality family footwear at affordable prices. And now Payless has arrived in Canada. The flagship store recently opened on Yonge Street, and there are four other locations in and around Toronto. All stores carry a wide assortment of footwear, including dress, casual, athletic, work boot and specialty categories.

Location: **237 Yonge Street (just south of Dundas Street), Toronto.**
Hours: M. to F. 10 - 9, Sat. 10 - 8, Sun. 12 - 6
Telephone: (416) 362-6415

Location: **Dixie Outlet Mall, 1250 South Service Road, Mississauga.**
Telephone: (905) 271-7077

Location: **Dufferin Mall, 900 Dufferin Street, Toronto.**
Hours: M. to F. 10 - 9; Sat: 9:30 - 6, Sun. 12-6
Telephone: (416) 531-6041

Location: **Oshawa Centre, 419 King Street West, Oshawa.**
Hours: M. to S. 10 - 9; Sun. 12-5
Telephone: (905) 571-7881

Location: **Square One Shopping Centre, 100 City Centre Drive, Mississauga.**
Hours: M. to F. 10 - 9; Sat. 10 - 6, Sun. 12-5
Telephone: (905) 273-7629

REEBOK - WAREHOUSE OUTLET

It seems as though the outlet has grown along with our children's feet! If you have some bare soles, you will be happy to know of great savings on active footwear - from children's size 1 to men's size 15. Also included are sweat suits, tennis outfits etc. for men and women, as well as children's sizes 4 to 18. Don't forget that this store also clears out Rockport shoes for men and ladies, although this stock does come and go.

Location: **201 Earl Stewart Dr. (north on Bayview Ave from Aurora Rd.), Aurora.**
Hours: M. to F. 9-7, Sat. 9 - 6, Sun. 12 - 5.
Summer hrs (Victoria Day to Labour Day) M. to F. 9 - 7, Sat. 9 - 6, Sun. 11 - 5
Telephone: (905) 727-0704

Location: **25 Benjamin Rd., Waterloo.**
Telephone: (519) 746-3666

Location: **7500 Lundy's Lane, Ste. Building A-3/4, Niagara Falls.**
Telephone: (905) 356-5924

Location: **3311 Highway 89, Ste. Building C-24, Cookstown.**
Telephone: (705) 458-2550

RHODES INC. - FACTORY OUTLET
A large outlet with many choices for the entire family. Manufacturer of footwear like shoes, winter boots, western boots, purses & leather garments can be found. Up to 80% off retail prices. They can make any style, size & type of leather garments.
Location: 21 Steinway Blvd. #1, (1 block W of Hwy 27 off Steeles Ave.) Etobicoke.
Telephone: (416) 674-8541

RUNNING FREE
Nick has scored some great buys from several suppliers including Nike, Adidas and Reebok so look for great savings on sports apparel and footwear for the whole family.
Location: 2084 Steeles Ave. E.(west off Hwy. 427), Brampton.
Hours: Call for hours.
Telephone: 416-410-FREE

THE SHOE CLUB
There's no membership fee here, only tremendous savings on imported shoes and bags from Spain for the entire family. Call to find out a location nearest you.
Telephone: (905) 820-3668

> Q. How do crazy people go through the forest?
> A. They take the psychopath.

Footwear

THE SHOE COMPANY

The buying power of 20+ Superstores means they can offer you 20% - 50% off brand name fashion footwear every day! They offer well defined women's, men's & kids departments in a no pressure environment. Shop on your own, or ask one of their well-trained service staff for assistance. Call 1-8888-Shoe-Co for hours and location nearest you.

Brampton
Trinity Common (905) 789-8181

Markham
Woodside Mall
Hwy. 7 & Woodbine Ave. (905) 477-2224

Mississauga
Dixie Value Mall Dixie Rd. & Q.E.W. (905) 274-3861

Heartland Centre
Mavis Rd. & Hwy. 401 (905) 712-4949

Dundas St. & Winston Churchill Beside Costco (905) 608-0266

Newmarket
17820 Yonge St. Dawson Blvd. & Yonge St. (905) 895-9161

Oakville
Oakville Town Centre II Dorval Rd. & Q.E.W. (905) 338-8285

Scarborough
Warden Power Centre St. Clair & Warden Ave. (416) 751-3290
Warden Ave & Eglinton Ave.(416) 751-1441

Thornhill
Thornhill Square John St & Bayview Ave. (905) 886-3997

Toronto
Lawrence Plaza Lawrence Ave. & Bathurst St. (416) 787-5136

Scotia Plaza
King St. & Bay St. (416) 360-7480
Yonge St. & Eglinton Ave. 2355 Yonge St. (416) 481-8448

Woodbridge Colossus Centre Hwy. 400 & Hwy. 7 (905) 850-8247

Other Locations in: London, Sudbury, Burlington, Kitchner, Nepean, Gloucester, Kingston, Ottawa, Barrie & Ancaster.

See advertisement on page A10

One tequila, two tequila, three tequila, floor.

SHOE HEAVEN WAREHOUSE OUTLET
It's not very big, but the stock does clear out quickly, and there are great bargains on family footwear.
Location: 51 Hurontario St., Collingwood.
Hours: M. to Thur. 9 - 6, Fri. 9 - 9 Sat. 9 - 6, Sun. 12 - 4
Telephone: (705) 444-2863

SHOE MACHINE - FACTORY OUTLET
Men's and women's styles manufactured from top quality leather, with Italian soles and fittings. The prices are hard to beat. No cheques.
Location: 130 Orfus Rd., 2nd floor (at Caledonia Rd.), Toronto.
Hours: M. to Sun. 7:30 - 4
Telephone: (416) 787-1451

If you can ...
...get going without caffeine,
... get going without pep pills,
... eat the same food every day and be grateful for it,
... understand when your loved ones are too busy to give you any time,
... overlook it when something goes wrong through no fault of yours and those you love take it out on you
... take criticism and blame without resentment,
... ignore a friend's limited education and never correct him,
... resist treating a rich friend better than a poor friend,
... face the world without lies and deceit,
... conquer tension without medical help,
... relax without liquor,
... sleep without the aid of drugs,
... say honestly that deep in your heart you have no prejudice against creed, colour, religion or politics,
Then, my friends, you are almost as good as your dog.

Footwear

TOOTSIES FAMILY SHOE MARKET
Canadian, family owned and operated, Tootsie's was established in 1992, Tootsies provides a unique blend of branded family footwear, specializing in Tender Tootsies and Clinic Footwear. A full service environment invites customers to browse through a large selection of men's, women's and children's styles with a keen eye on value. Tootsies seldom disappoints with factory direct savings. Tootsie's also caters to the hard to find widths and sizes. Women's Clinic Footwear is available in sizes 4-13 in up to 5 widths in full grain leather. (Two percent of net profits are donated annually to Breast Cancer Research and the Canadian Aids Foundation.)
Location: 298 Wayne Gretsky Parkway, Unit 6, Brantford
Tel: 519-754-4775
Location: 1508 Upper James Street, Unit C, Hamilton
Tel: 905-388-8466
Location: 28 Benjamin Road, Unit 15, Waterloo
          Tootsies Factory Shoe Market
Tel: 519-746-1050
Location: 370 Stone Road W., Unit 12, Guelph
Tel: 519-763-6343
Location: 18 Harwood Ave. S., Ajax
Tel: 905-427-6044
Location: 3657 Richmond Road, Unit 10, Nepean
Tel: 613-828-0363
Location: 130 Davis Drive, Unit 7A, Newmarket
Tel: 905-830-1405
Location: 102 Highway #8, Stoney Creek
Tel: 905-560-5012
Location: 200 Windflower Gate Unit 200
Tel: 905-856-0501
Location: 7500 Lunday's Lane, Unit 16, Niagara Falls
          Tootsies Factory Shoe Market
Tel: 905-371-1320

Two locations also in Winnipeg.   See advertisement on page A29

VARESE SHOES - OUTLET CENTRE
This outlet stocks mostly Italian imported men's/ladies shoes. Up to 70% off retail prices is being offered on seasonal and off-season merchandise.
Location: 51 Orfus Rd., North York.
Hours: M. to W. 10 - 6, Thu. & F. 9:30 - 9, Sat. 10 - 6, Sun. 11 - 6
Telephone: (416) 784-1330

for your family

Bridal Fashions & Accessories

BEA SHAWN BRIDAL FASHIONS
A huge selection of one-of-a-kind wedding gowns and dresses for bridesmaids, mothers and flower girls, is being cleared at up to 70% off retail prices. Call for specific warehouse sale dates.
Location: 389 Main St. N., Brampton.
Hours: M. to W. 10 - 6, Thu. & F. 10 - 9, Sat. 9:30 - 6
Telephone: (905) 457-3363

ELIZABETH STUART DISCOUNT BRIDAL - ONGOING OUTLET
Elizabeth would be happy to help you select that perfect gown from her racks of affordable wedding dresses, priced between $299 and $699.
Location: 1015 Matheson Blvd., Unit 9 (south-east corner of Tomken Rd. and Matheson Blvd.), Mississauga.
Hours: T., W. & F 11 - 6, Thu. 11 - 8, Sat. 10 - 3
Telephone: (905) 238-6856

FLOWERS & GIFTS BY WANDA
New wedding gowns at excellent prices, as well as cocktail dresses and accessories are offered. Wedding gowns can also be rented.
Location: 5 Waterbeach Cres., Etobicoke.
Hours: Please call for appointment.
Telephone: (416) 742-7433

LADY ANGELA GIFTS AND BOMBONIERE
This distributor of bombonieres, or wedding favors, carries hundreds of spools of ribbon, doilies and favors. If you like, the store can assemble and accessorize everything for you. It carries thank-you gifts for showers, ushers and bridesmaids.
Location: 260 Geary Ave. Toronto.
Hours: M. to W. 9 - 6, T. & F. 9-8, Sat. 9 - 6
Telephone: (416) 533-3568

Bridal Fashions & Accessories

LINA'S BOUTIQUE 💲
A one-stop shop for bargains on bridal wear. Nice selection of beautiful wedding gowns, and outfits for the bride's mother. January Warehouse Sale.
Location: 1901 Weston Rd. (north east corner of Lawrence Ave. and Weston Rd.), Toronto.
Hours: M. to Sat. 9:30 - 6, T. & Thu. 9:30 - 9
Telephone: (416) 241-8087

SATIN PARTY SHOES
This great little store carries a wide range of styles in satin and crepe wedding shoes and purses. Custom shoe dyeing to match your outfit is available.
Location: 184 Spadina Ave., (north of Queen St.), Toronto.
Hours: M. to Sat. 11:30 - 5:30
Telephone: (416) 504-8823

TUXEDO ROYALE 💲
New wool-blend tuxedos start at $249 and used ones at $99. All accessories are 20% off, with a few slashed by as much as 70%. October Warehouse.
Location: 185 Konrad Cres. (south of Hwy. 7 between Highway 404 & Woodbine Ave.), Markham.

VALERIE SMYTH BRIDAL FASHIONS
They offer new and used bridal gowns and accessories, evening and prom wear.
Location: Pickering.
Hours: By appointment only. Please call.
Telephone: (905) 839-5335

VILLAGE WEDDING BELLES
This bridal shop offers a lovely selection of new bridal wear at budget prices. The service is complete with bridal jewelry, shoes and attire for mothers and bridesmaids.
Location: 331 Dundas St. E. (east of Hwy. 6 on Hwy. 5), Waterdown.
Hours: M. to F. 10 - 5:30, Thu. 10 - 8:30, Sat. 9:30 - 4:30, Sun. 1 - 4 (seasonal from January to June).
Telephone: (905) 689-3150

It's frustrating when you know all the answers, but nobody bothers to ask you the questions..

for your family

Jewellery & Accessories

ACCESSORY CONCEPTS INC. 💰
Savings are up to 75% off and the selection is quite varied - from wallets, backpacks, luggage, travel accessories and handbags, to a wonderful assortment of cosmetic accessories and gift sets - many with great names like Samsonite, Oscar de la Renta and Fina. Warehouse sales in May and December.

Location: 5900 Keaton Cres., Mississauga.
Hours: Warehouse Sales 11 - 8; call for details.
Telephone: (905) 712-8343

COLONIAL JEWELLERY 💰
This manufacturer of designer jewelry holds an annual year end liquidation of current fashion jewelry samples and factory overruns. Savings are 60 - 80% off retail, and includes everything from necklaces to earrings and brooches. Prices include taxes. Warehouse sales; in Dec

Location: 70 Production Drive (south of Hwy 401, west off Markham Road), Scarborough.
Hours: Call for hours
Telephone: (416) 289-0911

FASHION ACCESSORIES - WAREHOUSE OUTLET 💰
It's small but packed with deals on hosiery, ladies socks and leggings, belts, slippers and some aerobic wear. There will be a big November warehouse sale. Cash and cheques with I.D. only. November and July Warehouse Sale.

Location: 65 Dufflaw Rd. (N. off Lawrence Ave., between Caledonia Rd. & Dufferin St.), Toronto
Telephone: (416) 256-5800

T.B.A. TO BE ANNOUNCED - DATES NOT AVAILABLE AT PRESS TIME

💰 THIS SYMBOL INDICATES WAREHOUSE SALES

GARBO GROUP
What a great treasure trove of fashion accessories and names that include Nine West, Anne Klein, and Point Zero. You'll find great jewelry, scarves, and hair accessories. Our teenagers love everything we buy here and so do we. Cash only. August & November warehouse sale.

Location: 34 Wingold Avenue (between Lawrence Ave. and Eglinton Ave., west of Dufferin Street), Toronto.
Hours: Thur. and Fri. 9 - 7, Sat., 10 ñ 4.
Telephone: (416) 782-9500

JES HANDBAG DESIGN
Beautiful leather handbags, evening purses and luggage are offered at 30 to 50% off.

Location: 53 Orfus Rd. (off Dufferin St., south of Hwy. 401), North York.
Hours: M. to Sat. 10 - 6, Sun. 12 - 5
Telephone: (416) 784-5266

LADY ROSEDALE - WAREHOUSE OUTLET
This Canadian manufacturer has a warehouse outlet open to the public. Large selection of pillows, baby products, placemats, fabric by the yard, travel accessories and baskets. All stock is priced to clear at 50 to 90% off suggested retail. Rear entrance.

Location: 120 West Beaver Creek Road., Unit 7, Richmond Hill.
Hours: M. to Sat. 9 - 6 Summer hours: M. - F. 8:30 - 4, Sat. 8:30 - 4
Telephone: (905) 881-7122

MAGGI-B LIMITED
You'll find this sale of discontinued and closeout products perfect for deals on cosmetic and travel bags, soft golf accessories, baby layette items as well as lots of fabrics by the yard. Merchandise is discontinued lines and fabrics, and is cash and carry. They are well-known for quality fabric, cosmetic, travel and baby accessories all manufactured in Canada. Excellent gifts for teachers, showers and moms, and all well-priced, too! Some fabrics by the yard. Please note - cash & VISA only.

Location: 410 Norfinch Dr. (just south of Steeles Ave., Norfinch runs parallel to Hwy. 400 on the east side), Downsview.
Hours: Thurs. & Fri. noon –2:00
Telephone: (416) 667-0808

MODERN WATCH CANADA
Perhaps a watch is in order for Dad - in which case, drop into the renovated premises of this company offering a wide variety of watches at the lowest price - guaranteed. Brand names include Seiko, Gucci, Movado, and many more. All watches come with a factory warranty. Batteries installed at discount prices. www.watchwholesale.com
Location: 835 Kipling Avenue (south of Bloor St.), Toronto.
Hours: M to Friday 10-7, Saturday 10-6....or visit them at
Telephone: (416) 236-1271
See advertisement on page A12

O'BORN PRODUCTS 💰
This manufacturer of high-quality cosmetics bags, travel accessories, decorations, placemats and baby products is clearing an excellent selection of items in unique fabrics and designs. Cash or cheque. April and November Warehouse Sales.
Location: 30 North Wind Place, (North of Scarboro Town Centre), Scarborough
Hours: M. to F. 9 – 5
Telephone: (416) 298-6750

PLEASANT PHEASANT 💰
Ruth Fox – award winning designer has lots of jackets and vests and tons of gloves for every occasion. They also have wonderful hats and caps. December Warehouse Sale.
Location: 401 Richmond St. W., Suite 124, Toronto.
Hours: M. to F. 8 - 6
Telephone: (416) 599-5408

PORTOLANO FACTORY OUTLET STORE
While you're in Prescott, drop in at this outlet store. You'll have to start thinking winter, however. The shop carries a selection of gloves and scarves at 50% or more off list price.
Location: 840 Walker St. (the store is located about three blocks from the Hathaway store. Follow signs posted at street corners) Prescott.
Hours: M. to F. 10 - 4:30
Telephone: (613) 925-4242

Jewellery & Accessories

> One of life's mysteries is how a two-pound box of candy can make a woman gain five pounds..

TILLEY OF CANADA

Lots of great gift giving ideas at this warehouse sale. Or maybe even some new luggage, or a briefcase for you! In addition to their well known leather products that include wallets, handbags, gloves and belts, you'll also find umbrellas, back packs, ties, accessories and more, all priced at up to 70% off retail. November Warehouse Sale.

Location: 1314 Blundel Road (north of The Queensway, west off Dixie Road), Mississauga.
Telephone: (905) 279-8844

TIMEX - CLEARANCE OUTLET

This small store - just a couple of counters actually - is located inside the company's repair depot. Discontinued styles at least 50% off retail prices.

Location: 445 Hood Rd. (W. of Warden Ave., N. off Denison St.), Markham.
Hours: M. to F. 8 - 4
Telephone: (905) 477-8463

VIVAH

Vivah has opened a second discount store and is offering discontinued items, as well as samples, seconds and special merchandise brought in for promotion. Great savings, with lots of earrings in the $2 - $6 range.

Location: Dixie Outlet Mall, 1250 South Service Road, Mississauga.
Hours: M. to F. 10 - 9, Sat 9:30 - 6, Sun. 12 - 6
Telephone: (905) 278-8418
Location: 995 Finch Ave. W.(at Dufferin), North York
Telephone: (416) 665-3444

> You're getting old when you get the same sensation from a rockingchair that you once got from a roller coaster.

for your family

Sportwear & Gear

B.Y. GROUP - FACTORY OUTLET 💰
Sports enthusiasts shouldn't miss these blow out sales of last year's and discontinued inventory. Less than wholesale prices on hiking & walking shoes, in-line skates & protective gear, golf clubs, bags & accessories, baseball gear, tennis rackets, outdoor games for adults and children, darts, table tennis equipment & assorted balls. Warehouse sales in month of November and May.

Location: **111 Barber Greene Rd. (north of Eglinton Ave., west off Don Mills Rd.), Don Mills.**
Hours: F. 12:30 - 6, Sat. 10 - 4 during sale months.
Telephone: (416) 391-3780

BANFF DESIGNS 💰
If warm weather clothing is something you either need or want to give as a gift, then this sale is a must. BANFF manufactures technical outerwear made from Gore-Tex and Protex - you know, that waterproof, windproof, breathable stuff - as well as high tech fleece and microfiber clothing. Lots of coordinated fleece accessories as well, and all items at least 50% off. November Warehouse Sale.

Location: **53A Fraser Ave. (two streets east of Dufferin St. south of King St.), Toronto.**
Hours: Please call for November warehouse hours.
Telephone: (416) 588-4839

Q. What lies at the bottom of the ocean and twitches?
A. A nervous wreck.

BIG CHIEF CANOE COMPANY
Not many places like this left where the family owned company that has been making canoes for 35 years still proudly crafts a product that is as Canadian as the loony. They manufacture canoes for various dealers, but sell their excess inventory as well as their seconds directly out of this location. In fact you can see them being manufacturered. Canoes are available in various lengths and colours, and prices range from approximately $500 for seconds that have a cosmetic blemish, to $625 for first quality - which is already considerably less than the retail price. Cash or personal cheques only.

Location: 5781 Hwy 7 (south side of 7, just east of Hwy 27 behind Leisure Marine), Vaughan.
Hours: M to Friday 7:00 a.m. - 6:00 p.m.,
Saturday 9:00 a.m. – 4:00 p.m. Closed Sunday.
Telephone: (905) 856-4301

BROWN'S SPORTS
Although this family-owned business sells new equipment, it also carries used ice skates for the entire family.
Location: 2447 Bloor St. W. (at Jane St.), Toronto.
Hours: M. to W. 9:30 - 6, Thu. & F. 9:30 - 8, Sat. 9:30 - 5:30
Telephone: (416) 763-4176

BRUZER FACTORY STORE
Boarders be aware! Whether you're on the snow slopes or into the wake you can see the whole line of street attire available from this Canadian manufacturer at this outlet. Not necessarily a 'discount' store we did pick up a couple of good deals on over run/discounted stock.
Location: 1203 Caledonia Rd., (same building as Discount Children's, Bruzer faces onto Caledonia)
Hours: M to Friday 10-7, Saturdays 10-5
Telephone: (416) 781-0011

CANADIAN SKI PATROL SKI SWAP
We are fortunate to have free ski patrolling in Canada - in some countries you have to negotiate a fee before being removed from the mountains after an injury! This huge ski swap is one way that they raise funds to continue their important work. It also presents an excellent way to pick up used equipment. There is a fee into the show but for enthusiasts, the Toronto Ski Show is a must. Ski show is mid-October.
Location: Exhibition Place on Toronto's waterfront.
Telephone: (416) 745-7511

COLLINGWOOD SKI CLUB SKI SWAP 💰
It's always well done with excellent bargains and always takes place during the Thanksgiving weekend. You can sell and buy everything from new and used equipment to clothing. The sale is in October.
Location: Central Base Lodge, Blue Mountain Resorts, seven miles west of Collingwood on Blue Mountain Rd. Collingwood.
Telephone: (705) 445-0231

CSA CANADA WAREHOUSE SALE
With all the emphasis on exercise and health, this outlet is a great spot to check out brand name exercise equipment. Up to 70% off on health walkers, alpine skiers, ab toners and Gold's gym accessories. We saw a health walker priced at $75.00, and an autobike at $150.
Location: 119 Franklin St. (take 401 to Bloomington Side Rd., go north to Uxbridge, turn right on Brock right on Franklin) Uxbridge.
Hours: M. to F. 9-4, Sat. 10-5
Telephone: (905) 852-8826

EUROPE BOUND
What does this travel outfitter do with last years rental gear in order to make room for the new - they sell it off half the regular retail. So should you be in the market for snowshoes, tents, sleeping bags, backpacks and other camping gear you, too, know where to go! Call for sale dates.
Location: 49 Front St. E
Telephone: 416-601-0854.
Location: 65 Front St. E.
Telephone: 416-601-1990
Location: 383 King St. W.
Telephone: 416-205-9992
Hours: M.-W. 10-7, Thurs.-F. 10-9, Sat. 9:30-6:30, Sun. 11-5

GEAR FOR SPORTS CANADA - WAREHOUSE SALE
Thanks to Sonia, we can mention this sale of sportswear which includes higher end/ better quality golf shirts, heavy weight sweatshirts from $20, spring jackets and tee shirts too. A well organized sale, with lots of stock and great prices on better quality items mainly for guys - young and old alike.
Location: 380 Bentley St. (north of Steeles Ave. E. on Warden Ave. go west of Denison St. and north on Hood Rd. to Bentley), North York.
Hours: T. to F. 11 - 6, Sat. 11 - 5
Telephone: (905) 470-0404

Sportwear & Gear

GEORGE BOND SPORTS
With 50,000 square feet of famous brand name ski outfits and various outerwear, we can strongly recommend this sale as being not only huge in size but huge on savings. Held over just four days, shoppers can expect great deals on warm outerwear, ski goggles, mittens, sweat and fleece tops, track suits and much more.

Location: 2345 Matheson Blvd. E., (west off Renforth Dr. or north off Eglinton Ave. E. to Orbitor Dr.), Mississauga.
Hours: Call for sale dates and hours
Telephone: (905) 602-4123

See advertisement on page A10

GREENHAWK HARNESS & EQUESTRIAN SUPPLIES 💲
Those in the know about all things related to horses will appreciate knowing of this excellent sale direct from their warehouse. Call for warehouse sale details.

Location: 5510 Ambler Drive, Unit #2 (Dixie Road and 401 area), Mississauga.
Telephone: (905) 238-5502

IN-LINE & ICE SKATE LIQUIDATION 💲
No better time than now to buy that pair of in-line skates you keep promising yourself you're going to try. This sale includes manufacturer's samples, overruns and odd colours all of first quality and with full warranty. Trained staff will help you with sizing and requirements. Skates will be 30 - 60% off retail, and include OXYGEN OZ series skates Abec 3 (it's a skating term for the bearings in the wheels!), Abec 1 hockey boots with aluminum chassies and high end children's skates starting at $29.95. The majority of skates are priced between $75 and $150.........as well, there will be a selection of new and used hockey equipment at heavily discounted prices. Wheelchair accessible. Call for warehouse sale(s) details.

Location: North York Centennial Centre Arena, 580 Finch Ave. W. (Bathurst St. and Finch Ave. area, opposite Branson Hospital), North York.
Hours: M. to F. 10- 8, Sat. & Sun. 10 - 5;
           please call for summer hours.
Telephone: (416) 663-5841

T.B.A. TO BE ANNOUNCED - DATES NOT AVAILABLE AT PRESS TIME

💲 THIS SYMBOL INDICATES WAREHOUSE SALES

JOTANI SPORTSWEAR - CATALOGUE OUTLET SALE
Ladie's golf fashion for on and off the course. Tee off with great savings - up to seventy per cent off retail - as this outlet clears out excess from their mail order company. Call for a free catalogue. Web Site: www.jotani.com
- **Location:** 604 Edward Ave. Unit 3, (west of Bayview Ave., north off Elgin Mills), Richmond Hill.
- Hours: Please call for hours and sale dates.
- Telephone: 1 (800) 431-9997

MR. BILLIARD
And now for something just a little different. If you're in the market for a pool table, there's no better selection. Happy cueing!
- **Location:** 55 Administration Rd., (northwest corner of Keele St. and Hwy. 7), Concord.
- Hours: M. to F. 9 - 5
- Telephone: (905) 660-3599

NATIONAL SPORTS EQUIPMENT REPAIR
This is a small facility with a tiny selection of used equipment. But is specializes in repairs that are important for players, who treasure the fine fit of their favourite gloves. For better quality equipment, repairs make economic sense. Cash or certified cheque only.
- **Location:** 1540 Lodestar Rd., Unit 5 (west off Dufferin St./ Allen Rd, north of Sheppard.), Downsview.
- Hours: M. to F. 8:30 - 5:30
- Telephone: (416) 638-3408

NEWSON'S BIKE AND SKATE EXCHANGE
Look here for new and used hockey equipment and ice skates during the winter, and bikes and in-line skates in the summer.
- **Location:** 612 Jane St. (at Dundas St.), Toronto.
- Hours: T. to Thu. 8:30 - 6, F. 8:30 - 8:30, Sat. 8:30 - 5
- Telephone: (416) 762-9976

NORTH FACE
Before you visit the North Pole or trip off to Katmandu do check out this new outlet featuring high tech, high quality outer wear, back packs and more.
- **Location:** Cookstown Manufacturers Outlet Mall, (south east corner of Hwy. 400 and Hwy. 89), Cookstown.
- Telephone: (705) 458-8400.
- Hours: M. to F. 10-9, Sat. and Sun. 9-6.

ON COURT SPORTS LTD.

With holidays on the horizon, there's no better time to buy a great pair of sunglasses at terrific prices. This outlet has over half a million dollars in inventory to clear out with discontinued styles, samples and overstocks. Brand names include Serengeti, Ray Ban, Reebok, DKNY, Hilfiger and lots more. Prices will range from 25 - 75% off - warranty on all products. Wheelchair accessible.

Location: 2601 Matheson Blvd. E., unit #3 (just north of Centennial Park near Renforth and Eglinton), Etobicoke

Hours: Weekdays noon to 7 pm, Saturdays and Sundays 11 - 4
Telephone: 905-629-8333 or 1 - 800 - 263-0100

SUNGLASS WAREHOUSE OUTLET

40-75% OFF SUGGESTED RETAIL

OVER 2000 STYLES ON DISPLAY!!
TOP QUALITY BRAND NAME
SUNGLASSES INCLUDING:

- DKNY
- H2OPTIX
- GUESS
- PGA TOUR
- SPYDER
- SERENGETI
- REEBOK
- TOMMY HILFIGER
- RAY BAN
- JONES NEW YORK

M - FRIDAY 12 NOON - 5 P.M.
ON COURT SPORTS LTD.
2601 MATHESON BLVD. E. UNIT #8
MISSISSAUGA (Near Renforth & Eglinton)
(905) 629-8333

PAVAN CYCLES INC.

If a high quality bike is on your Christmas list, be sure to check out this cycle shop. Pavan Cycles is well known for their personalized service on high quality performance bikes and accessories, and is currently offering a Christmas special on a number of their Italian mountain bikes at 25 to 40% off . If you are a biking enthusiast, you'll recognise the high-end names in gears, saddles and tires. Large clearance sale in November. Call for details.

Location: 2601 Matheson Blvd. East, Unit 24 (Renforth Road and Eglinton Ave.), Mississauga.

Hours: M. to F. 9:30 - 6, Sat. 9:30 - 5:30
Telephone: (905) 624-6614

I went to a bookstore and asked the saleswoman, "Where's the self-help section?" She said if she told me, it would defeat the purpose.

SI VOUS PLAY
With three stores and a clearance centre, this small chain carries big brand names in sports wearables and foot gear (but not "hard goods' such as hockey sticks etc.). Pricing is always at the very least 20% off regular retail, with the stores carrying current lines of merchandise and the outlet clearing the ends of lines.

Location: **(Warehouse Outlet) 6931 Steeles Ave. W (west of Hwy. 27), Etobicoke.**
Hours: W. to F. 10 - 9, Sat. 10 - 6
Telephone: (416) 675-9235

Location: **Lawrence Square, 700 Lawrence Ave. W., Toronto.**
Hours: M. to F. 10 - 9, Sat. 10 - 6
Telephone: (416) 256-1501

Location: **Westwood Mall, 7206 Goreway Dr., Malton.**
Hours: M. to F. 10 - 9, Sat. 10 - 6
Telephone: (905) 677-4596

Location: **York Gate Mall, 1 York Gate Blvd. (north west corner of Jane St. and Finch Ave.), North York.**
Hours: M. to F. 10 - 9, Sat. 10 - 6
Telephone: (416) 650-5665

Location: **902 Simcoe St. N., Unit # 1, Oshawa.**
Hours: M. to F. 10-8, Sat. 10-6
Telephone: (905) 725-3339

See advertisement on page A23

SILENT SPORTS - BICYCLING/ WINDSURFING/ SNOWBOARDING/ CROSS COUNTRY SKIING OUTLET
Bicycling/ Windsurfing/ Snowboarding/ Cross Country Skiing enthusiasts - check this out. They guarantee best value and satisfaction with stock that will boggle the technical types.

Location: **113 Doncaster Ave., Thornhill.**
Hours: M. to W. 10 - 6, Thu. & F. 10 - 9, Sat. 10 - 6
(May - July - Sundays 12 - 5)
Telephone: (905) 889-3772 or 1(800) 661-7873

Location: **2555 Dixie Rd., Mississauga.**
Hours: M. to W. 10 - 6, Thu. & F. 10 - 8, Sat. 10 - 6
Telephone: (905) 270-6635

Q. What do Eskimos get from sitting on the ice too long?
A. Polaroids.

SPORTING GOODS LIQUIDATION
We think two million dollars in brand name golf, hockey and baseball equipment just about says it all. Okay, let's add bats, clubs, sticks, balls, bags, gloves, factory authorized, bring your team and the biggest problem could be where to park

Location: 420 Denison St., (east off Woodbine Ave. between Hwy. 7 and Steeles Ave.), Markham.
Telephone: (905) 470-0974
Hours: Thurs. and Fri. noon to 9 p.m.,
Sat. 9 a.m. to 6 p.m. and Sun. 10 a.m. to 5 p.m.

SPORTS WORLD RENT AND SALES
Lots of equipment here ! Time to move the summer gear out, and the winter merchandise in ! They carry inline skates and protective gear at great prices and have special pricing on their newer models as well. Two locations to choose from.

Location: 2110 Bloor Street West (5 blocks east of Runneymede Ave.), Toronto.
Hours: M. to W. 11-6, Thurs. and F. 11-7, Sat. 10-6, Sun. 11-5
Telephone: (416) 762-7368
Location: 2229 Queen Street East (at Wineva), Toronto
Telephone: (416) 693-7368

SPORTSWAP
This shop deals in new and used downhill ski equipment, snowboards and bicycles. It caters to families with children, and offers a half-back program on new equipment, and trade-ins on used equipment. There is also a full service department.

Location: 2045 Yonge Street (between Eglinton Ave. and Davisville Ave.), Toronto.
Hours: M. to F. 10 - 9, Sat. 9 - 6, Sun. 11 - 6
Telephone: (416) 481-0249

TOMMY AND LEFEBVRE - WAREHOUSE SALE
All of Ottawa waits for this huge 9,000 square feet of warehouse space sale of sporting goods and wearables. Think off season and deep discounts as they clear out two million dollars in inventory from various store locations such as their nifty boutique at Mont. Tremblant. Warehouse Sales July to August and February.

Location: 2615 Lancaster Rd. (east off St. Laurent Blvd.), Ottawa.
Telephone: (613) 236-9731

for your family

Personal & Healthcare Products

A.G. LIQUIDATION
Save up to 50 - 70% off regular retail prices on brand name designer perfumes, cosmetics and health & beauty aids. We also carry houseware, books, stationery, jewelry and a wide range of gift items. One-stop x-mas shopping as you will find gift-wrap paper, stocking stuffers and something for everyone on your list Warehouse sale in Nov/Dec.
Location: 2565 Steeles Ave. E., Unit 27 & 28, Brampton. (S.E. corner of Steeles and Torbram Rd.)
Hours: Nov. 4 to Dec 24, 10 - 8
Telephone: (905) 799-0313

See advertisement on page A31

ACTION INVENTORY COSMETIC SALE
This cosmetic sale features all sorts of fragrances and cosmetics with names you'll recognise - unfortunately we can't tell you which ones, but you can certainly call them before you head out to the sale. Pricing is at least 35% off, with some products as much as 60% off.
Location: 1125 Kennedy Road (just north of Lawrence Ave.), Scarborough.
Hours: call for hours
Telephone: (416) 750-7778

BATHURST SALES
Basic cosmetics for the budget conscious, shampoos, fragrances, health care products and gift baskets are featured in this warehouse sale. December and April Warehouse Sales.
Location: 125 Norfinch Dr. (east of Hwy. 400, between Steeles and Finch Aves.), Downsview.
Hours: Call for details.
Telephone: (416) 663-8020

BEAUTY CLUB
When we first wrote about this new concept in total beauty care, many readers couldn't believe it; a yearly $10 club membership entitling them to discounts on beauty care. It's worth a try. There is also a full-service hair salon on the premises.
Location: 1170 Bay St. (south of Bloor St.), Toronto.
Hours: M. to W. 10 - 6, Thu. & F. 10 - 7, Sat. 9 - 5
Telephone: (416) 929-2582
Location: 74 Front St. E., Toronto.
Hours: M. to W. 10 - 6, Thu. & F. 10 - 8, Sat. 9 - 4;
call for summer hours.
Telephone: (416) 367-2582
Other Locations: Yonge/ Eglinton, Burlington, Oshawa, Courtice, Thornhill, Newmarket, Oakville and London.

BEAUTY SUPPLY OUTLETS
These outlets offer professional hair care products, sold only in the finest salons, at outlet prices. They carry state of the art professional tools of the trade with a full range of dryers that are accessible for customer demonstrations. Trendy and elegant hair accessories for all ages are offered. As of today they have 24 locations and are growing.
Location: 769 Yonge St.
Telephone: (416) 934-0911
Location: 1592 Bayview Ave.
Telephone: (416) 485-9005
Location: 494 Lawrence Ave. W. (Lawrence Plaza)
Telephone: (416) 782-1511
Location: 2293 Bloor St. W.
Telephone: (416) 767-6686
Other locations: Aurora, Markham, Richmond Hill, Thornhill, Barrie, Brantford, London, Streetsville, Burlington, Waterloo, Peterborough and Brampton.

BELVEDERE INTERNATIONAL FACTORY OUTLET SALE
This sale is always an excellent opportunity to stock up on haircare and bath products, with lots of well known names at terrific prices. In addition, you'll find sunglasses, sunscreen, cleaning products, fragrances and more. June & September warehouse sale.
Location: 5640 Kennedy Road (north of Matheson Blvd.), Mississauga
Telephone: (905)-568-1816

THE BODY SHOP OUTLET
Once a year this well known retailer clears out many of their successful products and accessories through a warehouse sale. Items include shower gels, body lotions, fragranced room sprays, candles, lots of soap and make-up as well as pre-made gifts. Perfect for pampering yourself, or stocking up on teacher's gifts. www.TheBodyShop.ca.
Location: Thornhill Square, 300 John Street, east of Bayview Avenue, Thornhill . Wheelchair accessible.
Telephone: (416)-441-3202

CLEARANCE WAREHOUSE
A variety of products that's perfect for teacher gifts, stocking stuffers and the hard-to-please. Brand name perfumes, housewares, chocolates, books and stationery items at 30-80% off retail is sure to help you with at least some of your Christmas shopping. Yearly sale mid November to mid December.
Location: 10 Bramhurst Avenue, unit 3 and 4 (second light north of Steeles Ave. off Torbram Road), Brampton.
Hours: M. to F. 9-8, S. - S. 9-6
Telephone: (905) 799-1694

COSMETICS 'N' MORE
Also located in Cookstown, this store combines deals from Upper Canada Soap and Candle with bargains from Revlon to provide savings on a wide assortment of personal care products. Wheel chair accessible.
Location: Cookstown Manufacturer's Outlet Mall, (south east corner of Hwy. 89 and Hwy. 400), Cookstown,
Hours: M. to F. 10-9, Sat. to Sun. 9-6
Telephone: (705) 458-4193.

COSMETIC WAREHOUSE
Three large warehouse stores that are crammed with excellent buys on Bob Mackie, Alfred Sung, Nicole Miller and Todd Oldham. They offer as well less than retail pricing on dozens of other famous names. They carry over 900 of the world's finest fragrances. Terrific buys on oils for the body and bath and a good line of cosmetics also.
Location: 1333 Kennedy Rd. (east side between Lawrence Ave. & Ellesmere, next to Future Shop), Scarborough.
Hours: M. to F. 10-9, Sat. 10-6, Sun. 12-5
Telephone: (416) 750-4619
Location: 30B Apex Rd., (north off Lawrence Ave. or west off Dufferin St.).
Hours: F. & Sat. 10-6, Sun. 12-5
Telephone: (416) 785-4506
Location: 275 Queen St. E. (Hwy 410 & Queen) Brampton.
Hours: M. to F. 10:30-8, Sat. 10-6, Sun. 12-5

See advertisement on page A4

Personal & Healthcare Products

DAREE IMPORT AND SALES LTD. 💰

GIANT warehouse sales TWICE a year! Lots of great buys on cosmetics, hosiery, hair care, bath products, kids' stuff and MORE! Terrific stocking stuffers for the entire family! A sale not to be missed. Save up to 70% off retail. November and April Warehouse Sales are held along with their sister company GIFT-Pak. These 2 companies, at one location are at the top of our list.

Location: 5486 Gorvan Dr. (south of Hwy. 401 and east off Tomken Rd. on Brevik Place to Gorvan Dr.), Mississauga.
Hours: M. to W. & F. 9 - 5, Thu. 9 – 7, Sat. 10-4
Telephone: (905) 624-3359

See advertisement on page A31

DESIGNER FRAGRANCES - OFF-PRICES PERFUMES

There is nothing like the smell of genuine designer perfumes at up to 70% off with more than 300 brands to choose from.

Location: 5635 Finch Ave. East, Unit 2, Toronto
Hours: M. to W. 10 - 7, Thu. 10 - 8, F. 10 - 8, Sat. 10 - 6, Sun. 12 - 5
Telephone: (416) 754-2693

GIFT-PAK 💰

This distributor of gourmet goods and basket supplies has everything for the do-it-yourself basket-maker; fine food, imported chocolate, candles and glassware, bath and baby products, baskets, designer ribbon and bows....ALL AT WHOLESALE PRICES! Save up to 50%. Great ideas for loot bags, bombonieres, teacher gifts, stocking stuffers, hostess gifts and hard-to-buy-for people on your list. Enjoy additional savings during their November and April Warehouse Sales(held along with their sister company Daree Imports and Sales Ltd.)

Location: 5486 Gorvan Drive, (south of Hwy 401, go east off Tomken Rd. onto Brevik Place and left onto Gorvan Dr.) Mississauga.
Hours: M. to W. & F. 9-4, Thur. 9-7, Sat. 10-3
           (Closed Sat. in the summer)
Telephone: (905) 624-3359

See advertisement on page A11

**Q. What do you call cheese that isn't yours?
A. Nacho Cheese.**

LISA COSMETICS / FRAGRANCES LTD. - WAREHOUSE SALE

If you visited this busy sale when they were on Granton Dr. then you'll know already what excellent buys they have on brand name cosmetic and skin products, bath and hair care, as well as some clothing accessories but most importantly Lisa's is famous for great savings on fine fragrances and wonderful boxed sets that make giving and even wrapping a joy.

Location: **NEW - 420 Passmore Ave., (west off Markham Rd. between Steeles and Finch Ave.), Scarborough**.
Hours: M. to F. 10 a.m. to 7 p.m., Sat. 9 a.m. to 4 p.m.,
Sun. 10 a.m. to 4 p.m.
Telephone: (416) 335-6505

MASSAGE THERAPY CLINIC - CENTENNIAL COLLEGE

Here's something to help soothe the aching muscles - especially if you've been shopping all day! This three year program includes as part of the curriculum a clinic where you can experience a wonderful relaxing massage for only $20. The one hour clinic includes an assessment by the student, so be prepared to discuss any specific areas you would like the staff to work on. (Opens August 28th)

Location: **Centennial College, Warden Woods Campus (Warden Avenue south of St. Clair Ave.), Scarborough. The clinic is held in the Annex, with an entrance right off Warden Ave. Look for the signs.**
Hours: 3rd Year Clinic, T. & Thu. 4:30 - 7:30 (focus is treatment of musculoskeletal problems);
2nd Year Clinic, M., W., F. & Sat. 4:30 - 7:30 during the week and 10:30 - 1:30 on weekend (focus on stress management and relaxation).
Telephone: (416) 289-5353

Q. What do you call four bullfighters in quicksand?
A. Quatro sinko.

Personal & Healthcare Products

MR. B'S
FACTORY OUTLET SALES
"New York has Macy's, London has Harrod's, Toronto has Honest Ed's, Mississauga has Mr. B's" Mississauga's best warehouse sale. Cosmetics, hair care, fragrances, health & fitness, clothing & more. National Brands at warehouse prices. Open to the public SIX times per year. Enjoy the Best Destination Sale anywhere. Call for the time and dates of our next huge event.
Location: Solution's Trading & Sales/Mr. B's Warehouse Sales – 1590 Matheson Blvd., Unit 12 (east of Dixie Rd.), Mississauga.
Hours: Regular Hours: M. to F. 8 - 5
Telephone: (905) 629-1500

Mr.B's Warehouse Sales
National Brands Warehouse Pricing
- Cosmetics
- Housewares
- Hair Care
- Bath & Body
- Fragrance
- Health/Fitness

6 Sales per year. Call for details.
1590 Matheson Blvd. E. Mississauga, Ontario
(905) 629-1500
www.retailreturnsolutions.com

PERFUME GALORE
You may have visited their retail outlets, which also offer discounts on the world's finest fragrances. Now they have a warehouse direct approach that is crammed with excellent buys on Bob Mackie, Alfred Sung, Nicole Miller and Todd Oldham, as well as offering less than retail pricing on dozens of other famous names. They have terrific buys on oils for the body and bath and cosmetics too.

Location: Two large warehouse stores: 1333 Kennedy Rd. (east side between Lawrence Ave. and Ellesmere), Scarborough.
Hours: M. to F., 10-9, Sat. 10-6, Sun. 12-5.
Telephone: (416) 750-4619
Location: 30B Apex Rd., (north off Lawrence Ave. or west off Dufferin St.),Toronto.
Hours: F. and Sat. 10-6 and Sun. 12-5.
Telephone: (416) 785-4506
Other locations:
    Yorkgate Mall
Telephone: (416) 661-7728;
    2640 Danforth Ave. E.
Telephone: (416) 698-8299;
    Pickering Town Centre
Telephone: (905) 831-4665 and
    700 Lawrence Ave. W.
Telephone: (416) 787-5040
Hours: M. to Sat. 11 a.m. to 7 p.m., Sun. noon to 5 p.m.

PROCTOR & GAMBLE 💲

From the number of faxes and e-mail inquiries that we have received we know many of you have been anxiously awaiting this sale! Take cash only. Leave the kids at home and save up to 75 per cent off regular retail on Cover Girl and Max Factor. Other various name brand products offered as well! T.B.A. Warehouse Sale.

Location: Call for location and dates.
Telephone: 1-800-668-0198

QHP/TRESSES - QUALITY HAIR PRODUCTS OUTLET

If you buy professional haircare products, you know how expensive they are compared to regular drugstore products. QHP brings a variety of products including Joico, KMS, Sebastian & Redken at excellent prices. On our recent visit, a product purchased was less than 1/2 the regular price. Every month QHP features different manufacturer specials above and beyond their every day guaranteed low prices.

Location: 1923 Avenue Rd. (south of Wilson Ave.), Toronto.
Hours: M. to F. 9:30 - 8, Sat. & Sun. 9 - 6
Telephone: (416) 787-0141

REVLON 💲

Loads of bargains with savings of up to 75% off retail on cosmetics, hair care products, fragrances and more. T.B.A. Warehouse Sale.

Location: Customers can call for address & exact dates.
Telephone: (905) 276-4500 x. 273

VIDAL SASSOON SALON

Willing to experiment with your hair? Can you spend three hours having it styled? A visit to this salon is in order. Licensed stylists take one-week courses here, and their curriculum involves working on models like you. Appointments are booked for Monday to Friday. The price is $17 plus GST and includes a wash, cut and blow-dry. Call several weeks ahead as this is a very popular service.

Location: 37 Avenue Rd. (two blocks north of Bloor St. at Yorkville Ave.), Toronto.
Hours: M. to F. 9:30 - 5, Call to book an appointment
Telephone: (416) 920-0593

Personal & Healthcare Products

Q. What do you call Santa's helpers?
A. Subordinate Clauses.

for your family

Food Fair

AMADEUS - FINE CAKES LTD.
This small family-owned establishment is presided over by a talented cake-master trained in Europe. He produces marvelous European-style pastries and cakes, and uses only fresh whipping cream and Belgian chocolate. The quality is first-rate and prices are competitive. We tasted his Éclairs, as well as the chocolate mousse cake, and decided we had to let the rest of you in on this secret. The best selection is from Thursday to Saturday.
Location: 7380 Bathurst St. (north of Steeles Ave.), Thornhill.
Hours: M. to Sat. 8 - 10, Sun. 8 - 9
Telephone: (905) 882-9957

AUNT SARAH'S - CANDY FACTORY OUTLET
Tucked near the end of Doncaster Ave. is this small chocolate and truffle factory. The day we dropped in they were making peanut clusters. We sampled some terrific truffles and they'll package your purchase ready for gift giving. Specialty orders also available.
Location: 140 Doncaster Ave., Unit 1, Thornhill.
Hours: Call for store hours.
Telephone: (905) 731-3900

BACKERHAUS VEIT
Once again, our thanks to the reader who wrote us about this German bakery. While it's definitely not budget bread, it is good value, with wonderful variety, German recipes, healthy ingredients and freshness. Cash only.
Location: 70 Whitmore Rd. (south of Hwy. 7 and west of Weston Rd.), Woodbridge.
Hours: W. to F. 10 - 6
Telephone: (905) 850-9229

BAKER'S HOUSE
Your guests will think you've cooked all week if you produce cookies, muffins, breads and more - that you've bought frozen and simply popped in the oven. As well, there are a number of items such as croissants and breads that are ready-made and require no baking. We have baked a number of items from this outlet and they've all been terrific.

Location: 3232 Steeles Ave. W., (between Jane St. and Hwy 400), Concord.
Hours: M. to F. 9 - 6:30, Sat. 10 - 5
Telephone: (905) 238-8786

BILLY BEE HONEY PRODUCTS LTD.
This has to be the smallest outlet we've previewed! Inside the front lobby is a wall with shelves, and some of the best deals around on this well known, brand name honey. The product varies and includes honeyed nuts, honey mustard and honey garlic sauce, as well as pails of honey. They do offer factory tours, which would make an inexpensive outing for Guides, Scouts, schools etc. Cash only.

Location: 68 Tycos Drive, (west off Dufferin St., south of Lawrence Ave.), Toronto.
Hours: M. to F. 9 - 4:30
Telephone: (416) 789-4391

BONCHEFF GREENHOUSES
We dropped in to visit, curious to know what fresh items were available. In addition to a mix of salad greens brought in fresh daily, there were baby zucchini, patty-pan squash, haricot vert beans and more. It's best to call ahead, as these vegetables come in only twice a week. Also hours vary, according to planting schedules. Fresh herbs and edible flowers are also available.

Location: 382 Olivewood Rd. (south of Bloor St. W., between Islington Ave. and Kipling Ave.), Toronto.
Hours: M. to F. 8 - 4, Sat. 9 - 4
Telephone: (416) 233-6922

THE BUTCHER SHOPPE
Not for the squeamish, but, you can pick up steaks, chicken, sausages and more at this meat producer's factory location. Call for warehouse sale dates that are held once a month.

Location: 121 Shorncliffe Rd. (south of Dundas St., north of North Queen St.), Etobicoke.
Hours: M. to F. 9 - 5
Telephone: (416) 234-2290

Food Fair

Food Fair

CADBURY OUTLET STORE
Unleash your passion for chocolate at these two outlet stores where you'll find an assortment of chocolate bars, gift items, sugar candy and seasonal products.

Locations: Cookstown Manufacturer's Outlet Mall at Hwy 400 and Hwy 89.

Hours: Monday to Friday 10:00 a.m. - 9:00 p.m., Saturday, Sunday and holidays 10:00 a.m. - 6:00 p.m.
Telephone: 705-458-4666

St. Jacobs Factory Outlet Mall - Waterloo

Hours: Monday to Friday 9:30 a.m. - 9:00 p.m., Saturday 8:30 a.m. - 6:00 p.m., Sunday noon - 5:00 p.m.
Telephone: 519-885-6298

See advertisement on page A2

CAMPBELL'S SOUP FACTORY OUTLET
MMmmmm, MMmmm good savings on a number of food products such as frozen vegetables. This is right at the factory and the best deals happen along with the various harvests when production is in full swing. Cash only.

Location: 1400 Mitchell Road South. (Hwy. 23, about 1 km south of Listowel Located inside a portable in the parking lot.).

Hours: Tues., W. & Sat. 9 - 5, Thu. 9 - 8, F. 9 - 6
Telephone: (519) 291-3410

CANDY OUTLET
This new outlet opened September 2000. They have the freshest bulk candy, nuts, chocolate, soft serve real ice cream, party and gift supplies around. Good opportunity to stock up for the fall.

Location: 991 Matheson Blvd. East, Unit #15 (north of Eglinton on corner of Tomken & Matheson) Mississauga

Hours: M. to F. 10 - 6, Sat. Closed Sat and Sun
Telephone: (905) 22-7762

CANADIAN HICKORY FARMS
Maybe a gift basket is what you really want to give to a special someone - and these baskets brimming with all sorts of food goodies as well as Valentine's treats may just be what you're looking for. This outlet store carries a wide variety of baskets in many price ranges, including specially made ones just for Valentines, as well as many items at clearance prices. Specials include cheese balls, summer sausage and turkey sticks. Annual clearance in Jan and Feb. Call for details. www.hickoryfarm.ca

Location: 10 Esna Park Drive (At Woodbine Avenue, 4 lights north of Steeles Avenue), Markham.

Hours: M. to F. 10 - 5, Sat. 10 – 4, Closed Sundays
Telephone: (905) 479-3199, Mail orders 1 (800) 845-4464

CARDINAL MEAT FACTORY OUTLET
Even if it's not barbecuing weather, this outlet has great burgers, ribs and steaks at mouth watering prices. We tried their ribs, and loved the kettle cooked ribs in sauce that simply needed to be baked in the oven. Roadhouse burgers are $12.99/box, and everything is manufactured and cooked on site.

Location: 2396 Stanfield Rd., (N. of The Queensway between Cawthra Rd. and Dixie Rd.), Mississauga.
Hours: M. to F. 9:30 - 5:30, Sat. 9 - 5, Sun 10:30 - 4:30
Telephone: (905) 279-1734

CILENTO WINES
The showroom is beautifully done with a tasting bar for sampling before you buy and tours of the winery are available. Using grapes from their vineyards in the Niagara Region, they produce house wines with 20 litres available for $90.25 – about $4.50 a litre. They also import and offer an international series that include Chilean and Italian wines.

Location: 672 Chrislea Rd., Woodbridge
Telephone: 905-264-9463

CJ - TEA IMPORTERS
As importers they bring in quantity and specialize in quality with a wide assortment of teas from India. This small shop is infused with the aroma of fine teas and are all very affordable.

Location: 230 Don Park Rd., Unit 1 (one block east of Woodbine Ave., off Dennison St.), Markham.
Hours: M. to F. 2 - 5, Sat. & Sun. 11 - 3
Telephone: (905) 947-0444

DAVID ROBERTS FOOD CORPORATION
Smell the nuts roasting as you enter this importer/distributor outlet of nuts, candy and baking ingredients. Lots of great ideas for gift giving for almost anyone on your list because they also make and clear out gift baskets at up to 50 per cent off.

Location: 426 Watline Ave. (south west corner at Kennedy Rd, just north of Matheson Blvd.), Mississauga.
Telephone: (905) 502-7700.
Hours: Tues. to F. 10 - 6, Sat. 10 - 5 and for December only Sun. 11 - 5.

See advertisement on page A4

Food Fair

T.B.A. TO BE ANNOUNCED - DATES NOT AVAILABLE AT PRESS TIME

THIS SYMBOL INDICATES WAREHOUSE SALES

Food Fair

DEL'S PASTRY LTD.
A delightful aroma greets you as you enter this bakery outlet, stocked fresh daily with muffins, tea biscuits, pies, cookies and buns. During the Christmas season, they have wonderful specials on Christmas goodies that include mince meat tarts, shortbread cookies, wonderful German loaf cakes and gingerbread houses that are all completely edible. Their chocolate chip cookies are also great! Drop in to visit, and you just may not need to bake!

Location: 344 Bering Ave., (between Kipling Ave. and Islington Ave. north of The Queensway), Toronto.
Hours: M. to F. 7 - 6, Sat. 8 - 3
Telephone: (416) 231-4383   See advertisement on page A9

DEMPSTER'S/ENTENMANN'S BAKERY OUTLET
We love stocking up for the cottage or freezer. Prices are tough to beat at this outlet for Entenmann and Dempster's products. Market returns are all $2.69 and include coffee cakes, cookies, cakes, strudels and more. Fresh bread is priced between 79 and 99 cents and a dozen bagels cost $1.29. The outlet carries pizza shells at 89 cents and frozen pizzas too. Try their pasta as well! Seniors receive a 10% discount off entire order (identification required).

Location: 3232 Steeles Ave. W. (between Jane St. and Highway 400), Concord.
Hours: Tues. to Thu. 10 - 6, F. & Sat. 10 - 5, Sun. 11 - 4
Telephone: (905) 669-0845
Location: 155 Nebo Rd., Hamilton.
Hours: M. to W. 8:30 - 6, Thu. & F. 8:30 - 7, Sat. 8:30 - 6, Sun. 8:30 - 5
Telephone: 905-387-3935

DICKIE DEE ICE CREAM WAREHOUSE SALE
It may be difficult to think of hot summer days, but stock up and save on ice cream novelties, tubs and yogurts at these semi-annual sales. Cash and carry or cheques with proper identification are accepted. May and October Warehouse sales.

Location: 680 Petrolia Rd., Downsview.
Hours: Call for specific dates and times of Warehouse sales.
Telephone: (416) 663-5525

DIMPFLMEIER BAKERY OUTLET
All of the fresh baked products here are made from natural spring water at prices that are tough to beat. Rolls start at .10 each, and they make beautiful cakes, cookies and pastries. Wedding cakes are also available for order. Go in, browse around, and enjoy a cup of German coffee for only $.50 while you shop.

Location: 26-36 Advance Road (south of Bloor St. between Kipling Ave. and Islington Ave.), Etobicoke.
Hours: M. to F. 7 - 9, Sat. 7 - 6, Sun. 9 - 5
Telephone: (416) 239-3031

DONINI'S CHOCOLATE OUTLET - FACTORY OUTLET
This small, family-owned business originally started in Italy, and they have been making their chocolates in Canada for the past 12 years. Using only natural ingredients and liqueurs ensures the best quality. Their specialty is a gianduia chocolate that is absolutely wonderful! They will also make wedding and specialty cakes.
Location: 335 Bell Blvd., Belleville.
Hours: M. to Thur. 9 - 5:00 ; F. 9-5:30
Telephone: (613) 967-4463

DOVER FLOUR MILLS
Bread, pastry and cake flour, and mixes are sold in bulk quantities at great prices.
Location: 14 William St., Chatham.
Hours: M., W. & F. 9 - 12, Sat. 1 - 4:30
Telephone: (519) 352-5950
Location: 140 King St. W., Cambridge.
Hours: M. to F. 9 - 5
Telephone: (519) 653-6267

EGLI'S MEAT MARKET
Egli's has very fresh, locally produced meats, with no preservatives. Custom freezer orders are better buys. Gay Lea cheese products has an outlet at the same location.
Location: 162 Snider Rd. E., Baden.
Hours: Tues. & W. 8 - 5, Thu. 8 - 5:30, F. 8 - 6, Sat. 8 - 2
Telephone: (519) 634-5320

EUROPEAN CHEESECAKE FACTORY LTD.
Resolved to lose a few pounds? You can wait until after a trip to this factory outlet. They manufacture more than 40 cheesecakes, pies and cakes with no preservatives or chemicals. We can personally tell you they are delicious, high-quality and perfect for a special occasion. Cash only.
Location: 110 Clairport Cres., Unit 2 (south of Steeles Ave., off Albion Rd.), Etobicoke.
Hours: M. to F. 8:30 - 5
Telephone: (416) 674-0606

EUROPEAN QUALITY MEATS & SAUSAGES
If you're planning any special meals, this shop will deliver quality meat at great prices. Two locations - both are wheelchair accessible.

Location: 16 Jutland Avenue, (north of the Queensway, west   of Islington Ave.), Toronto.
Hours: M. to W., 8 - 6, Thurs. and F. 8 - 7, Sat. 8 - 6
Telephone: (416) 251-6193

Location: 176 Baldwin Street (Kensington Market, Spadina Ave. just north of Dundas), Toronto.
Hours: M. to W. 8 - 7, Thurs. 8 - 8, F. 8 - 9, Sat. 8 - 7
Telephone: (416) 596-8691

FOOD DEPOT INTERNATIONAL
This delightful shop brims with European delicacies, coffee, biscuits and canned goods. Best of all is their fresh cheese, which is always competitively priced and exceptionally fresh. If you love to make raclette as we do, their raclette cheese is second to none. And try their truffles, which are an exceptional treat.

Location: 14 Jutland Rd. (north of The Queensway, west off Islington Ave.), Etobicoke.
Hours: M. to Sat. 9 - 6
Telephone: (416) 253-5257

FUTURE BAKERY - FACTORY OUTLET
If you've never tried Future Bakery's bread, you're in for a treat. This outlet, attached to the bakery in Etobicoke, offers wholesale prices on wonderful breads, quiches and even borscht!

Location: 106 North Queen St. (north of The Queensway, east of The East Mall), Etobicoke.
Hours: M. to F. 8 - 8, Sat. 8 - 6, Sun. 9 - 5
Telephone: (416) 231-1491

G. BRANDT MEAT PACKERS
This bright, spacious store sells everything from European foods and chocolates to meats and poultry, but it is mainly the meat that keeps shoppers returning. Prices are very competitive, and certainly less than other similar high-end stores. When we visited, the T-bone steaks were $11.90/kg. and sirloin was $ 9.90/kg.

Location: 1878 Mattawa Ave., (between Dixie Rd. and Hwy. 427, south of Dundas St.), Mississauga.
Hours: M. to W. 8 - 6, Th. Fr. 8 - 7; Sat. 7 - 2
Telephone: (905) 279-4460

GRANDE CHEESE COMPANY - FACTORY OUTLETS
There are 4 outlets featuring a wide selection of their own cheeses and an enormous range of Italian food specialty items, all deeply discounted. Bulk orders are welcome. Terms are cash and carry.

Location: 175 Milvan Dr., Weston.
Hours: M. to F. 3 - 6, Sat 8 - 5, Sun. 9 - 3
Telephone: (416) 740-8883

Location: 22 Orfus Rd., North York.
Hours: M. to Thu. 9 - 6, F. 9 - 7, Sat. 9 - 6, Sun. 9 - 5
Telephone: (416) 787-7670

Location: 468 Jevlan Dr., Woodbridge.
Hours: M. to Sat. 8:30 - 6, Sun. 8:30 - 3
Telephone: (905) 856-6880

Location: 9737 Yonge Street, Richmond Hill.
Hours: M. to W. 9:30 - 7, Thu. & F. 9:30 - 8, Sat 9 - 6, Sun. 10 - 5
Telephone: (905) 882-6444

Location: 9929 Keele Street - south of Major Mackenzie
Hours: M. to W. 9:30 - 7, Thu. & F. 9:30 - 8, Sat 9 - 6, Sun. 10 - 5
Telephone: (905) 832-6189

GROCERY WAREHOUSE - CLEARANCE CENTRE
Often referred to as the working man's Food Bank, this outlet stocks canned and packaged food items at prices from 20 - 70% off regular price. Stock changes constantly, and satisfaction guaranteed or money refunded.

Location: 1266 Queen Street West (near Dufferin St.), Toronto.
Hours: W. & Thu. 10 - 5, F. 10 - 8, Sat. 9 - 5
Telephone: (416) 535-7243

HERSHEY CANADA INC.
If you head to Ottawa via Smiths Falls, this factory is a wonderful stop, especially if you have kids in the car. Not only do you get to purchase peanuts, candy, chocolate and more, you can also take a self-guided tour and watch some of your favourite Hershey products being made. Tours are best from M. to F. before 2:30 as the production lines are working at that time. Cash only.

Location: 1 Hershey Dr. (take Hwy. 401 east to Kingston, then Hwy. 15 north to Smiths Falls, follow the signs to the outlet), Smiths Falls.
Hours: M. to F. 9 - 6, Sat. 9 - 5, Sun. 10 - 5
Telephone: (613) 283-3300

Q. How do you get holy water?
A. Boil the hell out of it.

Food Fair

HONOR'S PASTRIES
Always a wonderful spot for delectable desserts. Special desserts can be ordered with a minimum of 36 hours notice. Specials include very berry dacquoise, chocolate raspberry mousse, chocolate banana layer cake, tiramisu bombe and many more. If there's a wedding in your future, be sure to ask about their wedding cakes.

Location: 1085 Bellamy Rd. N., Unit 22 (north of Ellesmere Rd), Scarborough.
Hours: Tues. to Thu. 12 - 5, F. 12 - 6:30, Sat. 11 - 4
Telephone: (416) 439-6031

KRUG'S MEAT MARKET
We have made the trek to Krug's several times to stock the freezer with their great homemade garlic sausage, summer sausage and real bacon, all cured the old fashioned way using locally produced meats and no preservatives.

Location: 28 Woodstock St., Tavistock.
Hours: M. to F. 7 - 6, Sat. 7 - 3
Telephone: (519) 655-2221

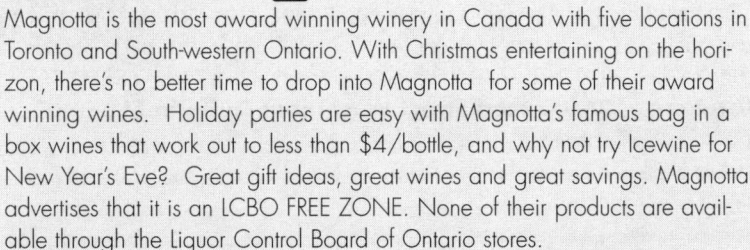

MAGNOTTA WINERY
Magnotta is the most award winning winery in Canada with five locations in Toronto and South-western Ontario. With Christmas entertaining on the horizon, there's no better time to drop into Magnotta for some of their award winning wines. Holiday parties are easy with Magnotta's famous bag in a box wines that work out to less than $4/bottle, and why not try Icewine for New Year's Eve? Great gift ideas, great wines and great savings. Magnotta advertises that it is an LCBO FREE ZONE. None of their products are available through the Liquor Control Board of Ontario stores.

All stores have tasting bars and most are open 7 days a week, year round with the exception of statutory holidays. M to Friday 9-9, Saturday 8:30 -6, Sunday 11-5.
Location: *Magnotta Winery Corp. Head Office, Wine Boutique, Brewery and Gallery*
Location: 271 Chrislea Road (H'wy 400 and H'wy. # 7 area), Woodbridge
Telephone: 905-738-9463; Toll Free: 1-800-461-9463
Web site: www.magnotta.com
Location: Magnotta Vineyards, 2555 Dixie Road, Mississauga

Telephone:	905-897-9463
Location:	**Magnotta Cellars, Brewery and Distillery 4701 Ontario Street, Beamsville**
Telephone:	905-563-5313
Location:	**Magnotta Wines, 1760 Midland Avenue, Scarborough**
Telephone:	416-701-9463
Location:	**Magnotta Vintners, 1585 Victoria Street, Kitchener**
Telephone:	519-571-0084

See advertisement on page A14 & A15

MAPLE LODGE FARMS LTD.
Purchase fresh and frozen chicken at wholesale prices. The farm also carries a line of frozen fish, fresh salads by the pail and frozen meat pies. It's really the chicken they're best known for. Be prepared to buy in large quantities either by the case or in 5 kg bags. A 25-pound case of chicken legs, backs attached, is 55 cents/pound - so shop with a friend.

Location: 8301 Winston Churchill Blvd. (Hwy. 401 west to Winston Churchill Blvd. and north over Steeles Ave.), Brampton.
Hours: M. to Thu. 9 - 8, F. 9 - 9, Sat. 8 - 6, Sun. 10 - 5:30
Telephone: (905) 455-8340

MAPLE ORCHARD FARMS & THE CHOCOLATE FACTORY
Visit this factory outlet, and you may even end up on a tour of their chocolate factory! The shop features maple syrup and sugar, jams, cheese, wood carvings and of course, chocolate. Try their maple cappuccino - it's delicious. Tours are at 10 and 2 and by appointment.

Location: 14 Gray Rd, Bracebridge.
Hours: M. to F. 9 - 4:30
July and August: Sat. 10 - 5; Sun. 12 - 5
Telephone: (705) 645-3053

MARKHAM WAREHOUSE OUTLET - NUTRITIONAL PRODUCTS
Inside this large, spacious store is a huge selection of vitamins, nutritional products, cereals, beauty aids and more - at prices lower than most of the smaller health stores. Swiss Herbal Remedies are always 30% off suggested retail prices. Granola bars and cereals are also discounted. Once a year this 4000 foot store clears out inventory which includes vitamins, sports nutrition products, natural foods, herbal and homeopathic products. For one day only, all items in the store will be 10-50% less than their already low prices.

Location: 330 Steelecase Rd. E. (east of Hwy. 404), south of Denison St.), Markham.
Hours: M. to Sat. 10 - 6
Telephone: (905) 475-5366   See advertisement on page A9

NABISCO/CHRISTIE FACTORY OUTLET STORES
When we think back to school, we inevitably think about packing lunches - so finding an outlet that stocks cookies, crackers and snacks at outlet prices is a treat for both kids and Moms. These locations feature a variety of products manufactured by Nabisco, and include stock that changes often. Look for granola breakfast bars, chocolate chip cookies, crackers and more. Cash only.

Location: **370 Progress Avenue (south of the 401, west of Brimley Road), Scarborough.**
Hours: M. to F. 8:30 - 4:30 2150
Telephone: 416-291-3713.

Location: **Lakeshore Blvd. W. (corner of Parklawn and Lakeshore), Etobicoke.**
Hours: M. to F. 8-5
Telephone: 416-503-6000.

Location: **5 Bermondsey Road (between Eglinton and O'Connor), East York.**
Hours: M. to W. 7-5, Thur. and F. 7-7, Sat. 9-6.
Telephone: 416-751-7120.

NATIONAL CHEESE COMPANY LTD.
You'll recognize the name Tre Stelle as you walk into this retail shop located in the factory. There are extra savings on cheese you know has to be fresh!

Location: 675 Rivermede Rd., Concord.
Hours: M. to F. 8:30 - 5, Sat. 8 - 5, Sun. 8 - 1
Telephone: (905) 669-9393

OAK GROVE CHEESE FACTORY - OUTLET STORE
This outlet specializes primarily in European cheeses.

Location: **29 Bleams Rd. E. (north off Hwy. 7/8 on to Peel St.), New Hamburg.**
Hours: M. to F. 9 - 5, Sat. 9 - 1
Telephone: (519) 662-1212

PASTA INTERNATIONAL
When it's time to think of something other than ham or turkey, pasta often comes to mind. This manufacturer of quality fresh pasta has a small gourmet pasta outlet that always sells their sauces and pasta at less than retail prices.

Location: **5715 Coopers Ave., Unit 8 (north of Matheson Blvd. and east off Kennedy Rd.), Mississauga.**
Hours: M. to F. 9 - 5:30
Telephone: (905) 890-5550

have fun and find bargains!

25 Outlet Stores Including ...

- BLACK & DECKER®
- PROUDLY CANADIAN Cambridge TOWEL & BEDDING MILL OUTLET
- FLORSHEIM SHOES FACTORY OUTLET
- CORNING
- JONES FACTORY FINALE
- KODIAK
- PADERNO Cookware Factory Store

Plus 30,000 sq. ft. of Antiques and Collectibles at ...
Southworks Antiques

Southworks
OUTLETS · ANTIQUES

**Located in the Cambridge Factory Outlet District ...
right next door to the Tiger Brand Factory Outlet!**

64 Grand Avenue South, Cambridge, Ontario N1S 2L8
Phone (519) 740-0380 • Fax (519) 740-8616
E-mail: swom@cwd.on.ca

Monday to Wednesday - 9:30 am to 6 pm
Thursday & Friday - 9:30 am to 8 pm
Saturday - 9 am to 6 pm • Sunday - 11 am to 5 pm

Cadbury
FACTORY STORE
Chocolate
Candy
Treats
Seasonal Favourites
Gifts
2 Locations in Ontario
Cookstown Manufacturer's
Outlet Mall
Hwys 400 & 89
(705) 458-4666
St. Jacobs Factory Outlet Mall
Conestoga Parkway
(Hwy 86) exit Road 15
(519) 885-6298

Colours
Exchange
LADIES' FASHION
ON
CONSIGNMENT
(RESALE)
NEW ARRIVALS DAILY
Take-ins by appointment
3 Brentwood Rd. N.
239-0559
1 blk west of Royal York, north off Bloor.
Closed Mondays

Caulfeild
Outlet Store
30-80% off
Men's
& Ladies
Golfwear,
Casualwear,
Samples,
Seconds,
End of
Lines
60 Bellfarm Rd., Barrie 737-0743

# IRON
Beauty in Strength

Quality crafted wrought iron ❖ *Handmade in Canada*
291 Jane Street Toronto • www.artiniron.net • 416 762 7777

CANADA • ENGLAND • AUSTRALIA

They have now opened a flower Shop and carry giftware and cards.
Hours: M-F 10:30 - 7 Sat 10 - 6 Sun 12 - 4

3 WAYS TO SHOP

1 IN-STORE
APPROACHING 200 STORES AND GROWING!

2 CATALOGUE
CALL 1-800-668-6888

3 INTERNET
SHOP ONLINE 24 HOURS A DAY!

Business DEPOT
Office Supplies • Warehouse Prices
www.businessdepot.com

**CHECK YOUR LOCAL DIRECTORY
FOR THE LOCATION NEAREST YOU!**

David Roberts
food corporation

FACTORY OUTLET STORE

NUTS • CANDIES • BAKING INGREDIENTS

Gourmet GIFT BASKETS — UP TO **50% OFF**

BUY DIRECT FROM THE MANUFACTURER

Open: Tues. to Fri. 10:00am - 6:00pm
Saturday 10:00am - 5:00pm
and
Sundays in December
11:00am - 5:00pm

David Roberts
food corporation
426 Watline Ave., Mississauga (905) 502-7700

COSMETICS WAREHOUSE

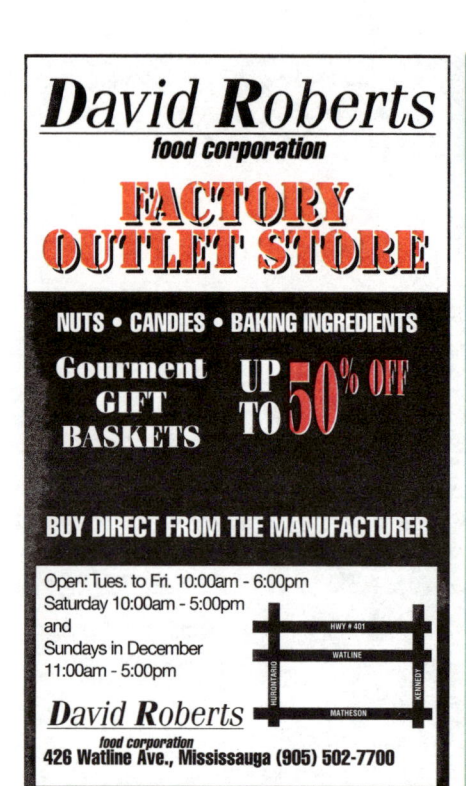

DESIGNER DISCOUNT OUTLETS

Save up to 80%
on the world's finest designer
fragrances and cosmetics
Over 900 Brand names including:

- Alfred Sung
- Givenchy
- Elizabeth arden
- Giorgio Beverly Hills
- Oscar de la Renta
- Nina Ricci
- Mackie
- Hugo Boss
- Dior
- Versace
- Dolce & Gabbana

York Gate Mall (Jane & Finch) Tel (416) 661-7728

700 Lawrence Ave. W. Tel (416) 787-5040

Pickering Town Centre Tel (905) 831-4665

WAREHOUSE LOCATIONS

1333 Kennedy Rd. Tel: (416) 750-4619

275 Queen St. E. Brampton Tel (905) 7963379

30B Apex Rd. Tel: (416) 785-4506

100,000 Sq. Ft. of Fun!

Fantastic Flea Markets Limited

2 Locations

We're in the ™ Yellow Pages DIRECTORY

Downstairs at Dixie Outlet Mall
1250 South Service Rd.
QEW & Dixie Mississauga
(905) 274-9403
Sat. Sun. 10-5

The Steeles West Market Place
**2375 Steeles Ave. W.
North York
(416) 650-1090**
www.fantasticfleamarket.com
email fleaweb@sympatico.ca
Sat. Sun. 10-6

Levi's Outlet

Great Savings
Great Selection

Save 30-50% or More!

ON FIRST QUALITY ENDS OF LINES AND IRREGULARS

Levi's quality, selection and savings.

Central Parkway Mall
377 Burnhamthorpe Rd. E., Mississauga
(905) 270-7362

St. Jacobs Factory Outlet Mall
Waterloo, Ontario
(519) 886-0675

Cookstown Mfr's Outlet Mall
Hwys. 400 & 89
(705) 458-0544

Canada One Factory Outlets
7500 Lundy's Lane • Niagara Falls, Ontario
(905) 354-4049

ALL LOCATIONS OPEN 7 DAYS A WEEK

POWER Shop!
Outlet Style

Over 45 manufacturer direct outlet stores!

Cookstown
MANUFACTURER'S *Outlet Mall*

weekdays 10 - 9
weekends 9 - 6
holidays 9 - 6

Take Hwy. 400 to 89 and look for the water tower!
705-458-1371
website: www.cookstownoutletmall.net
e-mail: shop@cookstownoutletmall.net

A5

We Are All The Brands You Love – Direct To You!

pyrex	**Baker's Secret**	**CORNINGWARE**	**EKCO**
CHICAGO CUTLERY	**French White**	**CORELLE**	**REVERE** REVERE WARE
REVERE Electrics	**VISIONS**	**OXO**	**REGENT SHEFFIELD** KNIFE EXPERTS SINCE 1839
Revolution	**POP·INS** Microwave...Individual Sizes!	**EKCO AIR WARE** AIR INSULATED	**CORNINGWARE Electrics**

THE LARGEST SELECTION OF YOUR FAVORITE COOKWARE, BAKEWARE, DINNERWARE, SERVEWARE, CUTLERY AND ACCESSORIES AT FACTORY DIRECT DISCOUNTS EVERY DAY.

SHOW THIS AD AND RECEIVE $5 Off YOUR TOTAL PURCHASE OF $50 OR MORE INCLUDING SALE MERCHANDISE

OFFER EXPIRES 7/31/2001 Not Valid On Prior Purchases. Limit one coupon per customer. Not valid in combination with any other coupons, discounts or store offers. Good Only at CORNING REVERE Factory Stores IN CANADA. ENTER CODE $4194

CORNING REVERE
FACTORY STORES

Join Our PURCHASE PLUS CLUB & Save!

Pickering Home and Leisure Centre, Pickering, ON
TEL: 905-428-9530 HOURS: Mon, Tue, Wed & Sat: 10:00 AM - 6:00 PM; Thu & Fri: 10:00 AM - 8:00 PM; Sun: 12 NOON - 5:00 PM

Factory Outlet Mall, Downsview, ON
TEL: 416-633-5636 HOURS: Mon, Tue, Wed & Sat: 10:00 AM - 6:00 PM; Thu & Fri: 10:00 AM - 8:00 PM; Sun: 12 NOON - 5:00 PM

Southworks Mall, Cambridge, ON
TEL: 416-633-5636 HOURS: Mon - Wed: 9:30 AM - 6:00 PM; Thu & Fri: 9:30 AM - 8:00 PM; Sat: 9 AM - 6:00 PM; Sun: 11:00 AM - 5:00 PM

Cookstown Manufacturer's Outlet Mall, Cookstown, ON
TEL: 705-458-9998 HOURS: Mon-Fri: 10:00 AM - 9:00 PM; Sat: 10:00 AM - 5:00 PM; Sun: 9:00 AM - 6:00 PM

NEW! St. Jacobs Factory Outlet Mall, Waterloo, ON
TEL: 519-885-6665 NEW STORE - CALL FOR HOURS

DIXIE SOUTH OF THE QEW

How much did you pay?

At Dixie Outlet Mall, you'll find LOW OUTLET PRICES and a huge selection, at over 100 of your favourite national brand name stores.

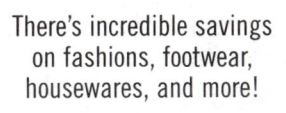

There's incredible savings on fashions, footwear, housewares, and more!

Pre-registered bus and group tours of 25 or more shoppers can experience our exclusive VIP treatment! Make a reservation today! Call (905) 278-3494.

Visit us, just minutes from downtown Toronto!

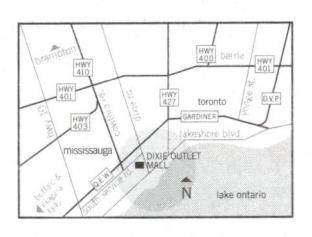

Dixie Outlet Mall
EXPECT ANYTHING AND EVERYTHING

1250 South Service Road, Mississauga, Ontario L5E 1V4 Open: Mon - Fri 10 a.m.- 9 p.m. Sat. 9:30 a.m.- 6 p.m. • Sun. Noon - 6 p.m. Telephone (905) 278-7492 Fax (905) 278-4283

New & Pre-rented Discount Furniture Deals

Aaron's
Executive Garage Sale
A Division of Executive Furniture Rentals

Your best destination for bargains!

Home & office furniture discounts with deals on many name brands!

Call now for times & details

416 785·2006

See our website for specials and upcoming sale dates!
www.aarons.ca

81 Tycos Drive,
Toronto, ON M6B 1W3

The official Clearance Centre for Executive Furniture Rentals

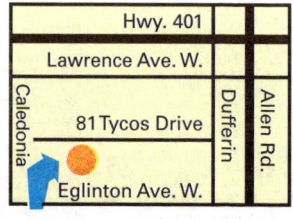

Hwy. 401		
Lawrence Ave. W.		
Caledonia	81 Tycos Drive	Dufferin / Allen Rd.
	Eglinton Ave. W.	

Aaron's Garage Sale is noted in the Toronto Life "Where to Get Good Stuff Cheap" guide.

A8

DEL'S PASTRY
experts in quality baking

Wholesale Bakery Outlet

344 BERING AVE. # 416-231-4383
Hrs: Mon-Fri 7-6pm Sat 9-4pm

PSST...'ETOBICOKE'S BEST KEPT SECRET'

Open to the Public !
Fresh from the oven !
*danish * muffins * cookies*
*donuts * croissants * pies*

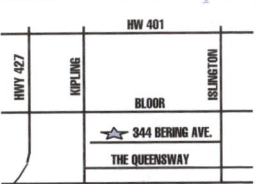

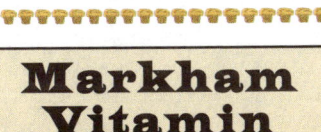

EBC GIFTS & COLLECTIBLES
NOVEMBER WAREHOUSE SALE

up to 70% OFF

Choose from our large selection of well-known crystal, lamps, silver plated giftware, stemware, brand name flatware, pots & pans

AN EXCITING CHOICE OF GIFT IDEAS FOR EVERY OCCASION

Telephone: (905) 764-0795
All sales final
Cash & Visa only   35 East Beaver Creek, Unit 1A (Rear)

Markham Vitamin
Warehouse Outlet

- Vitamins & Minerals
- Herbal
- Sports Nutrition
- Cosmetics
- Homeopathy
- Health Foods

Big Selection
Everyday low pricing
up to 20% off M.R.S.P.

- Certified Nutritional Therapist
- A.C.E. Certified Personal Trainer on Staff

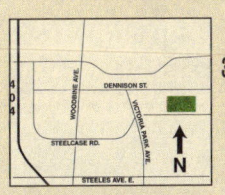

330 Steelcase Rd.
Markham, ON
(905) 475-5366

Concord Candle®
Factory Outlet

Concord Candle Factory Outlet is a unique shopping experience located just off the 400 south of Barrie.

Come and see our great selection of
- candles
- candlemaking supplies
- giftware and much, much more!

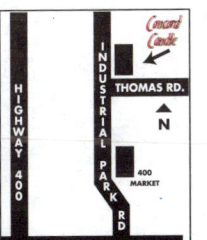

Tel: 705-431-7296
2315 Industrial Park Rd.
Thorton, Ontario
L0L 2N0

FREDA'S

Discover Toronto's best-kept secret. Designer/Manufacturer of exquisite ladies' suiting and evening wear made from the finest European fabrics available from size 4 to 20.
Buy direct and save! Freda's is the designer of choice for local and national TV personalities.

Additional warehouse clearance available with savings up to 80% off.

86 Bathurst St.,
Toronto, Ontario.
M5V 2P5
416-703-0304
www.fredas.com

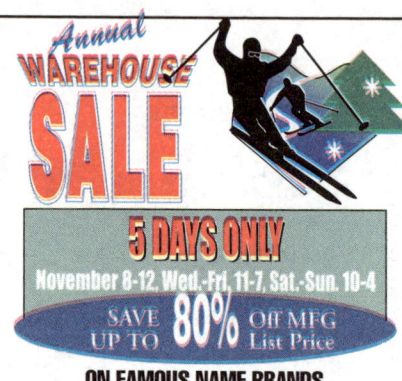

Annual WAREHOUSE SALE

5 DAYS ONLY
November 8-12, Wed.-Fri. 11-7, Sat.-Sun. 10-4

SAVE UP TO **80%** Off MFG List Price

ON FAMOUS NAME BRANDS
Ski Outfits and Various Outerwear
• WINTER & SPRING JACKETS • SNOWSUITS
• TRACK SUITS • SKI GOGGLES • SKI GLOVES/MITTENS
• SWEAT & FLEECE TOPS • SPORT AND GOLF APPAREL AND ACCESSORIES • AND MUCH MORE
• SAMPLES • ENDS OF LINES • SECONDS, ETC. •

FREE PARKING
All Sales Final
Personal Shopping Only
Sorry, no cheques

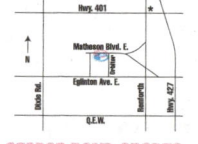

GEORGE-BOND SPORTS
2345 Matheson Blvd. E., Mississauga ON
905-602-4123

THE SHOE COMPANY
A DIVISION OF TOWN SHOES

Quality Brands up to 50% off Everyday
MENS • WOMENS • KIDS

Call 1-88-88-SHOE-CO for a store near you.

GOURMET FOOD & BASKET SUPPLIES WAREHOUSE OUTLET

The finest:
- Gourmet Food
- Chocolate & Candies
- Candles & Glassware
- Bath Products
- Baby Products
- Baskets & Bags
- Xmas Decorations
- Stocking Stuffers
- Gift Baskets

All at wholesale prices: Save up to 50% off retail

OPEN:
Mon, Tues, Wed. & Fri: 9-4
Thurs: 9-7
Sat: 10-3
(Closed Sat. in July & Aug.)

GIFT-PAK
IMPORTERS & DISTRIBUTORS
5486 GORVAN DR.,
MISSISSAUGA
Tel: (905) 624-9560

FABRIC CLEARANCE CENTRES

BEST PRICES ON:
UPHOLSTERY, DRAPERY, VINYL (NAUGAHYDE), NYLON, PLASTICS, LEATHER & FOAM

4884 Dufferin St. Unit 6
Toronto, Ont. M3H 5S8
(3 lights north of Finch)
Canada

Tel; (416) 665 - 4647
www.fabricclearance.com

Images that Suit

Business & Business Casual Wear at 1/2 Price to 75% off Sizes 4-22

Designer Warehouse Sale in women's wear brand-name labels such as Jones New York, D'Oraz, Olsen, Jax, Louben, Rino Rossi, Conrad C, Mac & Jac, Ross Mayer, and many more!

Locations:
260 Richmond St. West
Suite 201
Toronto, ON
(416) 593-5187

Meadowvale Court II
6511A Mississauga Road
Mississauga, ON
(905) 814-7933

IRWIN TOY FACTORY OUTLET

VISIT OUR WEBSITE
www.irwintoy.com

- Ends of Lines & Samples
- Games • Dolls • Sports Equipment
- Huge Asst. of Toys

Plus a host of brand names products, all reduced to clear.

Mon Oct 2 to Thur Dec 21
Monday to Saturday
9 a.m. - 4 p.m.

IRWIN
We remember when we were kids!

IRWIN TOY LTD.
43 Hanna Ave.,
Toronto, Ontario M6K 1X6
Tel: (416) 533-3521

- Cash or Carry
- Limited Quantites
- Cash, Debit Card, VISA, Mastercard
- Sorry NO Cheques
- Manufacturers Warranty in effect where applicable

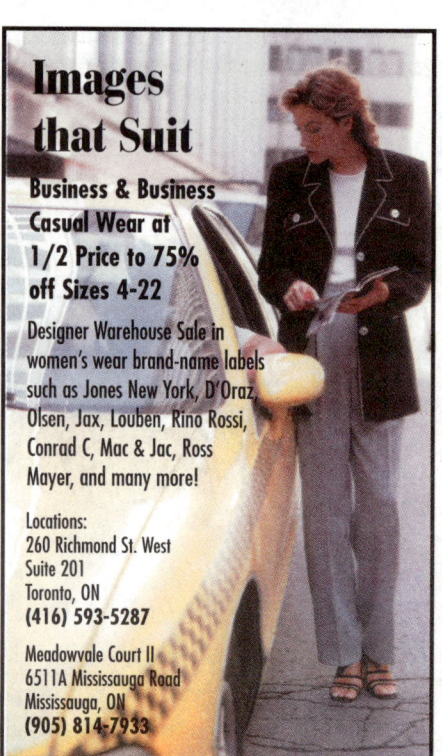

G. H. JOHNSON'S TRADING
• FURNITURE •

TEL: 416-532-6700   950 DUPONT STREET, TORONTO

---

visit: check with us before large selection. Lowest prices
www. high-grade watches
WATCHWHOLESALE.com

TAX FREE COUPON

UP TO 50% OFF

MOVADO CONCORD
OMEGA BREITLING BAUME & MERCIER ESQ
RAYMOND WEIL
SEIKO

Solid gold watches and many more

835 Kipling ave.,
Toronto Ont   (416)236-1271

IBM® WAREHOUSE OUTLET

Award-winning IBM technology at prices you can afford.

The IBM Warehouse Outlet offers a wide range of PCs and peripherals at great low prices.

Come visit us today to check out:
- used, refurbished, demonstrator, overstocked and new IBM PCs, monitors and printers.
- PC peripherals including hard drives, system memory, scanners and much, much more.
- software titles designed for fun, education and productivity.

4175 - 14th Avenue

MARKHAM
HWY. 404 | Warden Ave. | HWY. 7 | 14th Ave | Kennedy
Steeles Ave E

Mon.-Fri: 10:00-6:00
Sat: 10:00-5:00

VISIT THE IBM STORE WEB SITE AT:
www.ibm.ca/store

IBM is a registered trade-mark of International Business Machine Corporation and is used under license by IBM Canada Ltd.

MAKE BETTER WINE, USE BETTER JUICE.

exclusive new

fresh pasteurized juice

FERMENTS WHEN YOU'RE READY...NOT BEFORE

Every year wines made with Festa juice win awards at the InterVin International Amateur Wine Competition. Now you can make your own award-winning wine for as little as $1.20 per bottle (based on 28 bottles per pail). Festa offers varietals from around the world. All fresh pasteurized by an exclusive process so you can make your wine when you're ready.

Call your Festa Juice representative today.

Festa ♥ Juice
juice for great wine

Distributed across Canada. For the Festa Juice outlet nearest to you call toll free:

1-800-461-WINE
Tel: 905-738-5550   Fax: 905-738-5551
www.magnotta.com

MAKE AWARD-WINNING WINES FOR AS LITTLE AS $1.20 PER BOTTLE
(based on 28 bottles per pail)

Having a Party?

LOOT BAG EXPRESS

Loot Bags for all occasions.

Mention this ad and receive 10% off your purchase

🏆 Choose from hundreds of loot bag items for boys and girls of all ages.

🏆 Our party consultants will create loot bags to make your party a huge success.

🏆 Order your Loot Bags and all your party supplies by phone, fax or e-mail.

Visit our NEW location

44 East Beaver Creek Road, Unit 6, Richmond Hill

905-709-4370 or 1-877-LOOT BAG (566-8224)

www.lootbags.com

LCBO FREE ZONE

WINERY-DIRECT PRICES

NO $1.50 PER LITRE DISTRIBUTION CHARGE

NO 58% LCBO MARKUP

MAGNOTTA WINERY

CANADA'S MOST AWARD WINNING WINERY...BY FAR

VISIT ONE OF THESE "LCBO FREE ZONES". CALL TOLL FREE: 1-800-461-WINE

MAGNOTTA WINERY STORE AND HEAD OFFICE: 271 Chrislea Rd, Vaughan, ON 905-738-WINE (9463)

Magnotta Kitchener	Magnotta Mississauga	Magnotta Scarborough	Magnotta Beamsville
1585 Victoria Street N.	2555 Dixie Road	1760 Midland Avenue	4701 Ontario Street
519-571-0084	905-897-9463	416-701-9463	905-563-5313

Mississauga Bedding Superstore
Upper Canada Soap & Candle Makers

Tel: (905) 897-1710, ext. 3013

WESTPOINT STEVENS

UTICA, Spring maid, Sanderson, MARTEX, Fieldcrest, CANNON, DAN RIVER, AQUARIUS

STORE HOURS
Monday - Friday 10:00 am - 5:00 pm
Saturday 10:00 am - 4:00 pm
Sunday Closed

1310 Caterpillar Road
Mississauga, Ontario

MIKO TOY WAREHOUSE SUPERSTORE

60 EAST BEAVER CREEK RD.,
RICHMOND HILL L4B 1L3
KIDS WELCOME
OPEN TO THE PUBLIC SEPT. 27TH TO DEC. 24TH 2000
WED., SAT. 10-5; THURS., FRI. 10-8; Sun. 11-5
DEC 24 10-5; CLOSED MON. TUES.

TWO GREAT
1000'S OF BRAND NAM
LITTLE TYKES-MATTEL-HASBR
FISHER-PRICE-CRAYOLA-IRW

Please visit
(CASH, VISA, MASTER CAR
NO E

Snugabye
Factory Outlet Store
188 Bentworth Avenue, Toronto

Get all your baby's needs
at true factory prices...everyday!

- Sleepwear
- Bedding
- Cotton Underwear
- Socks, Tights
- Playwear
- Cloth Diapers

Monday to Saturday 10 am to 5 pm
(416) 783-0300

MasterCard VISA Interac

Patrician LINENS

The linen you thought was difficult to find...
...we offer...
In best Style, Quality and discount Prices

Bedding Kitchen and Curtains

Leslie & York Mills
(416) 444 1100
1875 Leslie St., Unit 16
Toronto, Ontario M3B 2M5

Open Monday to Friday

ITALIAN SWEATERS
AVAILABLE DIRECTLY AT THE IMPORTER'S PRICE!
Casual or Dressy, Cardigans, Mock Necks, Turtle, Twin Sets, Crew, Fancies...

LANCE LORENTS LIMITED
Ladieswear European Imports and Manufacturing
Importer & Distributor for Several Exclusive European Lines
500 GLENCAIRN AVE. UNIT 2. TORONTO, ONT.
(North West Corner at Bathurst St.)
(416) 782-7864

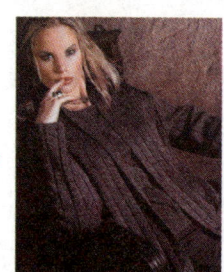

EMILIO BRAVINI
Elegant Business Suits
and Separates, Blazers, Pants, Skirts...

OCATIONS FOR
– BELOW WHOLESALE PRICES
-LEGO-TONKA-PLAYSCHOOL-NOMA-
ON BRADLEY-TYCO–KENNER-V-TECH

e: www.samkosales.com

C, NO CHEQUES ALL SALES FINAL;
ES/REFUNDS)

SAMCO SALES TOY WAREHOUSE SUPERSTORE

11 PEEL AVE., TORONTO M6J 1M3
(ONE BLOCK NORTH OF QUEEN & DUFFERIN
SORRY, NO INFANTS OR CHLDREN UNDER AGE 16
NOT OPEN TO THE GENERAL PUBLIC ADMITTANCE
FOR 2 PEOPLE BY UNION, SAMKO OR EMPLOYEE MEMBERSHIP
CARD OR BY COPY OF THIS AD
FROM SEPT. 28TH TO DEC. 24TH 2000 THURS. FRI. 10-8:30;
SAT. 9-4:30; Sun. 1O-4:30 CLOSED MON. TUES. WED.

PERFECT FLAME
CANDLE COMPANY

Candle & Gift Factory Outlet
Buy Factory Direct & Save!

- Huge & Unique Selection of Scented & Unscented Candles
- Great Gifts for under $20.00 • Candle Making Supplies
- Custom order available for Weddings, Showers, and other Special Ocassions

1616 Matheson Blvd. East, Units 25 & 26, Mississauga (905) 625-2521
Open: Mon. - Fri. 9:00am - 6:00pm   Sat. 10:00am - 6:00pm
Extended Hours September to December

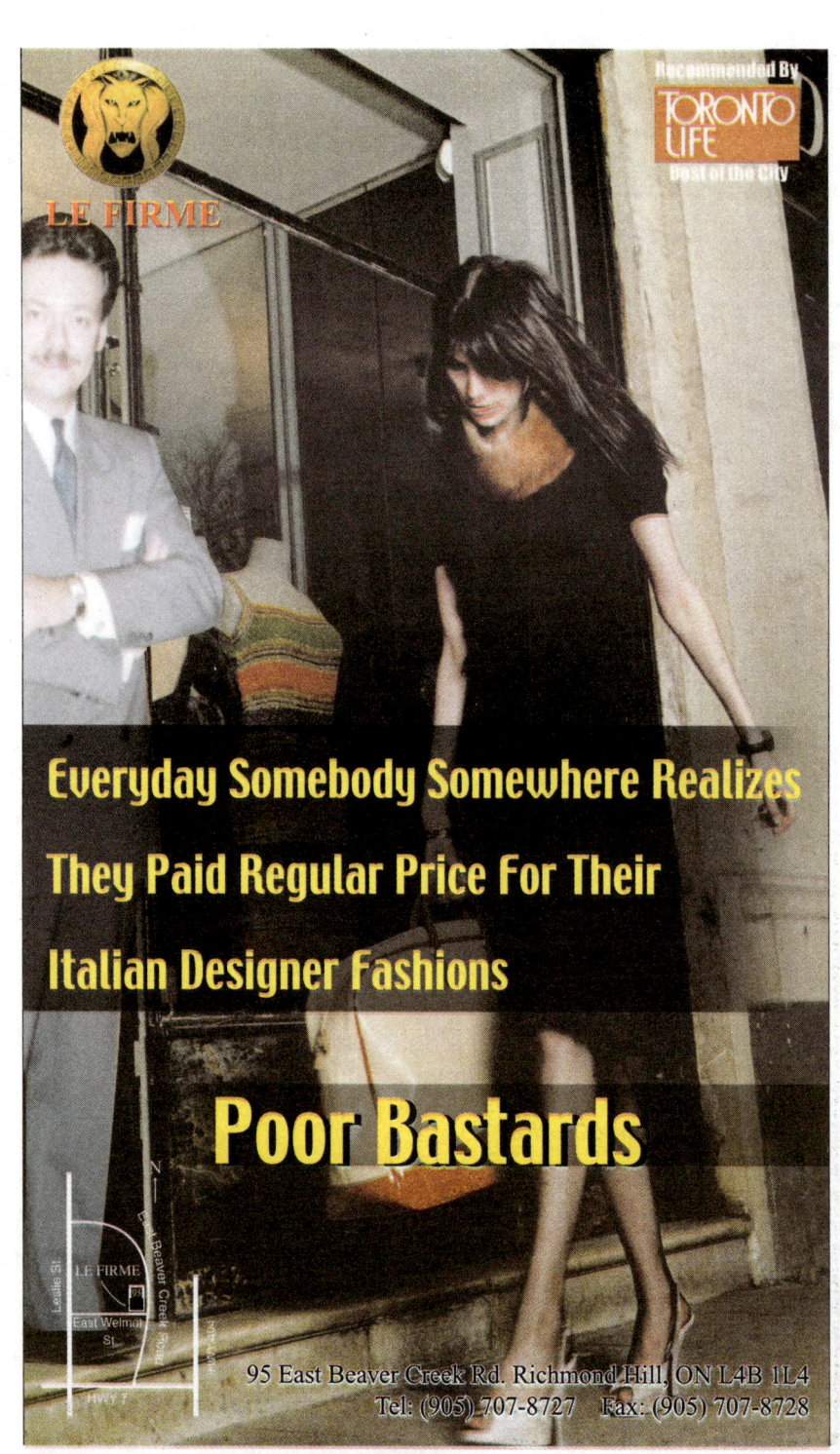

LE FIRME

Recommended By
TORONTO LIFE
Best of the City

Everyday Somebody Somewhere Realizes

They Paid Regular Price For Their

Italian Designer Fashions

Poor Bastards

95 East Beaver Creek Rd. Richmond Hill, ON L4B 1L4
Tel: (905) 707-8727   Fax: (905) 707-8728

silks PHANTOM OUTLET

8 LOCATIONS TO SERVE YOU!

Black Creek Super Value Centre
605 Rogers Rd. Toronto, ON Tel: 416-652-6256

Warden Woods Power Centre
725 Warden Ave. Scarborough, ON Tel: 416-750-924

Thornhill Square
300 John St. Thornhill, ON Tel: 905-889-2135

Lawrence Plaza
492 Lawrence Ave. W. Toronto, ON Tel: 416-785-4325

Dixie Outlet Mall
1250 South service Rd. Mississauga, ON Tel: 905-278-2147

Durham Centre
40 Kingston Rd. E. Ajax, ON Tel: 905-426-5735

Factory Outlet
7500 Lundy's Lane, Niagara Falls, ON. Tel. Fax: 905-371-3598

Trinity Commons Plaza
100 Great Lake Drive. (410/Bovaird East) Tel: 905-789-6976

Specializing in: • Hosiery • Swimwear • Tights • Bodywear • Socks • Casual Wear

---

The Rubbery WAREHOUSE STORE ®

Your Full-Line Rubbermaid Dealer!

North America's #1 Selling Store for

little tikes — 1,000 sq. ft. Little Tikes toy testing play area

toys that last.

Largest selection of **Rubbermaid** in Canada!

Now Two Locations To Serve You!

Hours of Operation: Mon.-Fri. 9:30-9:00 Saturdays 9:30-6:00 Sundays 11:00-5:00
Watch For Our Third Store Opening Fall 2000 - Durham Centre - Ajax

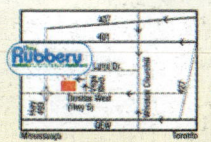

Rubbery — 905-820-5550
Located at Hwy 403 & 5
Erin Mills Centre, Mississauga

Rubbery — 905-850-4060
Located at Hwy 400 & 7
Colossus Centre, Woodbridge

Visit our Website at www.therubbery.com

roses only

Full-service Florist

We grow over 60 varieties of roses in a wonderful rainbow of colours. We also have a wide selection of cut flowers.

The Wedding Expert

Compare our prices:

24 Rose Bouquet
$75.00

Single Rose Boutonniere
$3.50

3 Rose Corsage
$10.00

&

We can create:
church hall &
table arrangements,
pew bows,
decorated arches,
presentation bouquets,
hair rings, etc.

Just for you & within your budget.

Call to make an appointment
416-594-6678

Next to the St. Lawrence Market,
8 Market Street
Toronto, Ontario, M5E 1M6.

A Tale of Things Past

...Of Things Past
Consignment Furniture Showroom
160 Tycos Drive Unit 2
256-9256   Mon-Sat. 10-5

voila

from one fine home to another.
a special place for buying & selling
your fine furnishings.

www.ofthingspast.com

NEW PRODUCTS WEEKLY • AMAZING STOCKING STUFFERS

RIZZCO TOY & GIFT
WAREHOUSE SALE

INCREDIBLE TEACHER'S GIFTS

GREAT GIFTS FOR OFFICE PARTIES

One stop Christmas shopping for everyone in your family and office!

Up to **70%** off retail

- Toys
- Educational Books
- Games
- Kids Books
- Novelty Gifts
- Stationery Sets
- Business/Travel Accessories
- Planners
- Plush Toys
- Kitchen Gadgets
- Gift Books
- Photo Albums
- Small Electronics
- Household Items

Terrific daycare/nursery books & toys

...and much, much more!

15 Locations Across Ontario

TORONTO • MISSISSAUGA
SCARBOROUGH • WINDSOR
LONDON • KITCHENER
NIAGARA FALLS • ST. CATHERINES
HAMILTON • BURLINGTON
OSHAWA / WHITBY • OTTAWA
NEWMARKET • BARRIE • NORTH BAY

Stores opening during October and remain open until December 24th. For Store locations, opening dates, hours and more information call toll free **1-877-305-3775** or visit our web site at **www.rizzco.com**

NEED FUNDRAISING PROGRAM? Call or visit our web site

RIZZCO TOY & GIFT OUTLET:
305 Supertest Road, North York
(Near Highland Farms)

Steeles Ave.
Supertest Rd.
Alness Ave. — RIZZCO TOY & GIFT OUTLET — Highland Farms — Dufferin St.
Finch Ave.

OCTOBER 23 TO DECEMBER 24
MON. - FRI. 10-6 • SAT. 10-5 • SUN. 10-4
Cash ■ Visa ■ Mastercard ■ Interac

Warehouse Outlet
KIDS WEAR
BOYS-GIRLS SIZE 6 MONTHS TO SIZE 10

frannie flowers™ **timmy tom tom™**

up to 50% OFF MSRP

Fleece, Leggings, Sweaters, T.Shirts, Dresses, Hats, Pants, Skirts, Polo Tops, Shorts, Tank Tops, Vests.

HOURS:
Mon.-Fri. 10:00 am-5:00 pm
Saturday 10:00 am-5:00 pm
Sunday Noon-5:00 pm
Cash, Visa, MC. Inter

Spotlite Kidswear
95 West Beaver Creek
Unit 15, Richmond Hill
(905) 882-1113

T-FAL® Factory Outlet

Visa, Mastercard, Interac, American Express

Markham Rd.	
	Tapscott Rd
Steeles Ave.	719 Tapscott Rd Unit B
Finch Ave.	

719 TAPSCOTT RD. UNIT B
MONDAY - SATURDAY 10:00AM - 5:00PM
SUNDAY 12:00 NOON - 5:00PM

Si Vous Play
SPORTS
Athletic Footwear & Leisure Wear

Always 20% - 60% off

- **Adidas**
- **Kappa**
- **CCM**
- **Converse**
- **Diadora**
- **Puma**
- **Fila**
- **Reebok**
- **Starter**
- **Nike**
- **Lotto**
- **Champion**

WAREHOUSE OUTLET
6931 Steeles Ave. W., Unit #2
Rexdale, ON M9W 6K7
416-675-9235
Wed-Fri 10:00am - 9:00pm
Sat 10:00am - 6:00pm

OSHAWA
902 Simco Street N. Unit #1
Oshawa, Ontario L1G 4W2
905-725-3339
Mon-Fri 10:00am - 8:00pm
Sat 10:00am - 6:00pm

Lawrence Square
700 Lawrence Ave. W.
North York, ON M6A 3B4
416-256-1501
Mon-Fri 10:00am - 9:00pm
Sat 10:00am - 6:00pm

Westwood Mall
7205 Goreway Dr.
Malton, ON L4T 2T9
905-677-4596
Mon-Fri 10:00am - 9:00pm
Sat 10:00am - 6:00pm

York Gate Mall
1 York Gate Blvd.
North York, ON M3N 3A1
416-650-5665
Mon-Fri 10:00am - 9:00pm
Sat 10:00am - 6:00pm

More New Stores!

Now more than 32 stores offering great quality, selection and savings, every day of the year*!

OPEN DAILY & WEEKNIGHTS TILL 9
Monday - Friday 9:30 - 9
Saturday 8:30 - 6, Sunday 12 - 5
* *Open every day except Dec. 25 and Jan. 1.*

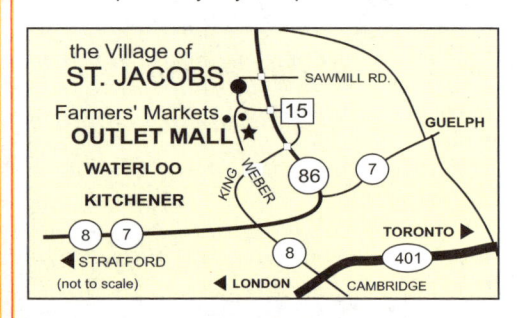

ST. JACOBS
OUTLET MALL

NORTH EDGE OF WATERLOO
From Conestoga Parkway (Hwy. 86) exit Rd. 15
left to Farmers Market Road   519-888-0138
www.stjacobs.com

- LEVI'S OUTLET
- REEBOK
- TOOTSIES
- LEGO
- JONES FACTORY FINALE
- ROYAL DOULTON
- FLORSHEIM SHOES
- CAMBRIDGE TOWEL & BEDDING
- CORNING REVERE
- PADERNO COOKWARE
- LIZ CLAIBORNE
- KODIAK
- WARNER'S INTIMATE APPAREL
- CADBURY

and more!

McGREGOR SOCKS® OUTLET STORES

*Stock up with McGregor Socks.
Great Brands. Great Value. Great Savings.*

DOWNTOWN
30 Spadina Ave.,(at Wellington St. West)
Telephone: (416) 593-5353 Ext. 344
Hours: Mon. to Sat., 10-5

ETOBICOKE
70 The East Mall,(at the Queensway)
Telephone: (416) 252-3716 Ext. 450
Hours: Mon. to Fri., 10-5

SCARBOROUGH
1360 Birchmount Rd.,(just north of Lawrence Ave.)
Telephone: (416) 751-5511
Hours: Tues. to Fri., 11-6 & Sat.10-5

Our Discount Policy:

3 Items 10% Discount
6 Items 20% Discount
12 Items 30% Discount
24 Items 40% Discount
36 Items or more 50% Discount

For additional savings ask for your club card membership!

Cash, Mastercard, Visa and Interac Accepted.

---

american essentials®

Calvin Klein

Levi's

essentials by McGregor

HAPPYFOOT®

DOCKERS

McGREGOR® PREMIUM

McGREGOR® SUPERSTAR®

McGREGOR® weekender®

Tom's Place

Since 1958

Men's & Women's Discounted Quality Business Fashions

Men's & Women's Suits from $149.99
Topcoats from $199.99
Men's & Women's Jackets from $74.99
Dress Shirts & Blouses from $49.99
Pants from $75.99
Leather Coats from $199.99
Ties & Accessories from $9.99

Save 20% to 60%

Tom's Place

190 Baldwin St.,
Kensington
Market
(just off Spadina Ave.)
TEL. 416-596-0297

HOURS:
Mon.-Wed. 10-6
Thurs.-Fri. 10-7
Saturday   9-6
Sunday   12-5

TONI+ PLUS

DESIGNER FASHIONS SIZES 14-22

SIZES 14-22

WAREHOUSE OUTLET

Save

30 to 90*

PERCENT OFF WOMEN'S DESIGNER LABELS

JONES NEW YORK • ELLEN TRACY • NYGARD • BRIAN BAILEY • RALPH LAUREN • VOTRE NOM

ANNE KLEIN II • DANA BUCHMAN • STUDIO JAX • EMANUEL • RALPH LAUREN • VOTRE

ASK ABOUT OUR FREQUENT BUYER CARD!

Monday to Saturday 10a.m. - 6p.m.
Sunday 12p.m. - 5p.m.

1140 SHEPPARD AVE. W. UNIT # 16
Telephone: (416) 633-9331 ext: 34
Just West of Allen Road.

*Sale at Toni Plus Warehouse Location Only.

Map: HWY 400, Kodiak Cr., TONI PLUS / Idomo Centre, Sheppard Ave. W., Allen Road, Downsview Subway Station, HWY 401

A27

Vendables Warehouse Sale

Great Savings! Great Giftware!!

- Kosta Boda
- Cristal J.G. Durand
- Fitz and Floyd
- Royal Worcester
- Schmid
- Spode

- Bowls • Platters • Brass
- Cannisters • Mugs
- Trays • Dinnerware
- Cookie Jars • Glasses
- Candlesticks • Planters
- Wind Chimes • Music Boxes • Candles • Bird Houses • Figurines
- Vases • Picture Frames
- and much, much more!

2000 Sale Dates
October 24-29
November 21-26
December 12-17

Sale Times: Tues., Wed., Thurs., Fri., 10-8 Sat., 10-5 Sun., 12-5

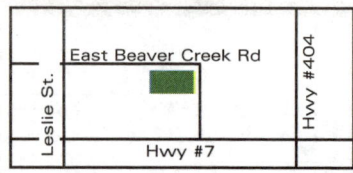

55 East Beaver Creek, Richmond Hill, ON
Entrance & Parking at rear
905-731-3187

The Comeback
Nearly New Ladies & Children's Wear

GREAT PRICES! FREQUENT REDUCTIONS!

Designer Fashions
Name Brands
Sizes Newborn to Ladies Plus

Mon. Tue. Wed. & Sat. 9:30am-5pm
THURSDAY 9:30am-8pm
FRIDAY 9:30am-6pm

4893 DUNDAS W
(at Burnhamthorpe)
ETOBICOKE
(416) 231-0381

MasterCard VISA Interac

Pasta Quistini — European Noodles

The Largest Selection of Pasta Products Under One Roof!

Your one stop Fresh Pasta House Specializing in Gourmet Pasta, Sauces, Spreads & Casseroles

Producers For Retail - Private Label - Wholesale & Industrial Sales

551 Jevlan Drive, Woodbridge, Ont. L4L 8W1 905-851-2030
email: PastaQueenPQI@AOL.com

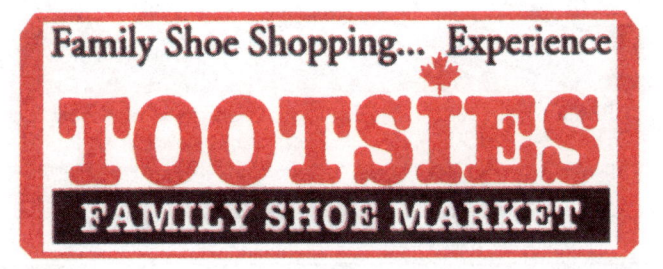

Try our Service & Prices on for Size... **They're a Great Fit!**

Family Shoe Shopping... Experience
TOOTSIES
FAMILY SHOE MARKET

C'om on In!
And
See Why We Let Our Shoes Do The Talking.

12 LOCATIONS TO SERVE YOU! SEE PAGE

SAVE up to 50%
on Bed, Bath & Linens

Get true outlet prices on - Bath Towels • Comforters • Sheets • Table Linens
Bedspreads • Bed Sets® • Sheets that fit extra thick mattresses • T-Shirt Sheets
Hypo Allergenic Bedding • Duvets • Quilts • Decorator Pillows • Mattress Pads
Throws • Bath Rugs • Kitchen Textiles • Shower Curtains • Much More!

MARTEX • LADY PEPPERELL • STEVENS • UTICA • VELLUX • OTHER FAMOUS BRANDS

10% Off your entire store purchase!

LAST NAME   PLEASE PRINT   FIRST   Expires September 15, 2001

ADDRESS

CITY/PROVINCE

POSTAL CODE

EMAIL ADDRESS

STORE USE ONLY
DATE   STORE   AMOUNT OF PURCHASE

NO ADJUSTMENTS MADE ON PREVIOUS PURCHASES. LIMIT ONE PER FAMILY. NOT GOOD WITH ANY OTHER OFFER OR DISCOUNT

015598

WestPoint Stevens
BED BATH & LINENS
FACTORY OUTLET

MISSISSAUGA, ONTARIO
HWY 401 • HWY 10 • HWY 401 • BRITANNIA RD.
WESTPOINT STEVENS FACTORY OUTLET • AVEBURY RD. • HOLIDAY

5800 Avebury Road • First Street West Of Hwy 10 Off Britannia
Phone: 905-712-8999 • We Accept Competitors' Coupons!

AG LIQUIDATION
NAME - BRANDS AT NO - NAME PRICES

SAVE up to **50 - 70 %** off Retail on NAME - BRAND Designer Perfumes, Cosmetics and Health & Beauty Aids. We also Carry Houseware, Books, Stationary, Jewellary and a wide range of Gift Items.

One-stop X-mas shopping as you will find gift-wrap paper, stocking-stuffers and something for everyone on your list.

Location: 2575 Steeles Ave. E.
Unit 13, Brampton
Southeast corner of Steeles & Torbram Rds
Telephone: (905) 799-0313
Open year round
Starting September 1st.

GIANT
WAREHOUSE SALES TWICE A YEAR

Cosmetics & Accessories
Great Gift Ideas for the whole family

☆ Witchcraft Nail Care Products
☆ Shower Gels & Sponges
☆ Lipstick & Nailpolish
☆ Cosmetic Pencils
☆ Cosmetic Bags
☆ Kids Products
☆ Shampoos
& Much more...

DAREE SALES LTD.
5486 Gorvan Dr.
Mississauga
905-624-3359

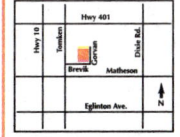

SAVE UP TO 70%

Bath n' Bedtime
your decor store

CROSCILL • FIELDCREST • ROYAL VELVET • SPRINGMAID
WAMSUTTA • SEALY • REYMAN • MARTEX • LAURA ASHLEY • DAN RIVER

Ontario's Largest Selection of Designer Bedding & Bathroom Accessories

GUARANTEED LOWEST PRICES ANYWHERE IN CANADA

TORONTO:
Lawrence Plaza, Bathurst & Lawrence **(416) 781-8600**
PICKERING:
Pickering Home & Leisure, 401 & Brock Rd. **(905) 428-0007**
LONDON:
Crossroads Centre, Exeter & Wellington **(519) 686-1759**
STONEY CREEK:
410 Lewis Rd., Unit #15, Stoney Creek **(905) 643-2114**

Shop Us On The Net at www.bathnbed.com

Notes

PASTA QUISTINI INC.
This outlet is small but the savings are huge with pasta seconds (edges may be cut slightly crooked or they produced too much of one style) selling at $4.99 for 2 kilos! Product is manufactured on the premise from top grade, hard durham wheat with both fresh and flash frozen for purchase. It's Kosher and much is suitable for diabetics. Producing about 215 varieties of pasta (not all at once!) they can do large custom orders and normally supply restaurants, hotels and grocery stores. Sauces are also made and sold in small containers and up to 4 litre pails. Note that it is cash or cheque witgh ID only.

Location: 551 Jevlan Drive (south off Langstaff betweek Hwy 400 and Weston Rd.) Wood bridge
Telephone: (905) 851-2030

See advertisement on page A28

PASTACO
Another family owned and managed business, supplying top quality noodle and pasta dishes to smaller high-end restaurants and cooking schools. The small outlet offers some specialty dietary dishes as well. Save on bulk orders. Cash only.

Location: 1140 Sheppard Ave. W., Unit 14 (west of Allen Rd.), Downsview.
Hours: M. to Sat. 8:30 - 6
Telephone: (416) 630-3635

PFALZGRAF CANADA INC.
This company makes and supplies those high-quality, proportioned, quick-frozen cakes to the hospitality industry. At this outlet, you can go in and select one for yourself.

Location: 90 Saunders Rd., Units 4 & 5, Barrie.
Hours: M. to F. 7 - 6
Telephone: (705) 739-8980

QZINA WAREHOUSE SALE
Who can resist the lure of delectable Belgium chocolates? Especially at wholesale prices. This company distributes a wide line of chocolates that includes Belgium truffles, seashells, chocolate bars and those delectable hedgehogs........open for a limited time only. As well, they also import olive oil and pasta which you'll find at the sale. No credit cards. December warehouse sale.

Location: 110 Woodbine Downs Blvd, Unit 3 (north of Finch Avenue, west of Hwy 27), Etobicoke.
Telephone: (416) 675-2282
Hours: Call for sale hours

REINHARDT FOODS - FACTORY OUTLET
Located in the town of Stayner and a major employer for a very long time, this company produces several types of vinegar as well as distributing for Jaffa and Dalton. Product is in 'food service' sizing and includes seventeen types of pie filling in 6 and 12 kilo pails; coconut in 4.54 kilo bags for approx. $12 each; glace fruits; raisins and dates and several types and sizes of vinegars. You do need to pre-order, pickup either Tuesday or Thursday and it's cash or cheque with ID.

Location: 214 King St. N., (northwest corner at Hwy. 26 and Airport Rd.), Stayner.
Hours: Office is open M. to F. 8-5 for ordering with pick ups on Tuesday or Thursday.
Telephone: (705) 428-2422. Call for a price list.

RENEE'S GOURMET
Brand names such as Renee's Gourmet & Excelle fat-free, no-oil dressings & numerous private label salad dressings & sauces, are being cleared at up to 80% off. Cash only.

Location: 1880 Ormont Dr. (3 blocks N. of Finch Ave. and W. off Weston Rd.), Toronto.
Hours: M. to F. 8:30 - 5
Telephone: (416) 744-2124, 1-888-4-RENEES

THE SALAD KING
Why not try some of the wonderful salads, lasagnas, chicken pot pies and more, available through this small factory outlet. Located on the manufacturing premises, this spotless outlet offers fresh food attractively priced. The three-pound chicken pot pie is stuffed with more chicken than we'd ever seen. Vegetarian, chicken or meat lasagnas are also available in five pound sizes. Coleslaws, desserts and ready-to-bake natural muffin mixes are also sold.

Location: 896 Lakeshore Rd. E. (between Dixie and Cawthra Rds.), Mississauga.
Hours: M. to F. 9-5 (Summer hours open Sat. 9 - 1)
Telephone: (905) 891-1912

SARA LEE - BAKERY OUTLET
This outlet carries the complete line of Sara Lee cake and pastry products at discounted prices. Savings fluctuate depending on inventory levels. It is mainly seconds that are sold in the outlet locations, but there is nothing wrong with either the quality or the ingredients: generally they have been classified as seconds because of minor cosmetic glitches! Cash only.

Location: 379 Orenda Road, Bramalea.
Hours: M. to F. 9:30 - 5, Sat. 9 - 5
Telephone: (905) 791-3147

SEAFOOD DEPOT
If you've ventured to the Eddie Bauer Outlet, you might also want to check out the awesome selection of seafood at this huge warehouse which is next door. It's the variety, freshness and quality that make it 'shoestring' material with pricing on your basic live lobster between $7.99 and $8.99 a pound.
Location: 81 Aviva Park Dr., Woodbridge.
Hours: M. & Sat. 9 - 5, T. & W. 9 - 6, Thu. 9 - 7, Fri. 9 - 8.
Telephone: (905) 856-2770 or 1-800-563-6222

SIENA FOODS/COLIO WINES - OUTLET STORE
Definitely not your usual outlet, but a rather fabulous shopping experience that still offers good value. This outlet offers traditional favourites like salami, as well as specialty cuts, pasta, specialty cheese and olive oils. Meats are available cut and vacuum-packed, with the best savings in bulk products. There are a number of unique products, as well as a cappuccino, espresso bar, and a wine bar where the sales professionals will advise you by letting you taste the wines.
Location: 2300 Haines Rd. (north of the Queensway between Cawthra and Dixie Rds.), Mississauga.
Hours: M. to F., 9: 30 - 6, Sat. 9 - 5
Telephone: (905) 275-0044

SIMON'S SMOKEHOUSE - FACTORY OUTLET
This manufacturing plant in Brampton has opened a factory outlet store, specializing in naturally wood-smoked hams, bacon, European salami and fresh frozen meat products. Prices are usually lower than advertised grocery meat specials and the quality and variety are first-class.
Location: 220 Clarence St. (between Steeles Ave. and Queen St., east of Kennedy Rd.), Brampton.
Hours: M. to W. 9 - 5, Thu. & F. 9 – 7; Sat. 9-5
Telephone: (905) 453-1822

TOMEK's NATURAL PRESERVES
This tiny outlet carries great specialty food products which are homemade and very fresh. We tried the dill pickles and thought they were terrific, and husband Brian who loves herring pronounced it one of the best ever. Dill pickles are $3/kilo, sauerkraut is $2.20/kilo and perogies are $2.99/dozen. Red and white borscht is ready to eat and reasonably priced at $2.50 for a large jar. Maybe your mother in law will think you cooked all day!
Location: 9 Advance Road (south of Bloor St. between Kipling Ave. and Islington Ave.), Toronto.
Hours: M. to F. 8-6, Sat. 8-4, Closed Sun.
Telephone: (416) 234-1943

TRE MARI BAKERY - FACTORY OUTLET
This commercial bakery has an outlet on the premises that sells overruns from the day. All products are fresh and selection varies daily. Advance notice is required for large orders. Cash only.

Location: 41 Shorncliffe Rd. (south off Dundas St. and west of Kipling Ave.), Etobicoke.
Hours: M. to Sat. 9 - 6, Sun. 10 - 4
Telephone: (416) 233-3800

VANHORN SEAFOOD WHOLESALE - FISH DISTRIBUTORS
Harry the inspector is there to make sure all products are grade A. As one of Canada's largest distributors of fresh and frozen seafood, this outlet has almost every imaginable type of fish, from shark to sole. Prices are excellent and their inventory includes many other types of food products, from frozen vegetables and chicken to dressings and pasta, but may only be available in large quantity or bulk packages. Terms are cash and carry.

Location: 2101 Lawrence Avenue E., Scarborough, Ontario
Hours: M. & Sat. 9 – 6, Tues to Fri. 9 - 7; Sun. 10 - 5
Telephone: (416) 288-9286

VOORTMAN COOKIES
To many of us, Voortman cookies are a household staple. If you're entertaining this weekend, particularly if you'll have a house or cottage full of kids, why not stock up at the retail store, which offers a complete range of freshly baked cookies at discount prices. Prices are generally discounted 25%, but may be even less if you buy in bulk.

Location: 4455 North Service Rd. (exit from the Q.E.W. at Appleby Line), Burlington.
Hours: M. to F. 8:15 - 4:30
Telephone: (905) 335-9500

Isn't it a bit unnerving that doctorscall what they do "practice?"

WESTON BAKERY OUTLET -FACTORY OUTLET STORE
Overruns, day olds, production seconds and bulk bakery goods are sold at least 50% off retail prices. Inventory changes frequently and there are often daily specials. Terms are cash only.

Location: **1425 The Queensway (east of Hwy. 427), Etobicoke.**
Hours: M. to F. 8 - 6, Sat. 8 - 5
Telephone: (416) 252-7323
Location: **462 Eastern Ave. (at Logan Ave.), Toronto.**
Hours: M. to F. 9 - 6, Sat. 8 - 4
Telephone: (416) 465-5601
Location: **also in Peterborough (705) 742-4211, Orillia, Kitchener, Kingston and Sudbury.**

WILLIES MERCANTILE
Exclusive to Willies are the 2 kilo pails of Reinhardt pie filling and they carry the rest of their lines of glace fruit, vinegars etc. in family sizing - all at excellent pricing too. Willies is also a very neat craft store that is sure to have something of interest for everyone, and again well priced - perfect to fill in the après ski hours! A special "Garden Room" was opened this summer.

Location: **236 Huron St., (turn south off Hwy. 26/Main St. at the TD Bank), Stayner.**
Telephone: (705) 428-5722.
Hours: M. to F. 9:30 - 5:30, Sat. 9-5, closed Mondays in Jan/Feb.

Food Fair

> What do you do when you see an endangered animal eating an endangered plant?

T.B.A. TO BE ANNOUNCED - DATES NOT AVAILABLE AT PRESS TIME

THIS SYMBOL INDICATES WAREHOUSE SALES

for the home

- Home Furnishings & Appliances
- Home Decorating & Housewares
- Fabrics & Linens

for the home

Home Furnishings & Appliances

ADVANCE FURNITURE LTD.
Heads up university students and others furnishing homes on tight budgets - 14,000 square feet of used hotel furniture from some of the better names in the hospitality industry are gathered here for you to hunt through. Some items are very well used while other pieces need minor refurbishing. Hundreds of lamps with shades are just $20 each and pictures start at $10.
Location: 2500 Lawrence Ave. E., (both Advance and the Scarborough Door Factory are on the north side of Lawrence Ave. E., just west of Midland and accessed by going south under the east side of the bridge), Scarborough.
Hours: Weekdays 10-8:30, Saturday 9-5.
Telephone: (416)-757-2444

ANDERSON'S FINE FURNITURE
This terrific furniture store has great furniture, great prices and a commitment to customer service. Let Gary Anderson help you choose the right sofa, casual dining furniture, bedroom furniture or assessories as well as the right fabric.
Location: 2100 Bloor St. West, (North side of Bloor between Runnymede & High Park Ave.) Toronto.
Hours: Tues.- Fri. 10-7 Sat 10-6, Sun. 10-5
Telephone: (416) 762-2666

ART IN IRON - FACTORY OUTLET SHOWROOM
Art In Iron manufactures a wide range of affordable, quality wrought iron products, from beds and tables to candelabras, plus an extensive range of home furnishings. Reasonable prices. Custom work available. Take a look at the new flower shop recently opened which also carries giftware and greeting cards.
Location: 291 Jane St., (north of Bloor St.), Toronto.
Hours: M. to Sat. 10 - 6, Sun. 12 - 5
Telephone: (416) 762-7777

See advertisement on page A3

Home Furnishings & Appliances

BARRYMORE - FURNITURE MANUFACTURER 💲
Since 1919, Barrymore has been manufacturing some of North America's finest upholstered furniture right here in Toronto. It has supplied items to Canadian embassies around the world, and to such renowned retailers as Harrods of London. Once a year Barrymore sells their factory made sofas and chairs at up to 20% off their factory prices, and during this sale there will be no GST as well. Customize your furniture selection by choosing seat depth, the firmness of the cushions as well as size and you'll be sure to get exactly what you want. January Warehouse Sale.

Location: **1137 King St. W. (four blocks east of Dufferin St.), Toronto.**
Hours: M. to Sun. 10 - 6, Thu. 10 - 8 all year-round
Telephone: (416) 532-2891

BARTOLINI DESIGN STUDIO
The selection of plaster or concrete items is huge & varied with great pricing. Choose from hundreds of different designs for bird baths, planters, sconces, pedestals, candle holders, gargoyles & cherubs. This is the actual factory and it certainly makes the trip interesting. It is small, however, therefore some items may not be priced. August Warehouse Sale.

Location: **244 Brockport Dr., Unit 20 (first road west of Hwy. 27 and north off Belfield Rd.) Toronto.**
Hours: M. to F. 9 - 5:30, call for Sat. hours
Telephone: (416) 675-7249

THE BOMBAY COMPANY OUTLET STORE 💲
Discontinued and slightly damaged pieces of its British-inspired home furnishings are available at 35% or more off regular retail prices. The huge warehouse at Kennedy Rd., just north of Hwy. 401 in Mississauga also has a once-a-year warehouse sale that is to die for! August Warehouse Sale.

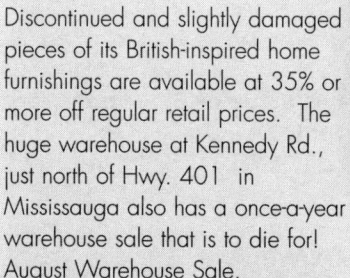

Location: Dixie Outlet Mall, 1250 South Service Rd. (Dixie Rd. and the Q.E.W.), Mississauga.
Hours: M. to F. 10 - 9, Sat. 10 - 6, Sun. 12 - 6
Telephone: (905) 278-5259

BOMBAY
OUTLET STORE

Discover fabulous finds in classic and timeless furniture, prints and home accessories! Special Purchase Outlet product along with discontinued, slightly damaged and/or overstocked home furnishings, all at wonderful prices!

DIXIE OUTLET MALL
1250 South Service Road, Mississauga
(Dixie Road and the QEW)

STORE HOURS: M - Friday 10am - 9pm
Saturday 9:30am - 6pm • Sunday 12 - 6pm

CAMCO TENT SALE 💲

Most of us recognize the CAMCO name as the company that manufactures and distributes GE, Hotpoint, Moffat and McClary appliances. Now is the time to visit them as they sell their factory uncrates, scratch & dent and end of line appliances at considerable savings. One year functional warranty on all products. Cash and carry.

Location: **5130 Dixie Road (north of Eglinton Ave., first plaza on the left), Mississauga. Back parking lot.**
Hours: Call for dates & time.
Telephone: (905) 602-5307

DANBY APPLIANCES - SCRATCH AND DENT WAREHOUSE SALE 💲

Danby is North Americas leader in compact appliances and will be clearing through the loading bays hundreds of microwaves, freezers, air conditioners, dehumidifiers, washing machines and dryers, stoves and refrigerators. Cash and VISA only. Wheel chair accessible. An extremely popular sale, its well worth the drive because of the excellent savings. This annual sale is traditionally held on the Mother's Day weekend. Call for confirmation of date and time.

Location: **Hwy. 24 and Whitelaw Rd., (Hwy 401 west from Toronto, north on Hwy. 6, left on Hwy. 24, right at 3rd stoplight), Guelph,**
Hours: M. to F. 10-3 Closed weekends and holidays.
Telephone: (519) 837-0920.

DESIGNERS WALK GARAGE SALE 💲

Forty different furniture, fabric and lighting companies are gathering together to clear out samples and overstocked items for the home. There will also be a silent auction in support of the Starlight Childrens Foundation. Cash and carry. June Warehouse Sale. Call for details

Location: **Designers Walk Bldg. #5, 160 Pears Ave. (one block north of Davenport Rd., go west off Avenue Rd.),**
Telephone: (416) 961-1211.

T.B.A. TO BE ANNOUNCED - DATES NOT AVAILABLE AT PRESS TIME

💲 THIS SYMBOL INDICATES WAREHOUSE SALES

Home Furnishings & Appliances

DISCOUNT INTERIOR DESIGN WAREHOUSE 💰

This outlet carries just about everything for the home, including furniture and accessories, fabric and wall coverings. They have a fantastic garage sale the first Saturday after Labour Day with bargains of 80 % off retail pricing.

Location: 4155 Fairview St., Unit 16 (south of the Q.E.W. between Appleby Line and Walkers Line), Burlington.
Hours: M. to Thu. 10 - 5:30, F. 10 - 8, Sat. 10 - 5:30
Telephone: (905) 634-3439

EXCELLENCE IN ART - WHOLESALE OUTLET

Why not a 'faux' for your wall? If you've a desire for a Degas, or maybe a Monet or Matisse, and are unable to afford an original, here's the spot. Prices run from several hundred to a couple of thousand dollars and you can pick up a replica of something famous. This outlet also carries those deep and decadent frames that are ideal for mirrors or framing your own masterpieces, and these are extremely well priced.

Location: 860 Denison St., Unit 6, Markham.
Telephone: (905) 305-0177

EXECUTIVE FURNITURE RENTALS

Perhaps you're decorating for a student, or simply need to fill in some empty spaces, but whatever the reason, now's the time to pick up some well used furniture from this rental shop. Lots of furniture, including sofas, loveseats, desks, dinettes, bedroom furniture and much more. All items priced at $199 or less.

Location: 81 Tycos Drive (6 blocks south of Lawrence Ave., west off Dufferin Street), Toronto.
Hours: M. to F. 9 - 5:30, Sat. 10 - 12
Telephone: (416) 785-0932

Closed on weekends throughout the summer (July to August). Please call for details.
See advertisement on page A8

THE GRACIOUS LIVING CENTRE

This company clears substantial quantities of high-end acrylic furniture, as well as acrylic tubs, shower bases and sinks. Prices range from 30% off bathware to 25% off acrylic furniture. Some glass tops are also available. Cash, MasterCard and Visa (on purchases over $200 only) accepted.

Location: 160 West Beaver Creek Rd. (near Hwy. 7 & Leslie St.), Richmond Hill.
Hours: M. to F. 10 - 6, Sat. 10 - 5
Telephone: (905) 731-4556

G H JOHNSON TRADING
Look for the 950 on the exterior to find 30,000 square feet of decor and furnishings on the interior. This treasure trove, long shopped by the design trade and not advertised any where, is crammed with well priced pieces suitable for any home.
Location: 950 Dupont St. Toronto
Hours: M to Saturday 10-5, Sunday 12-5.
Telephone: (416) 532-6700
See advertisement on page A12

HAUSER FURNITURE - FACTORY DIRECT 💰
This company, a well known name in patio furniture, has been manufacturing in their Waterloo factory for over 35 years. They have multiple locations, so please call for a complete list. They no longer sell through retail outlets, but offer a complete line of all-weather wicker, cast aluminum, extruded aluminum and wrought iron furniture at 40% off suggested retail prices. Once a year Hauser sells their high quality lawn and patio furniture at specially reduced prices. They do not carry resin or plastic
Location: 10815 Bathurst Street, (Bathurst St. & Elgin Mills Road), Richmond Hill.
Hours: T. to F. 10 - 6, Sat. 10 - 6, Sun. 12 - 5
Telephone: (905) 770-8742
Location: 1570 Clarkson Rd. N., Mississauga.
Hours: T. to F. 10 - 6, Sat. 10 - 6, Sun. 12 - 5
Telephone: (905) 855-5291

HERITAGE CASTING AND IRONWORKS - FACTORY OUTLET 💰
This manufacturer offers a wide selection of cast aluminum garden furniture, as well as lamp posts, benches, planters, fountains and much more. It also offers a unique service of custom finishing, with a rainbow of colours, including antique finishes. By selling directly from its manufacturing facility, it is able to price competitively.
Location: 1280 Fewster Dr., (Dixie Rd. & Eglinton Ave.), Mississauga.
Hours: M. to F. 8 - 4
Telephone: (905) 238-2648

HERITAGE INTERIORS
Bring samples of your own fabrics to match colours at this warehouse sale of designer sofas, chairs, tables, cabinets, dining suites, lamps & accessories. Many are one-of-a-kind. November Warehouse Sale.
Location: 1100 Sheppard Avenue West, Toronto.
Hours: M. to W. 10 - 6, Thu. & F. 10 - 8, Sat. 10 - 6
Telephone: (416) 398-5560

Home Furnishings & Appliances

IDOMO
Idomo is currently clearing out their warehouse and offering a number of furniture items at substantial savings. They are also Canada's largest retailer of rustic Mexican furniture, at prices that can't be beat anywhere in North America. Check out their 5-drawer Mexican CD tower for only $129.00. Wheelchair accessible. Website is www.idomo.com

Location: 1100 Sheppard Ave. West (at Allen Road, north of the 401, top of Spadina subway), Toronto.
Hours: M to Friday 10-9, Saturday 10-6, Sunday 12-5
Telephone: (416) 630-3622

LEDA'S ATTIC - FURNITURE MANUFACTURER'S OUTLET
To reach the 'attic' on the second floor, one strolls through the beautifully furnished showroom of Leda's various high quality furniture lines - pricing and current product is available through the regular retail dealers. Up the back stairs are dealer returns, discontinued pieces, market samples and various showroom accessory pieces - all available at great discounts.

Location: 350 Clayson Rd., (north off Wilson Ave., just west of Hwy. 400), North York.
Hours: T. to Thu. 10 - 3, Sat. 10 - 1
Telephone: (416) 745-9588

LEISURELAND
Reconditioned air conditioners are sold here for half the price of a new one with the usual full warranty.

Location: 418 Consumers Rd., North York.
Hours: Hours are seasonal, please call for details.
Telephone: (416) 492-2665

LITE KING
Need to light up your life? Or someone else's? These folks manufacture all sorts of lamps, ranging from table and floor lamps to torchieres - and need to clear out their older lines or discontinued styles. All lamps are at least 50% off regular price, and you'll find some really unique pieces - as space is really tight in this original factory location, please do not bring any children. Cash and Visa only

Location: 779 Richmond St. West (at the corner of Niagara St.), Toronto.
Hours: M. to F. 9 - 4:15
For weekend sales, please call for dates and times.
Telephone: (416) 504-LITE (5483)

MARBLE DEPOT
A builder friend, Bob, tipped us off to this outlet that has exceptional buys on slate, marble, granite and limestone. He emphasized that he really appreciates being able to browse and open skids to inspect the product before buying. They also carry 'feature strips' for that finishing touch, and inventory is always coming and going.

Location: 900 Caledonia Rd., (1 block south of Lawrence Ave.), Toronto.
Hours: M. to F. 8 - 5:30, Sat. 8 - 5
Telephone: (416) 787-0391 or 1-800-379-1111

MORETTE'S FURNITURE
Morette's has long been known for their quality funiture for 40 years. At Morette's you choose not only your fabric, but also your furniture option – for example, the shape of the arms or legs, as well as the stain. Their factory is located nearby. It's a wonderful drive, and to make it even more memorable, stop in for lunch at the Tea House right beside Morette's.

Location: West on the 401 to Trafalgar Road. North 35 km. To Hillsburg - can't miss it on the main street
Hours: M. to Sat. 9:30 - 5:30, F. 9:30 - 9:30
Telephone: (519) 855-4905 or (905) 846-2907

Morette's FURNITURE INC.

Makers of
Fine Upholstered Furniture

Re-Upholstering Service Available

Visit our showrooms
Wide selection of Fabrics

HILLSBURGH, ONTARIO • 1-519-855-4905
NORTH OFF HIGHWAY 401
AT TRAFALGAR RD. 35 KM.

Home Furnishings & Appliances

> If a man is standing in the middle of the forest speaking and there is no woman around to hear him...is he still wrong?

Home Furnishings & Appliances

MOSSMAN'S APPLIANCE PARTS LTD. - PARTS DISTRIBUTOR
Many repair people rely on Mossman's for parts, & the public can purchase here too! With 4 locations in the Metro area, another in Ottawa and one in Winnipeg, their computers (using your make, model & serial) will tell you in a minute what you need & the closest location. Their new location in Pickering is now 40,000 square feet.

Location: 2273 Dundas St. W., Unit 12, Mississauga.
Hours: M. to F. 8 - 6, Sat. 9 - 3
Telephone: (905) 569-8333

Location: 651 McCowan Rd., Scarborough
Hours: M. to F. 8 - 6, Sat. 9 - 3
Telephone: (416) 431-2222

Location: 922 Dillingham Road, (first street south of Bayly St. running off of Brock Rd.) Pickering.
Hours: M. to F. 8 - 6, Sat. 9 - 1
Telephone: (905) 831-2222

Location: 876 Bathurst St., Toronto.
Hours: M. to F. 8 – 6, Sat. 9 - 3
Telephone: (416) 532-2526

MUSKOKA FURNITURE OUTLET
This shop liquidates merchandise of all kinds, so you're likely to find anything from furniture to clothing.

Location: 195 Wellington St. N., Unit 7 (Wellington Place Mall), Bracebridge.
Hours: Regular Hours: M. - Thu. & Sat. 9 - 6, F. 9 - 9
Summer Hours: M. to F. 9 - 9, Sat. 9 - 6, Sun. 12 - 4
Telephone: (705) 645-8183

SEARS CLEARANCE CENTRES
Another place where stock comes and goes quickly and with the deals they offer on such things as major appliances it's no wonder! Scratch and dent, returns and floor models alike still come with a one year guarantee and in a wide range of price points and brand names. Good deals on furnishings and excellent deals on mattresses especially if you don't need the two pieces to match.

Location: 2200 Islington Ave., Rexdale.
Telephone: (416) 401-4545

Location: 253 Queen St. E., Brampton
Telephone: (905) 796-6450

Location: Dixie Outlet Mall, Mississauga.
Telephone: (905) 278-6400
Hours: Weekdays 10-9, Saturday 9:30-6 and Sunday 12-5.
Note: Rexdale location is open weekdays 10-9, Saturday 9-6 and Sunday 11-5.

SESCOLITE - LIGHTING CLEARANCE CENTRE
Look in the back of the regular showroom for a great selection of well-priced lighting fixtures and lamps.
Location: 4175 Fairview St., Burlington.
Hours: M. to W. 8:30 - 6, Thur. 8:30 - 9, F. 8:30 - 6, Sat. 9:30 - 6, Sun. 12 - 4 (closed Sundays during Summer)
Telephone: (905) 632-8659

SHAW-PEZZO & ASSOCIATES INC.
These are upscale, quality U.S. designer upholstered pieces with substantially reduced pricing on selected floor models at this unassuming warehouse. Their inventory varies with each sale occurring in July and January.
Location: 80 Wingold Ave. (south of Lawrence Ave. and west off Dufferin St.), Toronto.
Hours: M. to F. 9 - 5, Sat. 10 - 5
Telephone: (416) 784-4400

STEPTOE & WIFE ANTIQUES LTD. - ANNUAL SALE
Wonderful and eclectic decor pieces for the home and garden - everything from cast iron to Lincrusta wallcover to who knows what! Once a year, this shop holds its sale of interesting and offbeat home decor and architectural restoration products. These items are discontinued designs, samples, overstocks and seconds. Look for iron castings, garden torch lights, embossed wallcoverings, drapery hardware and other eclectic items. You might just find that perfect item that has eluded you so far. The warehouse sale is usually in May.
Location: 322 Geary Ave. (one block north of Dupont St., west off Dufferin St.) Toronto.
Hours: M. to F. 9 - 5
Telephone: (416) 530-4200 or 1-800-461-0060

ELTE CARPETS
The Summerhill Hardware display is a cabinet makersdream but the deals are in the Backyard room where everything is mainly 50 per cent off - more or less. Wall to wall savings on area rugs, furniture, bathroom fixtures, decorative hardware and more. Come in with your measurements and find great savings on broadloom remnants on the roll, as well as upholstered furniture pieces and flor models. Don't forget to visit the backyard at Ginger's with substantial savings on kitchen and bath items. Web site: www.elte.com
Location: 80 Ronald Ave., (two blocks west of Dufferin Ave., north off Eglinton Ave.) Toronto
Hours: M to Sat 9-6, later on Thurs until 9 and Sun 12-5
Telephone: 416-785-7885; Toll Free 1-888-276-3583

TERRACOTTA HOUSE AND SALTILLO IMPORTS
Our thanks to Ida who mentioned this fabulous find - especially noteworthy if you're building a villa or are mad about Mexico. There are excellent buys on Mexican tile of every description as well as good deals on a wide selection of rustic Mexican pine furniture, ceramic tableware, neat hand painted ceramic sinks and wonderful metal home accessories.

Location: **Saltillo Imports is at 132 Railside Rd., Unit 8, (2 blocks east of Don Valley Parkway and south of Lawrence Ave.), Toronto.**
Hours: M. to F. 9 - 6, Sat. 10 - 4
Telephone: (416) 441-2224
Location: **Terracotta House, 206 Dupont St., Toronto.**
Hours: M. to T. & Sat. 10 - 6, W. to F. 10 - 8, Sun. 12 - 5.
Telephone: (416) 966-1698.

THE URBAN MODE
Terrific buys on household furniture & accessories. You will realize up to 50% off retail prices on ends-of-lines & clearout merchandise during sales.

Location: **389 Queen St. W., (east of Spadina Ave.), Toronto.**
Hours: Hours change daily. Please call for hours.
Telephone: (416) 591-8834

VANI METAL ART - FACTORY OUTLET
You can see them hand forging and clipping pieces together into various home furnishings at this small factory without even a sign. Those who are familiar with craftsman quality will appreciate that the ends are actually forged and not just turned into a curl. Goran is also willing to do custom work and show you pictures of past projects. The place is tiny and the prices are not 'cheap' but are certainly good value for the quality.

Location: **6923 Steeles Ave. W., Units 56 & 57, (west of Hwy. 7, look for the wrought iron in the windows!), Etobicoke.**
Hours: Call for hours.
Telephone: (416) 213-0515

> Where do forest rangers go to "get away from it all?"

for the home

Home Decorating & Housewares

ACADIA CANDLE OUTLET STORE
We dropped in to this store en route to the African Lion Safari. Their store ships to countries around the world, and they pride themselves on their fragrant candle jars and votive candles. Buy five votives, and get one free. Buy two large jar candles and get one medium free. Lots of selection and good prices.

Location: Carlisle Road & Hwy. 6, Flamborugh. Take Hwy 401 and exit at Hwy 6 - go south approximately 4 km.
Hours: M to Fri 10- 6:00
           Sat 9 - 6, Sun noon - 5
Telephone: 1-905-777-9638

ALDERBROOK INDUSTRIES
Give new meaning to 'start early' when you shop and save from 30 to 70% off retail prices on a wide variety of Christmas ornaments, lights, decorations and artificial Christmas trees. Do bring your own large bags, although they will have some for sale, and don't bring the kids - children under 16 are not allowed in for safety reasons. No cheques are accepted, they do take VISA and debit cards but the cash lines are the fastest. T.B.A. Warehouse Sale.
Location: 885 Sandy Beach Rd., Pickering.
Telephone: (905) 420-0494

ARORA
There are two service centre locations that sell new and refurbished small electrical appliances and personal care products. All products come with a full warranty at prices 30 - 50% lower than suggested retail prices. Many brands are available.
Location: 488 Bloor St. W. (1 block E. of Bathurst St.), Toronto.
Hours: M. to F. 10 - 7, Sat. 10 - 6, Sun. 12 - 5
Telephone: (416) 532-8544
Location: 926 Bloor St. W. (1 block W. of Ossington subway), Toronto.
Hours: M. to Sat. 10 - 6
Telephone: (416) 588-9728

Home Decorating & Housewares

AURORA COLLECTIBLE FINE CHINA & CRYSTAL 💰
Clearance of brand name crystal and china such as Waterford, Royal Doulton, Baccarat and Wallace & International Sterling Silver. Aurora also carries many pieces of hard-to-find, discontinued lines with savings up to 90% off. October and November Warehouse Sale

Location: 1610 Midland Ave. (east of Kennedy Rd. and south of Lawrence Ave.), Scarborough.
Hours: M., T. & Sat. 10 - 6, W. & F. 10 - 8, Sun. 12. - 5
Telephone: (416) 752-9300 or 1-800-668-3333

BARTOLINI 💰
The plaster dust is always flying while this small manufacturer produces its wide range of items such as candle sticks, pedestals, planters and gargoyles. Shoppers will find excellent bargains on seconds and we invariably find something new in concrete or plaster to tuck in to the garden or home. Cash or cheques with ID. Call for warehouse sale dates and hours.

Location: 244 Brockport Dr., Unit 20, (first road west of hwy. 27, go north off Belfield Rd.) Toronto
Hours: M. to F. 9-5:30

BATH 'N BEDTIME DECOR STORE
This is the best location for bedding, bath, pictures, lamps and décor items. Choose form Fieldcrest, Springmaid, Martex, Dan River and many other well-known designer names, as well as a wide selection of bathroom accessories and tableware. Semi-annual warehouse sale mid May and mid November. For store hours please call the store or visit our Website www.bathnbed.com.

Location: 502 Lawrence Ave. West (Lawrence Plaza, Bathurst and Lawrence)
Telephone: (416) 781-8600
Location: 1755 Pickering Parkway (Pickering Home & Leisure, 401 and Brock Road)
Telephone: (905) 428-0007
Location: 765 Exeter Road (Crossroads Centre, Exeter & Wellington), London
Telephone: (519) 686-1759
Location: Stoney Creek Décor Centre, 410 Lewis Rd,, Unit 15, Stoney Creek
Telephone: (905) 643-2114

See advertisement on page A31

BENIX AND CO. - WAREHOUSE OUTLET STORE 💲
Benix and Co., an importer and wholesaler of fine china, housewares and chandeliers offers every day savings of 50 to 70%. The showroom is clean, the merchandise is well displayed and the service is excellent. T.B.A. Warehouse Sales.
Location: 127 Cartwright Ave. (south of Hwy. 401, west off Dufferin St.), North York.
Hours: M. to F. 10 - 9, Sat. & Sun. 10 - 6
Telephone: (416) 784-0732

BLACK & DECKER CANADA INC.
Occasionally the Black & Decker outlet stores lower their prices even more to provide real savings to the consumer and will have special pricing on power tools, lawn and garden items, housewares and accessories. A refurbished cordless 2 speed VersaPak drill kit - complete with batteries, charger and accessories is $39.95 - a savings of 50% and with a full warranty. Call for details.
Location: 1480 Dundas St. E. (one block east of Dixie Rd., south side of Dundas St.), Mississauga.
Hours: Please call for individual store hours.
Telephone: (905) 277-0011
Location: Cookstown Mall.
Telephone: (705) 458-2071
Location: Factory Outlet Plaza, 1150 Sheppard Avenue West (two blocks west of Allen Road), North York.
Telephone: (416) 635-6740
Location: Warden Power Center, 725 Warden Ave. (N. of St. Clair), Scaborough
Telephone: 416-285-5638
Location: Southworks Outlet Mall, 64 Grand Ave. S., Cambridge.
Telephone: (519) 624-8824

BOMBAY WAREHOUSE SALE 💲
Many of us have pieces of furniture purchased at this well know retailer, and now for two days you can save up to 60% off original prices. Choose from overstocks, discontinued or slightly damage merchandise that includes furniture, wall dÈcor, home accessories and more. Bring your own truck or van if you plan to buy any large pieces.
Location: 6100 Kenway Drive (Kennedy Road and Hwy 401), Mississauga.
Hours: Call for hours.
Telephone: (905) 795-8800

See advertisement on page 96

Home Decorating & Housewares

C.W. & ASSOCIATES
They offer gifts galore - with assorted Christmas merchandise, porcelain mugs, frames and pewter, at unbelievable prices. A wide variety of iron art. December Warehouse Sale.

Location: 6150 Dixie Rd., Units 2 and 3, (north of Hwy. 401, south of Courtney Park Dr., on the west side), Mississauga.
Hours: Call for details.
Telephone: (905) 564-8521

CAYNE'S SUPER HOUSEWARES
Housewares, small appliances, gadgets and more abound in this spacious shop. Cayne's boasts famous brand names at warehouse prices. They also hold weekly specials that feature good values.

Location: 112 Doncaster Ave. (one traffic light north of Steeles Ave., east off Yonge St.), Thornhill.
Hours: M. to W. & Sat. 10 - 6, Thu. & F. 10 - 9, Sun. 11 - 5
Telephone: (905) 764-1188

CANDLES BY MONTANNA
If you should be planning a party, especially a wedding, then do check out this smaller location for its wide assortment of elegant party accessories and candles, too. Now on is a clearance sale with many items less than wholesale.

Location: 2415 Holly Lane, Suite 220, (same industrial strip as McIntosh and Watts), Ottawa.
Hours: M. to Sat. 9:30 - 5
Telephone: (613) 739-3705

CONCORD CANDLE CORP. - FACTORY OUTLET
This is a stop you will want to make. They have a large selection of firsts as well as seconds, including a large variety of prints, candle holders, garden accessories and many other items to choose from. While browsing the store don't forget to say "hi" to their candle makers and take some time to watch them carve candles. Each candle is hand dipped and hand carved so each one is unique in design and colour.

Location: 2315 Industrial Park Rd. (Innisfil Beach Road Exit off Hwy. 400, turn left on Industrial Park Rd.), Thornton.
Hours: Seven days a week 9 - 5
Summer Hours M. – T. 9-5, Fri. 9-8, Sat. & Sun. 9-5
Telephone: (705) 431-7296

See advertisement on page A9

CORNING - OUTLET STORE SALE
At this outlet, you'll find pots and dishes by Corning, Pyrex and Revere at up to 70% off suggested retail prices.
Location: 60 Leek Crescent, Richmond Hill.
Telephone: (905) 771-3576
Location: Cookstown Manufacturers Mall (Hwy. 400 & 89), Cookstown.
Telephone: (705) 458-9998
Location: Factory Outlet Plaza, 1150 Sheppard Avenue W. (two blocks west of Allen Road), Downsview.
Telephone: (416) 633-5636
Location: Pickering Home and Leisure Centre, 1755 Pickering Pkwy., Pickering.
Telephone: (905) 428-9530
Location: Southworks Mall, 64 Grand Ave. S., Cambridge.
Telephone: (519) 624-9911
See advertisement on page A6

CONSOLIDATED BOTTLE COMPANY
If you are interested in doing some canning or preserving, this is the place for you. This store is stocked with thousands of different types of containers and closures for just about anything. Preserving jars are their specialty, but they also have lots of food, cosmetic, chemical and pharmaceutical containers with separate lids. Stock up now. Lots of free parking.
Location: 77 Union Street (one block northwest of Old Weston Road and St. Clair Ave. W.), Toronto
Hours: M to Friday 8:30 a.m. - 4:00 p.m. Closed weekends.
Telephone: 416-656-7777

COUNTRY FLOORS
Attention designers and home renovators - here's a quickie sale of tiles imported from the four corners of the earth - from Peru to Portugal, from Spain to Japan. Discontinued and overstocked floor and wall tiles at up to 80% of regular pricing.
Location: 321 Davenport Road, Toronto.
Hours: M. to F. 9 - 5
Telephone: (416) 922-9214

T.B.A. TO BE ANNOUNCED - DATES NOT AVAILABLE AT PRESS TIME

THIS SYMBOL INDICATES WAREHOUSE SALES

Home Decorating & Housewares

DANSK FACTORY OUTLET 💰
Save up to 75% at this annual sale, which will feature dinnerware, glassware, home accessories, kitchen items, patio candles and more. Great ideas for shower and wedding gifts. Don't miss the Clearance Corner featuring ends of lines, samples and discontinued items as well. Wheelchair accessible. November & December Warehouse Sales.

Location: **60 Horner Ave. (S. of Q.E.W. between Kipling & Islington Ave.), Etobicoke**
Telephone: (416) 259-1127
Location: **166 Princess St., Kingston.**
Telephone: (613) 531-9999
Location: **91 Queen St., Niagara-on-the-Lake.**
Telephone: (905) 468-2614
Location: **Cookstown Manufacturer's Outlet Mall (Hwy. 400 & 89), Cookstown.**
Telephone: (705) 458-2967
Location: **Riverworks, 9 King St., St. Jacob's.**
Telephone: (519) 664-2700

THE DOOR FACTORY
We were impressed with not only the sheer number and variety of doors available but the prices as well- solid wood interior French doors were just $49. They do installation and service work too, not just sales.

Location: **114 Kennedy Rd. S. in Brampton.**
Hours: M, Tue and Fri 9-6; Wed and Thu 9-8 and Sat 9-3.
Telephone: (905) 796-3373

EBC GIFTS & COLLECTIBLES - WAREHOUSE SALE 💰
This is always a good sale if you love crystal either for yourself, or for giving. Lots of vases, candlesticks, stemware and other crystal items, as well as a selection of frames, ceramics and giftware at prices of 50 – 70% off.

Location: **35 East Beaver Creek Road, Unit 1A at the rear (Hwy 7 and Leslie Street area), Richmond Hill**
Hours: Vary by season call for details and pre-christmas warehouse sale dates.
Telephone: 905-764-0795

See advertisement on page A9

EGLINTON WHOLESALE PAINT & HARDWARE
Hardware and paints are plentiful. Those in the know will recognize the best: Pratt and Lambert, Sikkens, Para, Minwax.

Location: **536 Eglinton Ave. W. (2 blocks W. of Avenue Rd.), Toronto.**
Hours: M. to F. 9 - 6, Sat. 9 - 5
Telephone: (416) 485-2352

EUROPEAN HOTEL & RESTAURANT IMPORTS LTD.
This commercial kitchenware supplier is open to the public year-round, offering excellent quality and wholesale prices on flatware, china, glassware and commercial-grade kitchenware.
Location: 343 Horner Ave. (off Kipling Ave., three blocks south of Evans Ave.), Etobicoke.
Hours: M. to F. 8:30 - 5, call for weekend hours
Telephone: (416) 253-9449

EUROPEAN
Hotel and Restaurant Imports Ltd.

"Where the Chefs come to shop"

343 Horner Avenue,
Etobicoke, Ontario M8W 1Z6
Tel: 416-253-9449
Fax: 416-253-9552
www.starpages.com/european~hotel

GIFTS THAT MAKE A DIFFERENCE
This non-profit organization carries handmade crafts, including Xmas decorations, wooden mobiles, wrought iron candelabras and hand-painted ceramics, all from craft co-ops in Southeast Asia. No cheques. T.B.A. Warehouse Sale.
Location: 388 Carlaw Ave., Unit W-11, (at Dundas St. E.), Toronto.
Telephone: (416) 720-2223

GOODMAN'S CHINA
A family owned & operated business for years, they bring their customers back time after time with their personal service, selection & everyday reduced sale prices. Save 20% - 60% everyday on dinnerware, stemware, flatware, figurines, giftware & more. Bridal and gift registries, personal and corporate gift baskets and bonbonieres. Phone orders & delivery service also available.
Location: 221 Wilmington Ave., Downsview.
Hours: M., T. & Sat. 9:30 - 6, W. & Thu. 9:30 - 8, Sun. 12 - 5
Telephone: (416) 638-2630 or 1-800-665-8187

GRAND REGAL INTERNATIONAL LTD. - WAREHOUSE SALE
The name is almost bigger than this little spot with wonderful deals on porcelain dolls, great buys on silverplate, a small selection of ceramic pots and other odds and ends. Cash and VISA only. T.B.A Warehouse Sale in the fall until Christmas.
Location: 1255A Unit 2, Reid St., Richmond Hill.
Telephone: (905) 886-6817

GRANNY TAUGHT US HOW
This wonderful country store carries ladie's clothing – Woolrich, Royal Robbins, Susan Bristol, Sigrid Olsen, Catherine Steward, Bellepointe and Eric Alexandre. Beautiful 100% cotton fabric and quilting, home décor items, Christmas items, beanie babies and other country apparel. Great sales in July and the end of November.

Location: RR#4, Shelburne - go west on Hwy 89, and the store is between Airport Road and Hwy 10
Hours: M. to Thur., 10-6, Fri. to Sat. 10-9, Sun. 10-6.
Telephone: (519) 925-2748

IDEAL PAINTS - WAREHOUSE OUTLET
Not only do they manufacture house paints but they are middlemen supplying smaller locations with other product such as Sikken and Miniwax paint and stains. The outlet carries a variety of painting accessories and most items are not priced, so you do have to ask.

Location: 172 Belfield Rd. (east of Hwy. 27), Rexdale.
Hours: M. to F. 7 - 5:30
Telephone: (416) 243-7578

JOBSON AND SONS LTD.
Lots of great home decor items in this sale including lamps, chairpads, cushions, baskets, silk flowers and more. Stock consists of end of lines, seconds and overstocks, and are priced for at least 50% off. Bring in an old lamp that needs a new shade and match it up for size and colour.

October warehouse sale
Location: 5925 Tomken Road, Unit 9 (north of Hwy 401, south of Brittania Road), Mississauga
Hours: M. to F. 10 - 7, Sat. 10 - 6
Telephone: (905)795-1019

MADAWASKA DOORS INC.
Oh dear, need a door? For the past 25 years, this Canadian company has manufactured high quality doors and now they clear out canceled orders, returns and over-runs with over a thousand various stain grade, solid wood doors in stock to choose from. Actual prices run from $80 up to $1000 which is 50% off list with GST/PST included if you pay cash. Inventory changes daily and is computerized so you can call ahead to check on a particular size. Website: www.madawaska-doors.com

Location: #7405-17th Sideroad. Off Hwy #27, North of Nobleton
Hours: M. to F. 10 - 4, Sat 9 - 1. Call for appointment.
Telephone: (905) 859-4622, 1-800-483-2358,

MCINTOSH & WATTS - WAREHOUSE OUTLETS
Perfect for gift giving or pampering yourself; they clear stock from their twenty regular retail locations from these two outlets and feature all the best names in china and crystal.

Location: (off the 401 Hwy. south of the border with Quebec), Lancaster.
Hours: M. to Sat. 9:30 - 6, Sun. & holidays 11 - 5
Telephone: (613) 347-2461

Location: 2379 Holly Lane (at the junction of Walkley Rd. and Heron Rd.), Ottawa.
Hours: M. to W. 9:30 - 6, Thu. & F. 9:30 - 9, Sat. 9:30 - 5:30, Sun. 11 - 5
Telephone: (613) 532-7240

MIKASA
This well-known name in table settings makes dining an art and very appetizing too - at up to 80% off. You'll find dinnerware, giftware, flatware and crystal just in time for holiday toasting and gift giving. November and May Warehouse Sale.

Location: 233 Alden Road, Markham.
Telephone: (905) 474-0880

MIRAGE - FACTORY WAREHOUSE SALE
This will be their first ever sale, the space is limited but the product - discontinued and sample clocks, picture frames, mirrors, little coat racks and hooks, some stationery - is decidedly neat and funky, well priced at wholesale level and perfect for gift giving.

Location: 746 Warden Ave., Unit 3, (west side between Eglinton Ave. and St. Clair Ave.), Scarborough,
Hours: F. 9 a.m. to 6 p.m.,
Sat. and Sun. 11 a.m. to 6 p.m. Sun.
Telephone: (416) 285-7991.

MONARCH PAINTS LIMITED
If all you really want to do is paint, then you'll want to check out Monarch Paints, which offers up to 35% off retail prices. Monarch carries Benjamin Moore, Pittsburgh, Pratt and Lambert as well as Sikkens and Olympic stains.
Location: **3620 Dufferin St. (Dufferin St. and Wilson Ave., just north of Hwy. 401), North York.**
Hours: M. to W. 7 - 6, Thu. & F. 7 - 7, Sat. 8 - 5
Telephone: (416) 635-6560

MOUNT 'N SEAL
You've never tried shrink-wrap framing? Consider it an affordable alternative to traditional framing. This shop does an excellent job of framing everything, from posters and prints to tea towels and even jigsaw puzzles.
Location: **10 Brentcliffe Rd. (south of Eglinton Ave.), Leaside.**
Hours: M. to F. 9 - 5, Sat. 11 - 2
Summer Hours: M. to F. 9 - 5
Telephone: (416) 423-9975

NEO-IMAGE CANDELIGHT LTD.
Nothing evokes the Christmas spirit more than soft candlelight, especially scented ones that fill the home with warmth and Yuletide scents. This outlet carries a wide variety of candles, votives, mini jars and gift sets at prices that are tough to beat - their small scented mini jars are only $1.75. Open year round, but especially nice at Christmas.
Location: **1331 Blundell Road (one light south of Dundas Street, west of Dixie Road), Mississauga.**
Hours: M. to Sat. 9 - 4
Telephone: (905) 273-3020

ONTARIO PAINT AND WALLPAPER
Many a bolt of wallpaper has been cleared out of this long-standing establishment (since 1913). Not only do they offer excellent value on discontinued papers, but you'll find Evans pastes at far less than regular retail prices. The staff really know their stuff and they're just finishing off the first major expansion in 40 years.
Location: **275 Queen Street East, (east of Sherbourne St.), Toronto.**
Hours: M. to F. 7 - 6, Sat. 8 - 5:30
Telephone: (416) 362-5127

ONEIDA FACTORY OUTLET
You'll find bargains galore in silverplate, stainless flatware and hollowware. The stock consists of factory imperfects, discontinued patterns and other cash and carry specials.
Location: **8699 Stanley Ave. S. (take the Q.E.W. west to McLeod Rd., go south and turn right on to Stanley Ave.), Niagara Falls.**
Hours:	M. to Sun. 9:30 - 5
Telephone:	(905) 356-9691

OLD COLONY CANDLE FACTORY OUTLET
On your way to cottage country don't forget to stop and browse all our gift giving ideas. Candles galore at great discounted prices. Savings of up to 50% off. While you shop the candle makers will be producing candles. Don't be shy stop and say "hi".
Location: **66 Line 15 South, RR #1 (Oro-Medonte, Line15 off Hwy. 11) Orillia.**
Hours:	Open 7 days a week 10-5
	Summer hours:	M. – T. 10-5, Fri. 10-8, Sat. & Sun. 10-5.
Telephone:	(705) 325-0349

PAINT, WALLPAPER AND FABRIC SOURCE
If you want to be inspired to re-decorate then this is the place to start. Not only do they have 50% off the retail book price for all in-stock wall paper, 80% off on discontinued in-stock paper, a nice selection of current fabrics and savings on brand name paint by Para and Pittsburgh but all the knowledgeable help a person might need to get started.
Location: **85 Doncaster Ave. (North of Steeles Ave., east off Yonge St.), Thornhill.**
Hours:	M. to F. 7 - 6, Sat. 9:30 - 5
Telephone:	(905) 881-8828

PADERNO FACTORY STORE
This marvelous cookware is actually crafted in a small factory on Prince Edward Island, but you can drop in to the factory store and save 40 to 50% off the suggested list price on all the pieces and sets. This cookware is made from stainless steel and has a 25-year warranty. Some seconds are available with small imperfections that will not affect cooking performance.
Location: **Cookstown Manufacturers Mall, (building B) Hwy 400 & 89, Cookstown.**
Hours:	M. to Sat. 9 - 5, Sun. 12 - 4
Telephone:	(705) 458-2197
Location: **Prescott. (The store is in the train station at the north end of St. Lawrence)**
Telephone:	1-800-808-7687

Home Decorating & Housewares

Location: Southworks Mall, 64 Grand Ave. Cambridge.
Telephone: (519) 623-8652
Location: St. Jacob's Factory Outlet Mall, St. Jacob's.
Telephone: (519) 884-6486
Location: Warden Power Centre, 725 Warden Ave., Unit 65, Scarborough.
Telephone: (416) 757-4303

PIONEER STAR (CANADA) LTD
This wholesaler of giftware, including decorative wood items, candles, willow baskets, plush toys, etc., clear discontinued items in an upcoming warehouse sale. Items like small wooden jewelry boxes, bookends, towel holders and wooden Xmas decorations are at savings of 50% or more. Cash or Visa only. T.B.A. Warehouse Sale.
Location: 55 West Beaver Creek, Unit 8, (Leslie St. & Hwy. 7 area), Richmond Hill.
Telephone: (905) 709-0909

PERFECT FLAME CANDLE
Makers of unique hand-poured candles, highly scented votive pillars, jar candles, floaters, tapers etc. They also carry select giftware and gift ideas under $20.00. Special candles for custom wedding orders, showers, baptism and corporate functions. For hobbyists or do-it-yourselfer's they are one of the rare locations where you can find a wide selection of candle making supplies. Save up to 70%.
Location: 1616 Matheson Blvd. E., units 25, 26, Mississauga
Hours: M.-F. 9-6; Sat. 10-6; Extended hours Sept. -Dec.
Telephone: 905-625-2521

See advertisement on page A17

PRECIDIO INC WAREHOUSE SALE
If your Dad's idea of fun is lounging outside on the patio or by the pool sipping a favourite beverage, you should drop into this sale which features high quality acrylic glassware, trays, pitchers and more. They also carry a good selection of frames and other giftware all priced to sell during this sale.
Location: 35 Precidio Court (north of Queen St. at the corner of Corporation Drive and Torbram Road), Brampton.
Hours: June 15-17. Thursday and Friday noon - 7:30 p.m., Saturday 8:30 a.m.- noon.
Telephone: (905) 790-0790

PREMIER CANDLE CORP.
Those who delight in candlelight will find quite a selection of candles at definitely less than retail pricing - perfect for the holiday atmosphere
Location: 6200B Tomken Rd. (west side, north of 401), Mississauga.
Hours: M. to F. 9-5, Sat. 9-12, and for holiday season only, Sun. 10-5
Telephone: (905) 795-8833

THE PICTURE PICTURE CO.
Draw a blank or is that just your wall? While this location certainly would not appeal to fine art aficionados, it will provide inexpensive, fun prints and posters perfect for those university-bound or others with fiscal restraints. They laminate and frame pictures as well and sell frames and mats too.
Location: 122 Cartwright Ave. (between Dufferin St. and Caledonia Rd., just north of Bentworth Ave.), Toronto.
Hours: M. to F. 9 - 6, Sat. 10 - 6, Sun. 12 - 5
Telephone: (416) 787-9342

POSTERS INTERNATIONAL
As representatives for a number of artists, poster carry every conceivable print and frames. You can find and frame almost everything but the clearance corner at the back of their beautiful new showroom is not only filled with great ideas and prints for your walls but the best deals, too. As well, their retail store will start having their summer sidewalk sales of framed prints.
Locations: New showroom is at 1200 Castlefield Ave., (north side, west of Dufferin St.), Toronto,
Hours: M. to F. 9-5
Telephone: (416) 789-7156.
Locations: Retail store is at 501 Eglinton Ave. W., Toronto,
Hours: M. to F. 10-7, later on Thurs. until 8, Sat. 10-6, Sun. 12-5.
Telephone: (416) 481-5127.

Home Decorating & Housewares

> Give a man a fish and he will eat for a day.
> Teach him how to fish, and he will
> sit in a boat and drink beer all day.

Home Decorating & Housewares

THE RUBBERY
If visions of Rubbermaid dance through your head, this 20,000 square foot store is sure to fulfill every dream. This is the only full line Rubbermaid dealer in Canada, and the stores are full of every conceivable piece of Rubbermaid you can imagine, with prices that range generally from 10 - 40% off retail prices. The stores also stock CRAYOLA products, V-TECH electronic learning toys, GRACO infant products, and LITTLE TIKES toys. Now two locations to serve you in Mississauga and Woodbridge, with a third store opening Fall 2000 in Ajax. www.therubbery.com

Location: 3050 Vega Boulevard (Dundas Street and Hwy. 403 area), Mississauga
Hours: M. to F., 9:30-9, Sat. 9:30 - 6, Sun. 11-5
Telephone: (905) 820-5550
Location: 7575 Weston Road, Unit 116, Woodbridge
Telephone: (909) 850-4060

See advertisement on page A19

ROYAL DOULTON - WAREHOUSE SALE 💰
For the perfect wedding gift or as family heirlooms you hope the next generation will appreciate as much as you do - this annual sale is worth a visit to Pickering for clearance prices on well-known dinnerware, collectibles and crystal. November Warehouse Sale.

Location: Metro East Trade Centre, 1899 Brock Rd. (north east corner of Hwy. 401 and Brock Rd.), Pickering.
Telephone: (905) 427-0744

RICH HILL CANDLES AND GIFTS - FACTORY OUTLET
Do you have holiday plans to visit the Muskoka area? A visit to this gift store & candle outlet is in order. Not only do they have a great selection, but you can also view candles being made. First and second quality candles come in a variety of sizes and scents. If you purchase four bundles, the fifth one is free.

Location: 9 Robert Dollar Dr. (outlet is located off Hwy. 118), Bracebridge.
Hours: M. to Sat. 9 - 5:30
Open Sundays on long weekends 10 - 4.,
Call ahead to confirm.
Telephone: (705) 645-3068

Women like silent men; they think they're listening.

SAMUEL HARRIS 1994 LTD.
This is an excellent find of solid vinyl, wallcoverings. Although the stock comes and goes, the price is unbeatable, and if you want to spruce up the family vehicle, they also have quite a selection of auto findings like upholsteries, seat belting, carpeting and trims.
Location: 7131 Edwards Blvd. Unit #2, Mississauga
Hours: M. to F. 7:30 - 4:30, Sat. 8 - 12
Telephone: (905) 795-9795

SIGMA GIFTS
Need a wedding or shower gift? Could your kitchen use a few more wares? Then this is the sale for you. There are lots of interesting china, flatware, ceramics, Mexican glass, linens and decorator accessories all at excellent prices.
Location: 95 Wingold Ave. (W. off Dufferin St., between Lawrence & Eglinton Aves. W.), North York.
Hours: M. to F. 9 - 4
Telephone: (416) 787-1257

SUNBEAM FACTORY OUTLETS 💲
At the risk of stereotyping the dads of the world perhaps a deal on barbecue or some other small electrical appliance is in the cards for Dads Day? These two outlets also clear out for Coleman with better pricing on tents, heaters, coolers, back packs and, oh yes, camp stoves. Warehouse Sale in April.
Location: 5975 Falbourne St., Mississauga.
Hours: M. to Sat. 10 - 6, Sun. 12 - 5
Telephone: (905) 501-0090
Location: Dixie Outlet Mall, 1250 South Service Rd. (Dixie Rd. and the Q.E.W.), Mississauga.
Hours: M. to F. 10 - 9, Sat. 9:30 - 6, Sun. 12 - 6
Telephone: (905) 278-0504
Location: Warden Power Centre, Scarborough.
Hours: M. to F. 10 - 9, Sat. 9:30 - 6, Sun. 12 - 5
Telephone: (416) 288-0352

SWISS OUTLET
Here we go name dropping again! Wenger Swiss Army knives, watches (which are refurbished) and household knives as well as high end European kitchen gadgets, wine accessories, copper moulds and cookware - all of which are being cleared at less than retail as they clean out their overstocked and discontinued merchandise.
Location: 35 East Beaver Creek Rd., Unit 6 side entrance (north of Hwy 7, east of Leslie St.), Richmond Hill.
Hours: M. to F. 8:30 - 5
Telephone: (905) 764-1121

Home Decorating & Housewares

T-FAL ELECTRICAL APPLIANCES
They feature electrical appliances and assorted non-stick T-fal cookware with discounts of 15 to 50%. Ends of lines, overruns and refurbished products are featured.
Location: 719 Tapscott Ave., Unit B, Scarborough.
Hours: M. to Thu. 8:30 - 4:30, F. 8:30 - 1
Telephone: (416) 297-4131

See advertisement on page A22

TEN THOUSAND VILLAGES - IMPORTER'S STORE
This is a volunteer-operated, non-profit Mennonite warehouse and store that imports and sells thousands of neat & unique items from 35 developing nations. Their Thrift Shop located in the same building is one of the nicest that we have seen. The shop has several quilts for sale as well as clothes and housewares.
Location: 65 Heritage Drive (south off Hwy. 7/8 at the Beams/Hamilton Rd. stoplight), New Hamburg.
Hours: M. to F. 9 - 5, Sat. 10 - 4
Telephone: (519) 662-1879
Location: 2599 Yonge St., Toronto.
Hours: M. to F. 9-5, Sat. 10-4
Telephone: (416) 932-163
Location: Stores also in Waterloo, Stratford and Niagara-on-the-Lake.

TERRACE GALLERY AND ART & FRAME - LIQUIDATION SALE
If 'cabin fever' is affecting your point of view may we suggest some new art work to brighten your four walls? Excellent discounts are offered on thousands of framed pieces with images from every category: signed prints by Group of Seven artists, to sports, Impressionists, country and farm style, classical etc. etc.
Location: Terrace Gallery Showroom 50 Esna Park Dr., (4 lights north of Steeles Ave. and east off Woodbine Ave.), Markham, VISA, Mastercard, Interac and cheques with ID accepted;
Location: Art & Frame 125 Ashwarren Dr., (east off Keele St., between Finch and Sheppard Ave.), Downsview, VISA, Interac, cheques with ID.
Hours: Call for hours

Brain cells come and brain cells go, but fat cells live forever.

THE VICTORIAN SHOPPE
Again, another great tip from one of our readers, Nicola, who let us in on this eclectic collection of indoor and outdoor wrought iron pieces with an emphasis on Canadian designers and artists. This very interesting location has three levels and is just crammed (and we mean crammed) with home decor pieces of metal, iron, ceramic and some smaller samples of Mexican pine furniture.

Location: **334 Kingston Rd. (north side, east of Woodbine Ave.), Scarborough.**
Hours: T., Thu. to Fri. 11 - 7, Sat. 11-6, and Sun.
Telephone: (416) 698-5547

THE UMBRA FACTORY SALE 💲
Umbra is well known for high-quality designer items that include fabulous frames, drapery hardware, clocks, and other accessory items. Prices at this sale are always excellent, so drop in and you just may be able to finish up your shopping in one spot! December Warehouse Sale.

Location: **Warehouse sale location T.B.A. please call**
Telephone: (416) 299-0088

UPPER CANADA SOAP & CANDLE MAKERS - FACTORY OUTLET
This terrific outlet is now open on Mondays, and continues to offer great ideas for gift giving at outlet store prices. Look for soap, sheets and towels, toiletries, bath/body products and of course candles and accesories with new inventory arriving daily.

Location: **1510 Caterpillar Rd. (north of The Queensway, off Dixie Rd.), Mississauga.**
Hours: M-F 10-6; Sat. 10-4
Telephone: (905) 897-1710   See advertisement on page A15

Home Decorating & Housewares

T.B.A. TO BE ANNOUNCED - DATES NOT AVAILABLE AT PRESS TIME

💲 THIS SYMBOL INDICATES WAREHOUSE SALES

Home Decorating & Housewares

VENATOR ELECTRONICS - CLEARANCE CENTRE
Combined with the DeLonghi Outlet, shoppers will find excellent pricing on a wide range of electronic items from Orio, Sansui, Emerson, Magnavox and Braun. A selection of products for those in the kitchen includes small kitchen appliances such as breadmakers and pasta makers, pots and pans, gadgets and more. As a clearance centre for refurbished and end of line products and a service depot this outlet is great for last minute gifts at every price point and age group with follow-up service repairs too. Look for competitive prices on kitchen appliances - either factory refurbished or discontinued lines. Products such as humidifiers, espresso machines, toaster ovens and more, are featured - all brand names.
Location: 55 East Beaver Creek, (northwest of either Leslie St. or Hwy. 7), Richmond Hill.
Hours: M. to W. 9 - 6, Thu. & F. 9 - 8, Sat. 9 - 5
Telephone: (905) 602-8400

VENDABLES - WAREHOUSE SALE 💰
Gift ideas abound with lots for the kitchen and the Martha Stewart types plus vases, picture frames, music boxes, brass and more, bearing better brand names such as Beatrix Potter, Evesham, Fitz and Floyd, Schmid, Spode and others. Call for warehouse sale details.
Location: 55 East Beaver Creek, (northwest of either Leslie St. or Hwy. 7), Richmond Hill.
Telephone: (905) 731-3187
See advertisement on page A28

VARIMPO-CANHOME- WAREHOUSE SALE 💰
Lots of housewares and giftware at this sale that includes candles, picture frames, cookware, ceramic platters - too much to name - you'll have to drop in.
Location: 5320 Timberlea Blvd. (west of Tomken Road and south of Matheson Road), Mississauga.
Hours: call for hours
Telephone: (905)-624-6262

Do pediatricians play miniature golf on Wednesdays?

WILLIAM ASHLEY 💰
Of all the warehouse sales we report, Ashley's sale is probably best known - for sheer size and variety, this is one sale you can't miss. This year the sale will offer savings of up to 90% on china, crystal, silver and gifts, as well as lots of Christmas items, housewares, frames and lots more. Specials are distributed equally throughout the sale, so you may want to make several visits. All sales are final - and we'd recommend not bringing your kids - it can get pretty crowded and busy. Be prepared for a lineup. November Warehouse Sale.

Location: 62 Railside Rd. (2 blocks E. of the Don Valley Parkway & S. off Lawrence Ave.), Don Mills.
Hours: Call for hours
Telephone: (416) 964-2900

WILLOW TREE COLLECTIBLES 💰
This distributor offers gifts for all occasions. Items such as sachets, pillows, pot pourri, baskets, glasswares and more, are priced well below retail prices. December Warehouse Sale.

Location: 3959 Chesswood Dr.(at Sheppard and Allen), North York.
Hours: Call for store hours.
Telephone: (416) 630-1227

WILTON OUTLET STORE
Here's a wonderful opportunity to stock up your gift cupboard with some terrific items - this sale includes a variety of COPCO tea kettles, picture frames from the Weston Gallery, housewares, pottery and more. Wilton is a name you probably associate with cake decorating supplies, and they'll have plenty of those as well, including molds, pans, etc. - prices range from 50-70% off retail.

Location: 98 Carrier Drive (south of Albion Road, west off Hwy. 27), Etobicoke.
Telephone: (416) 679-0790, ext. 200

WORLD OF GIFTS AND HOME DECOR
The new location has a selection of rustic Mexican pine furniture, clay chimneys and planters, as well as a large selection of cement products - generally for your back yard or garden. As well, they have a large selection of gift giving items, so you just may find something unusual here.

New Location: 6725 Pacific Circle, Mississauga. Entrance at rear of building.
Hours: M to Fri 8:30a.m. - 4:30 p.m.,
Saturday 10:00 a.m. - 2:00 p.m.
Telephone: (905) 670-3490

Home Decorating & Housewares

for the home

Fabrics & Linens

BATH N' BEDTIME DECOR STORE
These are the best locations for bedding, bath, pictures, lamps and decor items. Choose from Fieldcrest, Springmaid, Martex, Dan River, and many other well-known designer names, as well as a wide selection of bathroom accessories and tableware. Semi-annual warehouse sale mid-May and mid-November. Call for store hours, of visit web site at www.bathnbed.com.

Location: 502 Lawrence Ave. W., Lawrence Plaza (Bathurst & Lawrence)
Tel: 416-781-8600
Location: 1755 Pickering Parkway, Pickering Home & Leisure (401 & Brock Rd.)
Tel: 905-428-0007
Location: 765 Exeter Rd., Crossroads Centre (Exeter & Wellington) London
Tel: 519-686-1759
Location: 410 Lewis Rd., Unit 15, Stoney Creek
Tel: 905-643-2114

See advertisement on page A31

BOLTS HOME FASHION OUTLET
This 10,000 square foot warehouse offers a smorgasbord of home decorating items at 20 - 70% off the manufacturer's suggested retail prices. The staff is helpful and knowledgeable on a wide range of products. Designer fabrics, drapery hardware, headboard kits, wallpaper and self-adhesive Easy Shades you cover with your own fabric are on the floor.

Location: 701 Alness St. (between Steeles and Finch Avenues., west of Dufferin St.), Downsview.
Hours: M. to F. 10 - 6, Sat. 10 - 5, Sun. 12 - 5
Telephone: (416) 661-2765

CAMBRIDGE TOWEL MILL OUTLET
This company manufactures quality household linens & towels - firsts, seconds & toweling by the pound. No cheques, but debit cards are accepted.
Location: 1150 Sheppard Ave. W (Sheppard Ave. & 2 blocks west of Allen Rd.), Downsview.

Hours: M. to W. 10 - 6, Thu. & F 10 - 8, Sat. 10 - 6, Sun. 12 - 5
Telephone: (416) 398-1557
Location: 341 Ottawa St. N., Hamilton.
Hours: M. to Thu. & Sat. 9 - 5, F. 9 - 9, Sun. 12 - 4
Telephone: (905) 549-3056
Location: 64 Grand Avenue S., South Works Mall, Cambridge.
Hours: M. to W. 9:30 - 6, Thu. & F 9:30 - 8, Sat. 9 - 6, Sun. 11 - 5
Telephone: (519) 622-5542
Location: Cookstown Mfrs. Outlet Mall, (400 & 89 Hwy.) Cookstown.
Hours: M. to F. 9 - 9, Sat. & Sun. 9 - 6
Telephone: (705) 458-1371
Location: 25 Benjamin Rd., Waterloo (St. Jacobs Mall).
Hours: M. to F. 9:30 - 9, Sat. 8:30 - 6, Sun. 12 - 5
Telephone: (519) 746-9186

CANALITE HOME FASHION
We always love the high quality linens here at discounted prices, and currently their 12th anniversary sale is underway with 35 - 80% off bedding and bath products. Specially priced for the sale is a Canadian white goose down duvet, 260 thread count, baffle box queen size at $125.
Location: 52 West Beaver Creek Road, Unit 8 (one light west of Leslie Street north of Hwy 7), Richmond Hill.
Hours: M. to Sat. 10 - 6, Thurs. 10 - 7
Telephone: (905) 886-6737

CHU SHING TEXTILES
Just one of many in the area, this particular store is well organized and carries a large selection of laces, silk and bridal fabrics as well as (figure skaters take note) a huge inventory of spandex fabrics.
Location: 440 Queen St. W., (west of Spadina Ave.), Toronto
Hours: Monday to Saturday 9-7.
Telephone: 504-9069.

DEBLINS LINENS SUPERSTORE
Expect at least 15% off and up to 90% off on a few items, with a wide range of excellent quality bed, bath and table linens.
Location: 39 Orfus Rd. (south of 401, west off Dufferin St.), North York.
Hours: M. to Sat. 10 - 6, Thu. 10 - 9, Sun. 12 - 5
Telephone: (416) 782-2910

DESIGNER FABRIC OUTLET
A bastion for dressmakers, decorators and tailors alike, they offer some of the finest designer and dress fabrics in town. and an amazing selection of decor fabric, fringes and notions. This is our number one favorite find for fabrics in the city.
Location: 1360 Queen St. W. (west of Dufferin St.), Toronto.
Hours: M. to W. 9:30 - 6, Thu. & F. 9:30 - 9, Sat 9:30 - 6:30
Telephone: (416) 531-2810

DOWNTOWN DUVETS & LINENS
High quality Canadian made, American & European imported designer brand name linen, towels, comforters, duvets and more, all being cleared at 50% off & more. No cheques. May and December Warehouse Sale.
Location: 530 Adelaide St. W., Basement (H. Brown building, just east of Bathurst St.), Toronto.
Hours: Call for specific dates and times of Warehouse sales.
Telephone: (416) 703-3777

DOWN UNDER - WAREHOUSE OUTLET
As always, this outlet continues to be a great spot to stock up on linens, and right now they are also clearing out a wide variety of in-stock beds, as well as duvets. Their Canadian white goose down duvet with 35 oz. of down is currently priced at $139 - considerably less than the competition. As well, we saw a terrific collection of cotton duvet covers priced at $49.99 - regularly priced at up to $149. Caution, however - their prices are not always well marked, so it's wise to double check the price - it's often lower than you think! Two annual clearance sales: first week of November and May.
Location: 444 Yonge St. (College Park), Toronto.
Hours: M. to W. 9 - 6, Thu. & F. 10 - 8, Sat 10 - 6
       Sun. 12 - 5 (Fall and Winter only)
Telephone: (416) 598-2184
Location: 5170 Dixie Road (south of the 401), Mississauga.
Hours: M. to Sat. 10 - 6, Thu. & F. 10 - 8, Sun. 12 - 5
Telephone: (905) 624-5854
Location: 5221 Highway #7 (SW corner McCowan & #7) Markham.
Hours: M. to FRI. 10 - 8, Sat. 10-6, Sun. 12-5
Telephone: (905) 305–9496

DREAMS DOWNEY DUVETS - FACTORY OUTLET
They are known for great buys on down products, like duvets for $69.99. They will redo your old duvets & pillows, stock bed linens & ship across Canada.
Location: **215 Spadina Ave., Toronto.**
Telephone: (416) 596-8489 or 1(800) 265-7104
Location: **Thornhill Square, 300 John St. (at Bayview Ave.), Thornhill.**
Hours: M. to F. 10 - 9, Sat. 10 - 6, Sun. 12 - 5 Sat. 10 - 9
Telephone: (905) 707-0887
Location: **Warden Power Centre (Warden and St. Clair), Scarborough.**
Telephone: (416) 288-0388

DRESSMAKERS SUPPLY
Dressmakers Supply has supplied the dressmaking trade for years with all sorts of hard to find sewing products.
Location: **1110 Yonge St. (near Summerhill TTC station), Toronto.**
Hours: M. to W. & Sat., 9 - 6, Thu. Fri., 9 - 8
Telephone: (416) 922-6000

EASTERN TEXTILES
Tucked between the big manufacturers like Caldwell and Fieldcrest and the small bath boutiques, is Rocky, the bedding middleman. Need linens for the table, bath or bed? You'll find a tremendous selection here. However, nothing is priced, and basically it's self-serve, so be prepared to spend time hunting around. Seconds mean savings, but look for the flaw and don't expect department store return policies. No cards.
Location: **164 Bentworth Ave. (E. off Caledonia Rd., & S. of Hwy. 401), Toronto.**
Hours: M. to F. 8:30 - 4:30, Sat.10 - 2:30
Telephone: (416) 783-1119

THE FABRIC SOLUTION
Prices on fabrics and notions for home decor are discounted along with 50% or more off the already hugely discounted retail prices in the clearance section. Free parking.
Location: **953 Eglinton Ave. E., Toronto.**
Hours: M. to W. 10 - 6, Thu. 10 - 8, F. & Sat. 10 - 6, Sun. 12 - 5 (closed Sundays during summer)
Telephone: (416) 429-5300

Fabrics & Linens

FABRICS FOR THE GREAT OUTDOORS
Their outlet in Mississauga can also provide everything a home sewer would need to make outerwear - from patterns and zippers to all those specialized fabrics and insulation materials. Sewing up your own outerwear makes great economic sense and is a wonderful fall project, but if you are timid then consider taking one of their classes. Store birthday sale in September, call for details

Location: 4560 Dixie Rd., Miississauga.
Hours: M. to F. 10 - 6, Sat. 10 - 5
Closed on Mondays throughout the summer months.
Telephone: (905) 629-4694

FABRIC CLEARANCE CENTRE
Another great find in the city for fabric with a good assortment of home decor fabrics for drapery and upholstery as well as foam, leather and a huge assortment of vinyl with everything neat and arranged by colour too. www.fabric-clearance.com

Location: 4884 Dufferin St., Unit 6, (three lights north of Finch Ave., west side) Downsview
Telephone: 416-665-4647

See advertisement on page A11

FINE DESIGN FABRICS - DRAPERY AND UPHOLSTERY OUTLET
There's a nice selection of printed cottons & glazed chintz as well as other upholstery weight fabrics with most fabrics at less than $20/yard.

Location: 4100 Chesswood Dr. #A (west of Dufferin St. and south off Finch Ave.), Downsview.
Hours: M. to F. 9 - 5, Sat. 10 - 4
Telephone: (416) 636-4904

HALTON LINEN COMPANY
This small shop specializes in bedding you won't find anywhere else. At the back of the shop is a clearance room where, if you're lucky, you can pick up exquisite bedding at 50% off. Co-ordinating lamp shades are available, too. Helpful staff assist in co- ordinating fabric, paper and paint samples.

Location: 481 North Service Rd. (between Dorval Rd. and Fourth Line), Oakville.
Hours: M. to Sat. 10 - 6, Sun. 12 - 5
Telephone: (905) 847-2274
Location: 800 Queenston Rd., Stoney Creek.
Hours: M. to F. 10 - 9, Sat. 10 - 6, Sun. 12 - 5
Telephone: (905) 560-5823

JORDI INTERNATIONAL FABRICS - WAREHOUSE SALE 💰
Great chance to stock up on lovely fabrics at great prices while you're in the area. Featured will be holiday fabrics, velvets, sequins, stretch velours as well as stretch ottomans, chinos, chenille and more. Marvelous fabrics for the fashion conscious seamstress, this importer normally sells direct to manufacturers and some fabric stores. Expect excellent deals on high quality and unusual yardage in animal prints, Liberty-look alikes, stretch lames etc. For those who sew for skaters, this is a gold mine, but remember it is a warehouse and not a retailer, so have your own patterns and measurements with you. Cash, VISA or cheques with proper I.D accepted. May and October Warehouse Sales.

Location: 721 Petrolia Rd., (south of Steeles Ave, east of Keele St. on the south east corner at Wildcat St.), Downsview.
Hours: M. to F. 8:30 - 5
Telephone: (416) 665-0080

KOBE FABRICS OUTLET 💰
Those who are familiar with quality upholstery fabrics will recognize the Kobe name, and this outlet lets you buy the name without the big price tag. Essentially this wholesale fabric company offers discontinued lines at prices of up to 70% off regular retail prices. However, once it's gone - it's gone. Inventory is limited to what's on hand, and changes often. As well, they offer limited wallpaper, window covering hardware and other home accessories at great savings. It's a real haven for the do-it-yourselfer, or if you would prefer to have them upholster your furniture, their labour charges are extremely reasonable. T.B.A. Warehouse Sales.

Location: 5380 South Service Road (SE corner of Burloak and the QEW), Burlington.
Hours: M. to Sat. 10 - 5
Telephone: (905) 639-2730

LA CACHE - CLEARANCE STORE
This small jewel is tucked into one of Hamilton's shopping malls, and is a haven for those who love the colours and designs of La Cache's table and bed linens and clothing. All merchandise is at least 50% off their regular retail prices, and consists of ends-of-lines, leftover stock, damaged items and odds and ends. Stock changes constantly, and right now you'll find some spring clothes from last year, as well as children's winter clothing. All linens and clothing are 100% cotton made in India. We particularly like their tablecloths - and at this price, you can afford several! Last season's damaged goods, 75% off retail.

Location: Jackson Square Mall, 2 King Street West, Hamilton.
Hours: M. to Sat. 10 - 5; Sun. 12 - 5
Telephone: (905) 528-3270

Fabrics & Linens

THE LACE PLACE
This is a real find for anyone looking for high quality upholstery, fabric and trims. The latest fabric from VIP and Cranston Works starts at $4.99/yard, and trimming and fringes are 20% off retail. Beautiful Spanish tassels and fringe to match. Some upholstery fabrics were $15.00/yard, regularly priced at $45.00/yard. With over 7000 square feet of retail space in the warehouse, you should find what you are looking for - and their Christmas fabrics are just starting to arrive now.

Location: 1698 Bayly Street (take the 401 east to Brock Road south, and turn right on Bayly Street), Pickering.
Hours: Mon. to Fri. 10 - 9, Sat. 10 - 6, Sun. noon - 5
Telephone: (905) 831-5223

MISSISSAUGA BEDDING SUPERSTORE
-UPPER CANADA SOAP & CANDLE MAKERS
Grand Re-Opening Summer 2000 with a huge open concept design. Look for duvets, sheets and towels, kitchen and bathroom accessories, bath and body products, candles and accessories – with new inventory arriving daily. Great place for gifts at outlet store prices.

Location: 1510 Caterpillar Road (north of The Queensway, off Dixie Road) Mississauga.
Hours: M. – F. 10-5, Sat. 10-4, Sun. closed
Telephone: (905) 897-1710

See advertisement on page A15

T.B.A. TO BE ANNOUNCED - DATES NOT AVAILABLE AT PRESS TIME

THIS SYMBOL INDICATES WAREHOUSE SALES

PATRICIAN LINENS
When we dropped in to this warehouse, we were impressed with the high quality home textiles which are all linen and cotton. Usually this importer sells to exclusive US retailers, but is opening their warehouse for this sale which will include tablecloths, napkins, placemats, kitchen towels, tab curtains and some bedding. High quality at discounted prices.

Location: 1875 Leslie Street, Unit #16 (between the 401 and York Mills, east side).

Hours: M to Fri 10 - 6
             Sat 10 - 5, Sun noon - 5
Telephone: (416) 444-1100   See advertisement on page A16

SUREWAY TRADING - SILK WHOLESALERS
Sharons favorite for decades, this outlet imports a mind boggling array of silks with every quality, weight, texture and colour imaginable at excellent prices. At the end of the month they are moving just around the corner but keeping this phone number - call ahead.

Location: 111 Peter St., Suite 212, (east of Spadina Ave. and north off King St.), Toronto

Hours: M. to F. 10 - 5:30, Sat. 11 - 3:30
Telephone: (416) 596-1887

WESTPOINT STEVENS FACTORY OUTLET
To go with your new bed, you should really check out this outlet which is running an end of season inventory reduction on bedding and towels. Twin comforters start at $15, flannel sheets at $7, and open stock sheets and towels are also reduced. Great quality at very reasonable prices. Wheelchair accessible.

Location: 5800 Avebury Road (first street west of Hwy 10 off Britannia Road), Mississauga.

Hours: M.T. W. Sat 10 - 6
             Thur and Fri 10 - 8, Sun noon - 5
Telephone: (905) 712-8999

See advertisement on page A30

Fabrics & Linens

leisure time

- Arts, Crafts & Books
- Toys, Party Novelties & Packaging
- Florist, Gift Baskets

leisure time

Arts, Crafts & Books

THE BOOK DEPOT INC.
And now for those of you who get to the St. Catharines area occasionally, or need to find a reason to go, we have the Book Depot, one of Canada's largest book warehouses. With more than 2 million books on display, it's almost impossible not to find something worth reading. Most of these books are 'remainders,' which means they have been purchased from the publishers as overruns, returns, etc., and range in price from 30 to 70% off the original price. Categories run from Art to Sports, Crafts to Health, Children's and more. Take the scenic drive to St. Catharines, have a complimentary coffee and check it out!
Location: 340 Welland Ave., (QEW west, exit at Niagara St. and remain on the South Service Rd. - turn right Welland Ave.), St. Catharines.
Hours: M. to W. 9 - 6, Thu. & F. 9 - 9, Sat. 9 - 5
Telephone: 1-800-801-7193

THE BOOK SOURCE
Perfect for gift giving (and easy to wrap too!) at 40 to 80 per cent off regular retail on books for cooks, children, do-it-yourselves, romantics, puzzle fiends, and both fiction and non-fiction titles. No cheques please. June Warehouse Sale.
Location: 770 Birchmount Rd., Unit 17, Scarborough.
Telephone: (416) 750-3286

CRAFT TREE
When you hear the inevitable, 'Mom, I'm bored - what can I do?' - try a visit to this chain of craft stores. Carrying much the same line of merchandise as other craft outlets, Craft Tree is able to keep prices lower by careful buying and inventory management. Weekly specials are often featured on paints, yarn and more. Classes and birthday parties are regular features.
Location: 1060 Ontario St., Stratford.
Hours: M. to F. 9:30 - 9, Sat. 9:30 - 6, Sun. 11:30 - 5
Telephone: (519) 273-3397
Location: 51 Simcoe St., Tillsonburg.

Hours:	M. to F. 9:30 - 9, Sat. 9:30 - 6, Sun. 11:30 - 5
Telephone:	(519) 688-9688
Location:	**545 Niagara St., Welland.**
Hours:	M. to F. 9:30 - 9, Sat. 9:30 - 6, Sun. 11:30 - 5
Telephone:	(905) 732-4866
Location:	**550 Ontario St. S., Milton.**
Hours:	M. to F. 9:30 - 9, Sat. 9:30 - 6, Sun. 11:30 - 5
Telephone:	(905) 875-4917
Location:	**St. Thomas.**
Hours:	M. to F. 9:30 - 9, Sat. 9:30 - 6, Sun. 11:30 - 5
Location:	**Woodstock.**
Hours:	M. to F. 9:30 - 9, Sat. 9:30 - 6, Sun. 11:30 - 5
Telephone:	(519) 539-2802

CRAFTER'S CORNER

This small, quaint shop is a paradise for quality decorator pieces for the home. There's no better place than this charming shop to either purchase quality materials to make an arrangement yourself, or have them customize one for you. Simply bring in a swatch of fabric or wallpaper, and they'll do the rest. Ask about their craft classes as well. The day we were in we were amazed by their preserved roses which were truly awesome!

Location:	**167 Queen St. S. (south of Hwy. 401, take Mississauga Rd. exit, then left at third light), Streetsville.**
Hours:	T. & W. 10 - 6, Thu. & F. 10 - 7, Sat. 10 - 5, Sun. 12 - 4 open additional hours from September - December, call for details
Telephone:	(905) 567-9795

THE CRAFTERS MARKETPLACES

Imagine a craft sale with 350 crafters open 7 days/week, year-round with no admission or parking charges. Shoppers with lots of gifts to purchase will find something for almost everyone. Most locations operate on mall hours, but call for details.

Location:	**167 Queen St. S. (south of Hwy. 401, take Mississauga Rd. exit, then left at third light), Streetsville.**
Telephone:	(905) 632-1990
Location:	**1755 Pickering Parkway, Unit 32, Pickering.**
Telephone:	(905) 686-0714
Location:	**Home and Design Centre, 2575 Dundas St. W., #18 (N. side, E. of Winston Churchill Blvd.), Mississauga.**
Telephone:	(905) 828-6626
Location:	**Thornhill Square Mall, Thornhill.**
Telephone:	(905) 707-0900

Location: Warden Power Centre (Warden and St. Clair Ave.), Scarborough.
Telephone: (416) 755-0988
Other locations:
Hamilton (905) 574-3333, Kitchener (519) 748-2285, London (519) 685-9800; Windsor 519) 250-7880; Ottawa (613)829-6943 or Ottawa East (613) 749-0959,Barrie (705) 737-2699; Oakville (905) 337-8089

HAMPSTEAD HOUSE BOOKS - OFF-PRICE OUTLET
Here's yet another reason to explore the Doncaster Ave. area. While most of their business deals with book mail orders, it's the overstocks and returns that will grab your attention.
Location: 80 Doncaster Ave. (east off Yonge St, north of Steeles Ave.), Thornhill.
Hours: M. to F. 9 - 4
Telephone: (905) 881-0607

HARCOURT BRACE - EDUCATIONAL BOOK WAREHOUSE SALE
All sorts of books - from children's literature to lap books, theme books, professional development books, activity books and atlases - at up to 75% off. Cash or VISA only.
Location: 55 Horner Ave. (south of the QEW, west of Islington Ave.), Etobicoke.
Hours: M. to F. 9 - 4:30
Telephone: (416) 255-4491

INTICRAFTS - IMPORTERS' STORES
Do you want a quick shopping trip to South America or some other exotic locale? We visited the largest location, on Bloor St. W., and found better buys on an eclectic range of clothing, jewelry, loose beads, purses and unusual artifacts from around the world.
Location: 2305 Yonge St., Toronto.
Hours: M. to Sat. 11 - 6
Telephone: (416) 480-9629
Location: 372A Queen St. W., Toronto.
Hours: M. to Sat. 11 - 6
Telephone: (416) 979-1085
Location: 444 Bloor St. W., (east of Honest Ed's and Bathurst St.), Toronto.
Hours: M. to Sat. 11 - 7, Sun. 12 - 6
Telephone: (416) 539-0319

LYNRICH ARTS
Many students will appreciate every day low prices on brand name art materials and drafting supplies. The staff is knowledgeable and helpful. Enjoy savings of up to 50%.
Location: 73 Doncaster Ave. (Yonge and Steeles area), Thornhill.
Telephone: (905) 771-0411 Call for hours.

MALABAR
Are little toes heading to a dance class? Point them in this direction & you'll find dance shoes, dance/exercise wear, accessories, theatrical makeup & more.
Location: 14 McCaul St. (just N. of Queen St. W.), Toronto.
Hours: M. to F. 10 - 6, Sat. 10 - 5
Telephone: (416) 598-2581

MARY MAXIM CLEARANCE SALE
Mary Maxim is a well known name for any of you crafty folks who purchase yarn, patterns, fabric, cross stitch and crochet thread or rug kits. All the yarn is manufactured to their specifications, and cannot be bought anywhere other than their outlet store. What better excuse for an outing to Paris?? Ontario that is!
Location: 75 Scott Avenue (north of town off 24A Hwy), Paris.
Hours: M. to Sat. 9:30 - 5:30, Sun. and most holidays 11 - 5
Telephone: (519) 442-6342

MINNOW BOOKS
A major distributor of children's books is clearing popular authors such as Robert Munsch and Beverly Cleary, titles from the Goosebumps and Hardy Boys series and much more. May Warehouse Sale.
Location: 1251 Northside Rd. (north off Mainway Rd. between the Guelph Line and Walkers Line), Burlington.
Hours: M. to F. 8:30 - 4:30
Telephone: (905) 336-4003; toll free 1-800-263-5210

NATIONAL BOOK SERVICE SALE
Teachers & Librarians: This company is your best source for curriculum relevant print and multimedia material as well as classroom & library supplies all at educational discounts. You can shop in person at any of their four showrooms in Ottawa, Cambridge, London or North York, or by catalogue or website.
Location: 25 Kodiak Crescent (north of Sheppard Avenue, west of Allan Road), North York.
Telephone: (416) 630-2950 or 1-800-387-3178

PAPER PEDDLERS WAREHOUSE SALE

With over 7000 sq. feet of space packed with art and education supplies for kids, this is a great sale to stock up on gifts and craft items. Brand names such as Crayola, Playdoh, Roylco, Trend and much more at warehouse reduced prices. Art paper is half price, markers start at $.99 and even wooden stamps are as little as $.45 cents.

Location: 75 Dolomite Drive (west off Dufferin Street between Finch and Steeles Ave.), Downsview.
Hours: M. to Fri. 9-5
Telephone: (416) 665-4934

PAPER PEDDLERS
ART & EDUCATIONAL SUPPLIES

A great place for parents to find all kinds of interesting craft supplies and educational materials at low, low prices. Originally established in 1983 as a supplier to schools and day cares, Paper Peddler's 7,000 sq. foot warehouse is now open to the public offering parents the same low prices that teachers pay. From paint, markers and paper, to beads, googly eyes and feathers, the selection is endless. Brand name products. View some of Paper Peddler's specials on line at www.paperpeddlers.com.

Location: 75 Dolomite Drive in North York. Dolomite Drive runs west off of Dufferin Street one traffic light south of Steeles Avenue.
Telephone: 416-665-4934

Hours: Mon, Tues, Wed. 9 – 5,
Thursday 9 – 9:30, Friday 9 – 4:30

Sale Events: Semi-Annual Sale events take place in November and June. Call for details.

PATONS CLEARANCE CENTRE

Winter seems a long way away, but summer holidays give you extra leisure time to knit - so drop into one of these two clearance centres for their annual yarn clearance sale. Lots of selection at discount prices.

Location: 2700 Dufferin Street, Unit #1, (at Castlefield Ave.), Toronto.
Telephone: (416)782-3938

PSH - THE POTTERY SUPPLY HOUSE

Professional potters surely know about this huge supplier already but hobbyists should note that they have absolutely everything from clay bodies, tools, books to cones and kilns. As wholesalers they offer better pricing on volume, there is a catalogue available as well as delivery and you can check them out on the web at www.pshcanada.com. Now go throw something! (It's a potter's term).

Location: 1120 Speers Rd., (between 3rd and 4th Lines, on the south side), Oakville.
Hours: M. to F. 8:30 - 5, Sat. 9 - 1
(July and August closed on Saturdays)
Telephone: (905) 827-1129, 800-465-8544

Arts, Crafts & Books

Arts, Crafts & Books

SPINRITE FACTORY OUTLET
This outlet deserves top rating for knitting machine supplies. They also carry a good variety of cottons, wools, blends and synthetic yarns in balls, suitable for a wide range of crafts with lots of notions and patterns to get you started. "Tent" sales occur in the summer. Call for details.

Location: 230 Elma St. W., (at the stoplight take Wallace Ave. S. off Hwy. 86 to Elma), Listowel.
Hours: M. to F. 9 - 6, Sat. 9 – 5, Sun. 11-5
Telephone: (519) 291-3951

TANDY LEATHER COMPANY - OUTLET STORES
Most will recognize this Canadian distributor of leathercraft goods and assorted craft supplies - there are dozens of retail stores across Canada. At their distribution centres, shoppers will find extra savings on clearances of end-of-lines etc.

Location: 120 Brock St. (north of Essa Rd. and west off Anne St.), Barrie.
Hours: M. to F. 9 - 5, Sat. 9 - 4
Telephone: (705) 728-6501
Location: 1315 Merivale Rd., Ottawa.
Hours: M. to W. 9 - 5:30, Thu. 9 - 6, Sat. 9 - 5
Telephone: (613) 225-3550

TRINITY COLLEGE BOOK SALE
Biblio-techs will want to stock up for the coming winter with better buys on books during this annual event. Expect to find used books in just about every category imaginable. October Warehouse Sale.

Location: Seeley Hall, Main Building, 6 Hoskin Ave. (near Museum Subway stop, west off University Ave. and directly north of the Queens Park Circle), Toronto.
Telephone: (416) 978-6750

T.B.A. TO BE ANNOUNCED - DATES NOT AVAILABLE AT PRESS TIME

THIS SYMBOL INDICATES WAREHOUSE SALES

leisure time

Toys, Party Novelties & Packaging

ALIRON MARKETING
Chock full of gifts and toys with lots of brand name products that include books, toys, games, electronics, and novelty items. Nothing is over $20, and all prices include tax - prices are 60 - 80% off retail.
Location: 261 Trowers Road (south of Hwy 7, west of Hwy 400), Woodbridge
Telephone: (905) 264-9411 Call for hours.

BAGS OF FUN
You can either make up your own personalized bags, or choose from 95 different loot bags priced from $5 - $6. Lots of great stuff including balloons and cakes. They even have their own clown. Call direct for upcoming sales.
Location: 94 George Street (QEW to Trafalgar Road, south to the Lakeshore and west two blocks).
Hours: Closed Mon., T. to Sat. 9:30 - 5:30
Telephone: (905) 337-2247

CANADIAN HOBBYCRAFT - MANUFACTURER'S OUTLET
Canada's largest manufacturer & wholesaler of hobbies & toys opens its outlet annually until Xmas. With prices it boasts are the best, & ends of lines & discontinued items such as wooden boat kits, train sets, scenery, science kits & various radio controlled toys, this place is interesting to say the least. Call for Warehouse Sales.
Location: 140 Applewood Cres. (north of Hwy. 7., west off Jane St.), Concord.
Hours: M. to F. 8:30 - 5
Telephone: (905) 738-6556

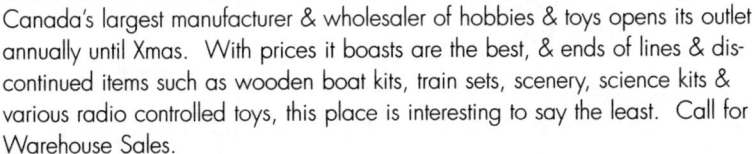

> **Do infants enjoy infancy as much as adults enjoy adultery?**

CREATIVE BAG
Gift wrapping is a delight if you have the right ingredients - and this outlet has them all! From festive bags and wrap, to ribbons, bows and boxes, you'll find everything you need at prices that won't break your Christmas budget. Beautiful tissue at .99, curling ribbon from $2.99/roll and beautifully patterned boxes help to make wrapping a breeze.

Location: 880 Steeprock Drive (Allan Expressway and Sheppard Ave. area), Downsview
Hours: M. to F. 9-6, Sat. 9-5 and Sun. 12-5
Telephone: (416)-631-6444

EVERGREEN PACKAGING INC. OUTLET SALE
This manufacturer is clearing out discontinued colours and designs of unique, high quality paper products that include giftwrap, gift boxes, gift bags, tissue, ribbons and just about anything you'd need to wrap an elegant gift. We particularly liked their wine and food boxes which are perfect for gift wrapping any time. Cash only. Call for November sale dates and times.

Location: 70 Clayson Road (north of Hwy 401, between Weston Road and Jane Street), Toronto .
Hours: M. to Sat. 9-5
Telephone: (416)-740-4345

GANZ WAREHOUSE SALE
Famous for their teddy bears, this sale also offers great savings on a wide assortment of gift giving ideas - from candles and ornaments to home and garden decor, collectibles and house wares too. It is cash only. November warehouse sale. Call for time and dates.

Location: 1 Pearce Rd., (north off of Steeles Ave. and just west of Weston Rd.), Woodbridge.

HENRY LIMITED
This company carries low, direct-from-the toy factory prices like swing sets, wagons and easels. Cash and carry. June and December Warehouse sales.

Location: 1 Head St., (west of Hamilton, south of Hwy. 5, north of Hwy.99), Dundas.
Hours: Please call for hours.
Telephone: (905) 628-2231

IRWIN TOY - FACTORY OUTLET
NOW SHOP ON-LINE at **www.irwin-toy.com** in our VIRTUAL TOY STORE. Toys and tons of them including: dolls, games, products for preschoolers and sports equipment too. Great savings on samples, ends of lines and over production.

Location: 43 Hanna Ave. (south of King St. W.), Toronto.
Hours: M. to F. 9 - 4
Telephone: (416) 533-3521 ext. 4111   See advertisement on page A12

LOOTBAG EXPRESS
Here's a great idea that will make having a party a lot easier and more fun - this Toy Superstore has just opened a new division called "LOOT BAG EXPRESS". Order professionally packaged loot bags and all your party supplies by phone, fax or e-mail and have them delivered for a small charge to your home. Lots of great bag fillers for both girls and boys of all ages or have them custom make them just for you.

Location: 145 West Beaver Creek Road
(Leslie St. and Hwy 7), Richmond Hill.
Hours: M. to W., 10 - 6, Thur. 10 - 7, F. 10 - 6, Sat. 10 - 5, Sun. 12-5
Telephone: 1-877-LOOT BAG, or visit their
web site at www.lootbags.com.

See advertisement on page A14

MARKA CANADA - CLEARANCE OUTLET
Their inventory is constantly changing and the prices are great on a wide range of items, including: Halloween supplies and make-up, watches, gift baskets, costume jewelry, bath accessories, stationery, giftware.

Location: 4500 Dixie Rd., Unit 11B, (south of Eglinton Ave.), Mississauga.
Hours: M. to F. 9 - 5
Telephone: (905) 238-6599

MATTEL TOY CLUB
In their huge distribution centre Mattel has created a store that offers almost the complete line of Mattel/Fisher-Price at retail pricing As well, they offer a wall of damaged boxes and discontinued items at great savings.

Location: 6155 Freemont Blvd., (2 lights west of Hwy. 10 on Britannia Rd.), Mississauga .
Hours: Tues. and W. 10 a.m. to 5 p.m., Thurs. and F. 10 a.m. tp.m., Sat. 10 a.m. to 5 p.m.
Telephone: 905) 501-5147 (Outlet Hotline)

MIKO TOY WAREHOUSE
What superlatives haven't we used to describe this place? It's the largest with 40,000 square feet that is packed to the rafters with the best brand name toys at the hottest prices. Celebrating their 25th year in business, they've added to the toy line with excellent deals on Mickey Mouse and Pooh Bear baby and children's fashion accessories, sweet savings on Hersey chocolates, lots of NOMA decor, bath and beauty sets and toys and gifts for adults too.

Location: 60 East Beaver Creek Rd., Richmond Hill.
Hours: W. and Sat. 10 to 5, Thurs. and F. 10 to
8, Sun. 11 to 5
Telephone: (905) 771-8714

See advertisement on page A16 & A17

NOAH'S ARK INDOOR PLAYLAND
Many busy parents are looking for alternatives to the traditional birthday party at home - if you're one of those, you may be interested in this new playland that has recently opened. The opening special offers a party for up to 24 kids, complete with invitations, 90 minutes of play, juice and pizza, an 8" birthday cake, a hostess and more for $175. Smaller packages are available from $99, and a 92 degree pool is also available. It may be cheaper to do at home, but this sure takes care of all the details and all the mess - plus the kids have a ball!

Location: 5004 Timberlea Blvd., Unit #9 & 10 (Eglinton Ave. E. to Tomken Road, right on Timberlea Blvd. and left at the first lights), Mississauga.
Hours: Parties are available weekdays after school and evenings, Sat. and Sun. morning and afternoons
Telephone: (905) 629-7946

NORAMPAC - BOX OUTLET
Summers coming which means moving season is on its way! Inside this huge factory is a wall with sample boxes that shoppers can choose from and the pricing is much better than retail. Here are some samples: cardboard wardrobe boxes are 5 for $52.20; 5 cubic foot boxes are 10 for $28.09 and file boxes for businesses are 20 for $41.00.

Location: 7700 Keele St., (west side just south of Hwy. 7), Concord.
Hours: M. to F. 7-4, closed holidays.
Telephone: (416) 663-6340

PACKAGING WORLD
Have you ever tried sending a parcel overseas, only to realize you lacked adequate packaging or the appropriate box? This small outlet will sell you everything you need - from boxes, bubble wrap, tape, corrugated wrap, labels to whatever it takes.

Location: 830 Steeprock Dr. (just off the Allen Expressway between Sheppard and Finch Ave.), Downsview.
Hours: M. to F. 9 - 5
Telephone: (416) 631-7441

If the #2 pencil is the most popular, why is it still #2?

PARTY CITY STORES
Having a party? Check out one of these huge stores. Halloween is a big deal with them, as they feature an amazing display. There are lots of 50% off stickers for real dollar stretching values. The convenience of having a tremendous selection of everything needed for a party; from cups to napkins, favours to decorations, saves you lots of time. Other locations in Barrie, Kingston, Kitchener, London, and Oakville.

Location: **280 Kingston Rd., Units 3 & 4, Ajax.**
Hours: M. to F. 9:30 - 9, Sat. 9:30 - 6, Sun. 11 - 5
Telephone: (905) 683-3532

Location: **1225 Dundas St. E, unit 20 (west of Dixie, north side), Mississauga.**
Hours: M. to F. 9:30 - 9, Sat. 9:30 - 6, Sun. 10 - 5
Telephone: (905) 275-3799

Location: **1250 Brant St., Burlington.**
Hours: M. to Sat. 9:30 - 9, Sun. 10 - 5
Telephone: (905) 331-1278

Location: **156 Chrislea Rd. (north of Hwy. 7 and east off Weston Rd.) Woodbridge.**
Hours: M. to F. 9:30 - 9, Sat. 9:30 - 6, Sun. 10 - 5
Telephone: (905) 856-2125

Location: **4 Kennedy Rd. S. Unit B1 (at Queen St.), Brampton.**
Hours: M. to F. 9:30 - 9, Sat. 9:30 - 6, Sun. 10 - 5
Telephone: (905) 457-4606

Location: **1448 Lawrence Ave. E. Unit 22, North York.**
Telephone: (416) 755-2552

Location: **7171 Yonge St., Thornhill.**
Telephone: (905) 771-9438

PARTY PACKAGERS
These folks have just opened another new 20,000-square-foot discount outlet in Ajax. These stores have over 800,000 discount toys, loot bags, and the best party supply items. They have everything you could possibly need for a party: loot bags, toys, games, crafts, puzzles, balloons, tableware, decorations, gift wrap and more! With highly discounted prices, savings are tremendous.

Location: **1225 Finch Ave. W., North York.**
Hours: M. to W. 10 - 7, Thu. & F. 10 - 9, Sat. 9:30 - 6, Sun. 11 - 5
Telephone: (416) 631-7688

Location: **3050 Vega Blvd., Unit 5 (Highway 403 and Dundas St.), Mississauga.**
Hours: M. to F. 10 - 9, Sat. 9:30 - 6, Sun. 11 - 5
Telephone: (905) 607-2789

Location: Durham Regional Centre (Hwy. 2 and Harwood Ave.), Ajax.
Hours: M. to F. 9:30 - 9, Sat. 9:30 - 6, Sun. 11 - 5
Telephone: (905) 619-9993

REGAL GREETINGS AND GIFTS
While most of us think of Regal as a company that sells merchandise through a catalogue, it has some stores as well. Selected current catalogue merchandise is priced at 25 to 30% off, with some liquidation items at 50% off or more. Most gift items are $25 or less, and we've listed the locations below.
Telephone: (905) 670-0066 - For more information call customer service.
Location: 1147 Bellamy Rd., Scarborough.
Hours: M. to W. & F. 9:30 - 5:30, Thu. 9:30 - 8, Sat. 9 - 5
Telephone: (416) 439-2939
Location: 1450 Hopkins St., Whitby.
Hours: M. to W. & F. 9:30 - 5:30, Thu. 9:30 - 8, Sat. 9 - 5
Telephone: (905) 666-3501
Location: 1126 Finch Ave. West, North York.
Hours: M. to W. & F. 9:30 - 5:30, Thu. 9:30 - 8, Sat. 9 - 5
Telephone: (416) 736-7535
Location: 335 Evans Ave., Etobicoke.
Hours: M. to W. 10 - 6, Thu. 10 - 8, F. 10 - 6, Sat. 9 - 5
Telephone: (416) 253-5560
Location: 939a Eglinton Ave. E., Toronto.
Hours: M. to W. 9 - 6, Thu. - F. 9 - 8, Sat. 9 - 5
Telephone: (416) 425-5871

Locations also in Kitchener, London, Kingston, Barrie, Ottawa, Windsor, Sudbury, Stoney Creek, St. Catharines, Peterborough & Hamilton.

RIZZCO TOY AND GIFT SALE
One stop shopping that is chock-a-block with savings, ideas and items for every one and every budget from your favorite aunt to THE boss and even Santa, ho, ho, ho.
Location: 305 Supertest Rd., (north of Finch Ave., west off Dufferin St.), North York.
Hours: Until Dec. 24th, weekdays 10-6, Saturday 11-5, Sunday 12-5.
Telephone: (416) 665-9595

See advertisement on page A21

ROYAL SPECIALTY SALES 💰
For all those aspiring witches and goblins, hop on your broom and zoom down to this sale - a great opportunity to pick up Haloween products that include costumes, makeup, masks, wigs, accessories and more. Most of the stock is discontinued merchandise, samples and seconds - no cheques. October Warehouse Sale. Call for dates and times.

Location: 11 Industrial St (five blocks south of Eglinton. Ave. and east of Laird Dr.), Toronto.
Telephone: (416) 423-1133

SAMKO SALES - TOY AND GIFT WAREHOUSE OUTLET
Shoppers can expect a vast selection of name brand toys and gifts at excellent pricing (most below wholesale) and the bright and cheery renovations in honour of their twenty fifth anniversary make it all even nicer. Not generally open to the public, this book will allow you entrance and please leave the kids at home.

Location: 11 Peel Ave. (turn N. on Gladstone Ave., off Queen St. W.), Toronto.
Hours: Until Dec. 24th Thurs. and F. 10 a.m. to p.m., Sat. 9 a.m. to 5 p.m. and Sun. 10 a.m. to 5 p.m. - doors close half hour before the store closes.
Telephone: (416) 532-1114

See advertisement on page A16 & A17

SANDYLION STICKER DESIGNS
This warehouse clears out stickers by the pound and in rolls. Window decals, sticker albums and wrapping accessories such as balloons and decals are also available. Cash and cheques only.

Location: 400 Cochrane Dr. (Hwy. 7 and Woodbine Ave.), Markham.
Hours: M. to F. 9 - 6, Sat. 9 - 4, Sun. 10 - 4
Telephone: (905) 475-6771

STUDIO SPECIALTIES 💰
Divine and decadent Christmas decor items at wholesale pricing are offered by the folks who supply window dressers and store display people with wonderful baubles, ribbons and garland to deck the retail halls with! Cash and Visa only. December Warehouse Sale.

Location: 289 Bridgeland Ave. (W. off Dufferin St., under the 401), Toronto.
Hours: M. to F. 9 - 5
Telephone: (416) 787-1813

Toys, Party Novelties & Packaging

leisure time

Florists, Gift Baskets

BASKITS WAREHOUSE SALE
From pots and mugs to gourmet foods, baby items and yes baskets, at 40 - 70% off. Fall Warehouse Sale. Call for details.
Location: 750 Birchmount Rd., Unit 51 & 52 (south of Eglinton Ave.), Scarborough.
Telephone: (416) 755-1100

FLOWER DEPOT
The six Flower Depot stores in the Metro area are full-service floral shops. They offer a wide selection of roses as well as cut flowers, floral arrangements and plants.
Location: 2400 Guelph Line, Burlington.
Telephone: (905) 336-8273
Location: 2902 Bloor St. W., Etobicoke.
Telephone: (416) 236-8273
Location: 3315 Fairview Street, Burlington.
Telephone: (905) 637-7673
Location: 4981 Hwy. 7 (across from Markville Mall), Markham.
Telephone: (905) 470-7673
Location: 666 Burnhamthorpe Rd., Etobicoke.
Telephone: (416) 622-8273
Location: 9255 Woodbine Ave., Unionville.
Telephone: (905) 887-8080

My inferiority complex is not as good as yours.

GIFT-PAK/DAREE IMPORTS AND SALES LTD.

Always a favourite when assembling a gift basket or stuffing a stocking. These two companies at one location are at the top of our list with a wide variety of cosmetics, bath and hair care products, as well as a fine lineup of portion packed gourmet foods, fine chocolates, candles, napkins and all the wrappings, bows and baskets to bring it all together. Warehouse sale in November. Call for details.

Location: 5486 Gorvan Dr.. (south of Highway 401, east off Tomken Rd. on to Brevik Place, left to Gorvan Dr.), Mississauga.
Hours: M. to Wed. and Fri. 9-4, Thurs. 9-7, Sat. 10-3. Closed on Sat. during the summer.
Telephone: (905) 624-3359   See advertisement on page A11

GRATRIX GARDEN LILIES

Tom's hobby of hybridizing lilies grew into a direct-to-consumer business that features over 500 varieties of day lilies and lily bulbs of the highest quality. Not inexpensive (between $4 and $15 a plant) this low-tech, farm-gate style operation is awesome - don't get whiplash if you drive by the thousands of plants still in bloom! Daylilies are ready for pick up in late August with bulbs available in early October and a price listing is available upon request.

Location: 3714 Vasey Rd., (take Hwy. 400 about 40 kms. north of Barrie, exit #141 and go west about 1 km., on north side), Coldwater.
Hours: Open daily 8 - 8 until September 30th.
Telephone: (705) 835-6032

LIB & IDO'S ROSE EMPORIUM

Grown in their own large greenhouses, this operation lets you pick a bouquet of roses that is not only good value, but they're fresh. Now choose up to 50 different colours of roses.

Location: 204 Dupont St., Toronto.
Hours: Please call for seasonal hours.
Telephone: (416) 922-9909

Florists, Gift Baskets

> To be intoxicated is to feel sophisticated, but not be able to say it.

Florists, Gift Baskets

ROSES ONLY
What Valentine's sentiment can be complete without roses? The quintessential time-honoured expression of love. We always buy our roses here, where both the quality and price are hard to beat. Boxed roses with baby breath and greens start at $30.00/dozen, and they have over 36 varieties of roses in colours ranging from traditional red to the exotic. If your beloved prefers tulips, why not order her a dozen long stem tulips in spring colours for $18.00? Banish those winter blues!

Location: 8 Market Street (across from St. Lawrence Market), Toronto M5E 1M6.
Hours: M. 9-1, Tues. to Thurs. 9-6, F. 9-7, Sat. 8-5.
Telephone: 416-594-6678, Fax: 416-594-3708

See advertisement on page A20

SWEET EXPRESSIONS 💲
Perfect for picking up gifts for those hard-to-buy-for people; they are open to the public before Christmas with good buys on gift baskets and other containers of edibles. November/December and April Sales.

Location: 266 Applewood Cres., (take Edgely Blvd. north off Hwy.7 and just east of Hwy. 400 to Applewood Cres.), Concord.
Hours: 6 weeks before Christmas, open M. to F. 8:30 - 4:30, Sat. 10 - 3
Telephone: (905) 660-1540

WHAT A BASKET!
There's still lots of time to order a customized basket for friends, colleagues or even yourself! We ordered several last year as gifts, and were delighted with the quality and price. Choose from dozens of baskets filled with gourmet treats, or find everything you need to make your own. Gift baskets also available at their Square One Christmas location on the lower level.

Location: 975 Pacific Gate, Unit 9 (Tomken & Derry Rds. area), Mississauga.
Hours: M. to F. 8:30 - 4:30, Sat. 10 - 3
Telephone: (905) 670-8056

> Men are from Earth, women are from Earth. Deal with it.

WHOLESALE FLORISTS

This superstore has an unusual concept. By becoming a member for $29.95 a year; you receive wholesale prices on all your floral purchases. Non-members also buy at competitive prices, but a membership allows your family exceptional value. The savings are particularly impressive if you are planning a wedding or other event where flowers are centre stage! Browse their 1000 sq. ft. walk in cooler for both imported and local flowers.
www.wholesalefloralgroup.com

Location: 55 Colossus Drive, Unit 128, (Hwy. 7 & Weston Road) Woodbridge.
Hours: M.- F. 9-5 , Sat. 10-6, Sun 10-5
Telephone: (905) 851-3001

WILD FLOWER FARM

A wonderful way to spend leisure time browsing in the country. Pick your own flowers, including unusual varieties. Most are priced at bouquet prices- 15 stems for $5 and 30 stems for $9, tax included. Some specialty flowers are priced separately. What a great idea if you're entertaining, planning a wedding, or just indulging yourself. The flowers bloom and change as the seasons do throughout the summer and fall.

Location: R.R.#3 (between Schomberg & Nobleton on the first road W. of Hwy. 27, just N. of the 17th Sideroad), Schomberg.
Hours: M. to Sun. 10 - 6
Telephone: (905) 859-0286

Practice safe eating -- always use condiments.

business

- Office Supplies
- Computers & Electronics

business

Office Supplies

BUSINESS DEPOT / STAPLES BUSINESS DEPOT
Business Depot / Staples Business Depot is Canada's largest office products superstore chain. With over 7,500 brand name office products, customers will find everything from pens and paper to furniture, business machines and computers, as well as Copy Centre and Business Services. We will provide customers with the lowest prices on national brand products, everyday, with associates who really care and provide friendly, knowledgeable service.
Customers can take advantage of three ways to shop: In any one of the 165 stores currently across Canada; Through the catalogue; And on-line, where we are open for business 24 hours a day, seven days a week. With every order of $50.00 or more (catalogue/on-line), we will deliver, free of charge to your home or business address. There are over 60 locations in Ontario to serve your personal or business needs. To determine the store location closest to you or shop online, we can be reached at: www.businessdepot.com., www.staples.ca or www.bureauengros.com.

Location: 1250 Steeles Ave. E., Brampton.
Hours: M. to F. 8 - 9, Sat. 9 - 6, Sun. 11 - 5
           Sat. 9 a.m. - 6 p.m., Sun. 9 a.m. - 6 p.m.
Telephone: (905) 796-2505

Location: 1750 The Queensway, Etobicoke.
Telephone: (416) 620-5674

Location: 180 Queens Plate Dr., Unit. 1A, Etobicoke.
Hours: M. to F. 8 - 9, Sat. 9 - 6, Sun. 11 - 5
           Extended hours during Back to School sales, call for details
Telephone: (416) 749-9932

Location: 1936 McCowan Rd., Scarborough.
Hours: M. to F. 8 - 9, Sat. 9 - 6, Sun. 11 - 5
Telephone: (416) 292-4570

Location: 1980 Eglinton Ave. E., Scarborough.
Hours: M. to F. 8 - 9, Sat. 9 - 6, Sun. 11 - 5
           Extended hours during Back to School sales, call for details
Telephone: (416) 752-1091

See advertisement on page A3

Office Supplies

Location: **2160 Steeles Ave. W., Concord.**
Hours: M. to F. 8 - 9, Sat. 9 - 6, Sun. 11 - 5
Extended hours during Back to School sales, call for details
Telephone: (905) 660-7051
Location: **250 Front St. E. (Front and Parliament), Toronto.**
Hours: M. to F. 8 - 9, Sat. 9 - 6, Sun. 11 - 5
Extended hours during Back to School sales, call for details
Telephone: (416) 368-3331
Location: **3150 Dufferin St., Toronto.**
Hours: M. to F. 8 - 9, Sat. 9 - 6, Sun. 11 - 5
Extended hours during Back to School sales, call for details
Telephone: (416) 785-5335
Location: **3175 Hwy. 7, Unit 200, Markham.**
Hours: M. to F. 8 - 9, Sat. 9 - 6, Sun. 11 - 5. Copy Depot open 24 hours a day, 7 days a week.
Telephone: (905) 479-3101
Location: **375 University Ave., Toronto.**
Hours: M. to F. 8 - 7, Sat. 9 - 6, Sun. 11 - 5
Extended hours during Back to School sales, call for details
Telephone: (416) 598-4818
Location: **5170 Dixie Rd., Mississauga.**
Hours: M. to F. 8 - 9, Sat. 9 - 6, Sun. 11 - 5
Telephone: (905) 602-5889
Location: **57 Northview Blvd., Woodbridge.**
Hours: M. to F. 8 - 9, Sat. 9 - 6, Sun. 11 - 5
Extended hours during Back to School sales, call for details
Telephone: (905) 856-6588
Location: **945 Eglinton Ave. E., Toronto.**
Hours: M. to F. 8 - 9, Sat. 9 - 6, Sun. 11 - 5
Telephone: (416) 696-0043
Location: **Heartland Town Centre, 5935 Mavis Rd., Mississauga.**
Hours: M. to F. 8 - 9, Sat. 9 - 6, Sun. 11 - 5
Telephone: (905) 712-4484
Location: **Plus locations in Oakville, Burlington and Hamilton. Call Head Office for addresses.**
Telephone: (905) 513-6116

See advertisement on page A3

DAY-TIMER OF CANADA
Memo, date and appointment books and organizational accessories are cleared through this very small outlet. The inventory changes frequently with specials offered on a regular basis.
Location: **9515 Montrose Rd., Niagara Falls.**
Hours: M. to F. 8 - 5
Telephone: (905) 356-8020 or 1-800-465-5501

business

Computers & Electronics

BEAMSCOPE - WAREHOUSE OUTLET
While they do carry electronics and such what we were most impressed with were the deals on computer software! Expect excellent pricing on a little less than current titles and programs and items that they are overstocked in.
Location: 33 West Beaver Creek Rd., (west off Leslie St. or north off Hwy. 7), Richmond Hill.
Hours: M. to F. 10 a.m. to 6 p.m. but closed Tuesdays.
Telephone: (905) 771-5100

CITIZEN ELECTRONICS
Consumer electronics, including microwaves, breadmakers, TV's, VCRs & portable stereos are being cleared at bargain prices. No cheques.
Location: 455 Gordon Baker Rd. (one light south of Victoria Park Ave. and Steeles Ave.), Willowdale.
Hours: M. to F. 8 - 5
Telephone: (416) 499-5611

THE ELECTRONICS OUTLET
This great ongoing outlet is filled with products by RCA, Proscan and GE. Knowledgeable and helpful staff! Inventory comes and goes and includes lots of video and audio equipment –TV's, VCR's, stereos and accessories - telephones, answering machines, cables and connections, some of which may be in damaged cartons or refurbished but still guaranteed.
Location: 7400A Bramalea Rd, (west side, between Steeles Rd. and Derry Rd.), Mississauga.
Hours: M. to F. 10 a.m. to 6 p.m. Closed Sat. & Sun.
Telephone: (905) 672-8616.
New Location: 6200 Edwards Blvd. Mississauga (North East corner of 401 & Hwy # 10)

Computers & Electronics

IBM WAREHOUSE OUTLET
It's not often you get a chance to pick up world class technology at outlet prices, but that's exactly what IBM is doing at this location - when we dropped in to the outlet store recently, we bought two systems absolutely loaded with memory and power for an unbelievable price - so drop in Big Blue's bargains on new and refurbished products that include computers, monitors, printers, peripherals, accessories, software and more. Quantities are limited but..... isn't it time to upgrade your system?

Location: 4175 - 14th Avenue, Markham East of Warden Ave., South of Highway 7
Hours: M - F 10 - 6 Sat. 10 - 5
Telephone: (905) 316-7777

See advertisement on page A13

IBM HOME COMPUTING STORE
Location: 3300 Highway 7 West Seven and 400 Centre, Vaughan.
Hours: Open 7 days a week – 10-6
Telephone: (905) 660-9333

See advertisement on page A13

> If all the world is a stage, where is the audience sitting?

T.B.A. TO BE ANNOUNCED - DATES NOT AVAILABLE AT PRESS TIME

THIS SYMBOL INDICATES WAREHOUSE SALES

LITEMOR
This wholesale operation should light up your life! Buy light bulbs, lighting fixtures and accessories at wholesale prices. For example - halogen lights by the case of fifteen are between $3.75 and $6.75 each, depending on the model.

Location: 325 Deerhide Cres. (west of Hwy. 400 on Finch Ave. take Arrow Rd. south), Weston.
Hours: M. to F. 8 - 5
Telephone: (416) 745-3806

MEI
If electronics are on your shopping list, this sale is one to check. Inventory will include car audio, car/home security, cellular phones & more, with up to 70% off retail prices.

Location: 310 Alden Rd., Markham.
Hours: M - F 8:30 - 5
Telephone: (905) 475-8444

PLAYBACK ELECTRONICS
With better brand name electronics at much better than retail pricing, this little industrial unit is packed with walkmans, TVs, VCRs, cordless phones, small kitchen appliances and much more. Warehouse Sales four times a year.

Location: 358 Flint Rd. (north of Finch Ave. west off Dufferin St. on Martin Ross Rd. to Flint), Downsview.
Hours: M. to F. 9 - 5
           Call for Warehouse times and dates.
Telephone: (416) 661-7781

Computers & Electronics

> If man evolved from monkeys and apes, why do we still have monkeys and apes?

Computers & Electronics

REPLAY ELECTRONICS
Another terrific spot for post-Christmas shopping is this electronics store that features new products, close outs and end-of-line brand name goods. Starting December 26, while supplies last, expect additional savings on final clearance items that include Toshiba big screen TVs and DVDs, Kenwood home theatre systems, RCA televisions and much more.
Location: 1120 The Queensway (just west of Islington Ave.), Toronto
Hours: M to Friday 10-6, Saturday 10-5 (open on Boxing Day, December 26 12-5)
Telephone: (416) 251-9096

street priced electronics™
Always up to 65% OFF

Check out our great selection - it changes con-

◀◀**REPLAY**▶▶
ELECTRONICS
■ New Products ■ Close-Outs ■
■ End of Lines ■ Re-Packaged ■
home theatre systems, big screens, loud speakers, telephones, dvd and vcrs, subwoofers and hdtv ready television sets.
■ brand name ■ satisfaction guaranteed ■
1120 THE QUEENSWAY, WEST OF ISLINGTON 416-251-9096

UPGRADE FACTORY
Perhaps you just need a little more memory - or maybe a hard drive - or even another computer for the kids or for home. In any case, drop in to this location where the knowledgeable staff can help you with whatever your hardware requirements might be. Product includes many brand names, as well as a number of end-of-line and used notebook computers. Extended and factory backed warranties are often included, and prices are very competitive. No cheques.
Location: 1515 Matheson Blvd. E., Unit B-11 (south of Hwy 401 and east off Dixie Rd.), Mississauga.
Hours: M. to Sat. 10 - 6
Telephone: (905) 625-5525

miscellaneous

- Resale Goods
- A Little Bit Of Everything
- Malls
- Duty Free

miscellaneous

Resale Goods

ARCH INDUSTRIES
Okay grunge-ites, here it is. Before this rag factory turns used jeans into something else, they are offered for sale at $5 a pair, complete with holes, rips and unwashed to boot! Also available are used workwear, coveralls and new fabric. Cash and carry

Location: **200 Bartor Rd., (west side of Hwy. 400 between Sheppard and Wilson Aves., for Bartor Rd. take Clayson Rd. north off Wilson Ave. or Arrow Rd. north off Sheppard), Toronto.**
Hours: M. to F. 7:30 - 5
Telephone: (416) 741-7247

BACK AGAIN
Back Again carries high end and brand name new and gently used clothing for ladie's and children. This well stocked store also sells maternity wear, plus sizes and petites.

Location: **Richview Plaza, 250 Wincott Drive, Etobicoke.**
Hours: M. to W. 10 - 6, Sat. 9:30 - 5, Thu. & F. 10 - 7
Telephone: (416) 249-2225

BEAN SPROUT
A resale shop specializing in kid's designer clothing and accessories. There is a large play area, free juice, cookies and coffee, a quiet area for nursing moms and free diapers.

Location: **616 Mount Pleasant Rd. (south of Manor Rd.), Toronto.**
Hours: M. to Sat. 10:30 - 5:30
Telephone: (416) 932-3727

BIG TIME
New and resale fashions sizes 14 - 4X. 50% off sales in August and February.

Location: **551 Eglinton Ave. W., Toronto.**
Hours: M. to W. 10 - 6, Thu. 12 - 8, F. 10 - 6, Sat. 10 - 5
Telephone: (416) 481-6464

CANADIAN SKI PATROL SKI SWAP
We are fortunate to have free ski patrolling in Canada - in some countries you have to negotiate a fee before being removed from the mountains after an injury! This huge ski swap is one way that they raise funds to continue their important work. It also presents an excellent way to pick up used equipment. There is a fee into the show but for enthusiasts, the Toronto Ski Show is a must. Ski show is mid-October.
Location: Exhibition Place on Toronto's waterfront.
Telephone: (416) 745-7511

CASH CONVERTERS
This chain's slogan is "a better way to sell....a great place to shop!" And indeed, with 28 stores in Ontario, there's no question you just may pick up a terrific item for a fraction of the price if bought new. Secondhand goods include jewelry, electrical appliances, sporting equipment, power tools, cameras and much more - it really is an "alternative department store." They also pay cash for any quality used item, and have a section in each store where you can bring in your used goods. Right now is a great time to trade in summer sports gear, and winter sports equipment is 35-50% off. There is a 30 day warranty on items purchased, which does provide you with a comfort level when buying second hand goods.
Location: 3003 Danforth Rd. Shoppers World Plaza
Telephone: (416) 693-2274
Location: #24 - 508 Lawrence Ave. W., North York.
Telephone: (416) 785 7797
Location: #4 - 263 Queen Street E., Brampton.
Telephone: (905) 796-7777
Location: 1370 Dundas St. East, Mississauga.
Telephone: (905) 279-9717
Location: 1620 Albion Road, Rexdale.
Telephone: (416) 747-5242
Location: 180 Harwood Ave. S., Ajax.
Plus other locations throughout Ontario.

CHIC REPEATS
They offer designer children's clothing, from infant to size 14. Also available are: maternity, quality toys and baby accessories.
Location: 115 Trafalgar Rd. (near the Lakeshore), Oakville.
Hours: T. to Sat. 10 - 5 Summer hours T. to Sat. 10 - 4
Telephone: (905) 842-0905

Resale Goods

THE CLASSY ATTIC
They offer new and used designer fashions for ladie's, as well as used furs in the winter only. Look for a good selection of business attire and accessories.
Location: **1051 Simcoe St. N., Oshawa.**
Hours: M. to W. 10 - 5, Thu. 10 -6, F. 10 - 5:30, Sat. 10 - 5
Telephone: (905) 432-1012

CLOTHES FRIENDS - FASHION BOUTIQUE
Shop for designer labels in ladie's fashions, business & casual wear, evening & party wear, shoes, accessories and jewelry. The bridal boutique has a good selection of gowns. For children, the Kids Closet is next door.
Location: **109 Brock St. S., Whitby.**
Hours: M. to W., Sat. 10 - 6, Thu. & F. 10 - 8
Telephone: (905) 668-4100

COLLINGWOOD SKI CLUB SKI SWAP
It's always well done with excellent bargains and always takes place during the Thanksgiving weekend. You can sell and buy everything from new and used equipment to clothing. The sale is in October.
Location: **Central Base Lodge, Blue Mountain Resorts, seven miles west of Collingwood on Blue Mountain Rd. Collingwood.**
Telephone: (705) 445-0231

COLOURS EXCHANGE
Another terrific consignment shop which is a favourite for quality in previously owned ladie's wear. Great selection of women's designer and high quality clothing, shoes and accessories. Prices are slashed even more during the off season. Appointments can be arranged to bring in seasonal items you wish to sell. New arrivals daily.
Location: 3 Brentwood Road North (one block west of Royal York Road north off Bloor St.), Etobicoke.
Hours: T. to F 10 - 6, Sat. 10 - 5:30
Telephone: (416) 239-0559   See advertisement on page A2

THE COMEBACK
The Comeback has been in business for 22 years and continues to offer a large variety of ladie's and children's clothing and accessories. Racks are filled with Designer and trendy store labels, plus they carry a special plus size section. This is a busy, well-stocked and organized store and right now most of the inventory is 25-50 % off. They have an annual end of season sale when everything is discounted even more. Shop now for a better selection.
Location: **4893 Dundas St. W. (south side and just east of Burnhampthorpe Rd.), Etobicoke.**
Hours: M. to W. & Sat. 9:30 - 5, Thu. 9:30 - 8:00, F. 9:30 - 6
Telephone: (416) 231-0381   See advertisement on page A28

CONTENTS CONNECTION
Here's a great consignment store with quality used furniture ranging from antiques to modern and collectibles. New shipments arrive daily, with 3,000 square feet of dining room and bedroom sets, couches, tables, light fixtures, china and more. A great way to upgrade or furnish without spending a lot of money.....and this is one place where prices are flexible!
Location: 3321 Bathurst St. (between Lawrence & Wilson Aves.), Toronto.
Hours: Open 7 days a week 10-5 (until 8 on W. and Thurs.)
Telephone: (416) 256-3566

DURHAM REGION PARENTS OF MULTIPLE BIRTHS ASSOC.
For the past 15 years, they have hosted a children's clothing & equipment sale. Proceeds go toward a network of support for parents of multiple births. The sales carry gently-used clothing in sizes from newborn to size 14, maternity clothes, baby equipment, toys & crafts. Cash only & no strollers are allowed. March and September Warehouse sales.
Location: Metro East Trade Centre, Brock Rd., (just north off Hwy. 401), Pickering.
Telephone: (905) 721-2238

THE ELEGANT GARAGE SALE
This everything/anything place is just as the name indicates and stacked to the rafters with new and used items to be sold at rock bottom prices. They take things on consignment, purchase items from individuals or buy bankrupt stocks.
Location: 1588 Bayview Ave., (south of Eglinton Ave.), Toronto.
Hours: M. and Tue 11-5, W. and Thur 11-8, F. 11-9, Sat and Sun 11-7
Telephone: (416) 322-9744.

ENCORE
This shop boasts high quality and great selection of gently used and new clothing. Right now they are taking in a lot of cruise wear, as well as party and wedding wear. Some very high quality ski wear is also available, as well as lots of accessories.
Location: 193 Bayfield Street, (400 north to Barrie - right on Bayfield approximately one mile. Parking in rear.), Barrie.
Hours: M. to Sat. 10 - 5, Thu. 10 - 7
Telephone: (705) 737-9623

Resale Goods

Resale Goods

THE FASHION GO ROUND
It's an interesting selection of ladie's and children's gently used clothing and accessories as well as baby needs, including strollers and playpens.
Location: 6 Brentwood Rd. (south off Bloor St., west of Royal York Rd.), Etobicoke.
Hours: T. to Sat. 10 - 5:30
Telephone: (416) 236-1220

THE FRUGAL SCOT
This small shop has expanded, and now offers even more good stuff! There's a large selection of quality used furniture, as well as an assortment of just about anything from small appliances to linen, household items, collectibles and even the odd antique. Consignments welcome with 60% of the selling price going to the consignor.
Location: 3783 Lakeshore Blvd. W. (at Brown's Line), Etobicoke.
Hours: T. to Thu. 10 - 6, F. 10 - 7, Sat. 10 - 5
Telephone: (416) 259-2149

FANTASTIC FLEA MARKET
At the Fantastic Flea Market you'll find lots of choice, bargains and savings. With 100,000 square feet of booths, this Flea Market prides itself in offering the most variety of items at the best prices. Lots of special events make this a fun location to shop for off-beat items for the whole family.
Location: 2375 Steeles Ave. W., North York
Telephone: 416-650-1090; Web site: www.fantasticfleamarket.com
Location: Dixie Outlet Mall (Downstairs) 1250 South Service Rd., Mississauga
Telephone: 905-274-9403

See advertisement on page A4

GOODWILL STORE
This bright, well-organized location has clothing for the whole family as well, everything is colour grouped, with lots of better names and very well priced.
Location: 382 Queen St. E. (north west corner at Hwy. 410 and Queen St. E.), Brampton.
Hours: M. to F. 9 - 9, Sat. 9 - 6, Sun. 10 - 5
Telephone: (905) 453-5252
Many other locations in Ontario.

HAND ME DOWNS
This is Canada's largest chain of resale stores specializing in children's clothing, maternity wear, toys, nursery furniture & equipment. Sellers are either paid for their belongings up front or once the items are sold. Visit their web page at www.handmedowns.com.

Location: 5051 Hwy. 7, Markham.
Hours: Hours vary. Please call for details.
Telephone: (905) 479-1869
Location: 545 Steeles Ave., W., Brampton
Hours: Hours vary. Please call for details.
Telephone: (905) 796-5437
Other locations: Oshawa, Peterborough, Collingwood, Courtice, Kitchener, St. Catharines, Oshawa, Barrie,

HAPPY HARRY'S
Harry is ready to strip out recyclables & sell the salvaged - everything from kitchen sinks to windows, studs & insulation. His associated company, the Environmental Recycling Group Inc., works not only with homeowners but also as brokers to large de-construction sites, and finding markets for reusable materials to meet provincial recycling regulations. Check out his web page at www.er-group.com! Cash or cheque with ID only.
Location: 4128 South Service Rd. (east of Walkers Line, north of Harvester Rd.), Burlington.
Hours: Call for hours
Telephone: (905) 631-0990

INESRA - I'LL NEVER EVER SHOP RETAIL AGAIN
From unique funky/classic vintage to elegant retro you can splurge without losing your shirt. All items in great condition. Generally $50 and under. Four shows; Spring, Summer, Fall and Winter or by appointment. A Host booking for small groups of 5 or more receive $25 off and complimentary wine and snack.
Location: 315 Albany Ave., 2nd Floor (E. of Bathurst St. & N. of Dupont Ave., off Bridgman Ave.), Toronto.
Hours: Call for specific dates and times.
Telephone: (416) 699-5242

IT'S WORTH REPEATING
This is a well displayed shop with a great selection of upscale children's clothing and accessories. It also carries high quality women's casual wear, maternity clothing, toys, baby equipment and country crafts. There's a children's play area as well.
Location: 3555 Thickson Rd. N. (north of Rossland Rd. E.), Whitby.
Hours: M. to F. 9:30 - 8, Sat 9:30 - 5, Sun 12 - 5
Telephone: (905) 579-9912

IDS KONSIGNMENT
This location has great quality merchandise - Patti checks every item carefully. Consignees can trust her to get a fair price on infant and children's clothing, equipment, furniture and maternity wear. Please note - they'll soon open in Georgetown as they too, are franchising.

Location: 66 Thomas St. Unit 26 (south of Britannia Rd. and between Queen St. and Erin Mills Pkwy.), Streetsville.
Hours: T. & W. 9:30 - 6, Thu. 9:30 - 8, F. 9:30 - 6, Sat. 9 - 5, Sun. 12 - 4 Call for Summer hours
Telephone: (905) 567-7890

L'ELEGANTE
High-end ladie's wear and accessories.
Location: 122 Yorkville Ave. (north of Bloor St. and east off Avenue Rd.), Toronto.
Hours: M. to Sat. 10 - 6, Sun. 11 - 5
Telephone: (416) 923-3220
Location: Sherwood Forest Shopping Village, 1900 Dundas St. W., Mississauga.
Hours: M. to W. 10 - 6, Thu. - F. 10 - 7, Sat. 10 - 5
Telephone: (905) 822-9610

NATIONAL SPORTS EQUIPMENT REPAIR
This is a small facility with a tiny selection of used equipment. It specializes in repairs that are important for players, who treasure the fine fit of their favourite gloves. For better quality equipment, repairs make economic sense. Cash or certified cheque only.
Location: 1540 Lodestar Rd., Unit 5 (west off Dufferin St./Allen Rd, north of Sheppard.), Downsview.
Hours: M. to F. 8:30 - 5:30
Telephone: (416) 638-3408

OF THINGS PAST - CONSIGNMENT FURNITURE SHOWROOM
Now in its 5th year, this store accepts and sells high quality home furnishings with good design and great value. With over 9000 square feet of space, both furniture and acessories show well and are displayed in a manner that delights the beholder. www.ofthingspast.com.
Location: 160 Tycos Dr., Unit 2 (between Caledonia Ave. and Dufferin St., south of Lawrence Ave.), Toronto.
Hours: M. to Sat. 10 - 5
Telephone: (416) 256-9256

See advertisement on page A20

OFF THE CUFF
Men's new and resale fashions are offered including shirts and ties. Things are always on sale. Layaway plans available.
Location: 5 Broadway Ave. (north of Eglinton Ave., east of Yonge St.), Toronto.
Hours: T. & W. 10 - 6, Thu. 12 - 8, F. 10 - 5 , Sat. 10 - 4
            Call for January and February Hours.
Telephone: (416) 489-4248

ONCE UPON A CHILD
These stores buy, sell and trade new and gently used children's clothing, toys, books, cribs, bedding, strollers, playpens, high chairs, and car seats. When you sell to them you are paid immediately.
Other locations: Hamilton, Burlington, Barrie, Ajax, Whitby, London,
Location: 16655 Yonge St., Newmarket.
Hours: M. to F. 10 - 8, Sat. 10 - 6, Sun. 12 - 4
Telephone: (905) 715-7939
Location: 1881 Steeles Ave. W., North York.
Hours: M. to F. 10 - 8, Sat. 10 - 5, Sun. 12 - 4
Telephone: (416) 661-0678
Location: 2555 Dixie Rd., Mississauga.
Hours: M. to F. 10 - 8, Sat. 10 - 6, Sun 12 - 5
Telephone: (905) 276-7799
Location: Oakville.
Telephone: (905) 257-5775

PETITES PLEASE
Product lines are: ladie's fashions for petites under 5 foot 4 and new accessories and costume jewelry.
Location: 3383 Yonge. St. (two blocks south of York Mills Rd.), Toronto.
Hours: M. to Sat. 10 - 6
Telephone: (416) 480-0844

PHASE 2 CLOTHING INC. - RESALE CLOTHING
Epitomizing the second generation of second hand clothing stores, this chain has scouts out picking up the best in designer/brandname fashions for the whole family. Every garment is cleaned and mended and shipped to one of their four locations - they do not take clothing on consignment and do offer a selection of off-price new items.
Location: 260 Lakeshore Rd., Oakville.
Hours: M. to F. 9:30 - 9, Sat. 9:30 - 6, Sun. 12 - 5
Telephone: (905) 337-0640

Resale Goods

Location: Bloor West Village, 2383 Bloor St., Toronto.
Hours: M. to F. 9:30 - 9, Sat. 9:30 - 6, Sun. 12 - 5
Telephone: (416) 762-0970
Other locations: Kingston and Ottawa

PLAY 'N' WEAR
Having now been seventeen years in the trade, this location is filled to the ceiling and the basement too, with quality toys, clothing (from infants to size 16 as well as maternity) and furniture - they also do some rentals. We purchased an almost new Ralph Lauren boy's dress shirt for $12 - a fraction of the original.
Location: 1722 Avenue Rd. (west side, north of Lawrence Ave.), Toronto.
Hours: T. to Sat. 9:30 - 5, Thu. 9:30 - 8
Telephone: (416) 782-0211

PLAY IT AGAIN SPORTS - SECOND-HAND SPORTING GOODS
There are more than 800 stores worldwide & 28 franchised stores have been opened or are planned in Southern Ontario. There is an extensive selection of used and new sports equipment for the entire family.
Location: 2055 Lawrence Avenue, Toronto
Telephone: (416) 285-7529
Location: 2488 Gerrard Street E., Scarborough.
Telephone: (416) 690-0666
Location: 258A Queen St. E., Brampton.
Telephone: (905) 456-1331
Location: 2625 Weston Road, Weston.
Telephone: (416) 244-9640
Location: 3055 Dundas St. W., Mississauga West.
Telephone: (905) 607-2837
Location: 3100 Dixie Road, Mississauga East.
Telephone: (905) 270-3731
Location: 3456 Yonge St., North Toronto.
Telephone: (416) 488-6471
Location: 697 Markham Rd., Scarborough.
Telephone: (416) 431-7113
Location: 773C The Queensway, Etobicoke.
Telephone: (416) 503-2288
Location: 9251 Yonge Street, Richmond Hill.
Telephone: (905) 763-0777
Location: 9275 Hwy. 48, Markham.
Telephone: (905) 471-9652
Location: Newbrook Plaza, 5863 Yonge St., North York.
Telephone: (416) 222-5713

Other locations: **Hamilton, Courtice, Sarnia, Barrie, Whitby, Guelph, St. Catharines, Burlington, Sault Ste. Marie, North Bay, Thunder Bay, Sudbury, Orleans, Ottawa, Arnprior, Nepean, Valleyfield, Cornwall and Oakville**

PROVIDENCE RETAIL OUTLET
One of our favorites, this 4,700 square foot location is jammed with better brand names, used clothing for the whole family. We spent over an hour and under sixty bucks purchasing a huge bag of clothes. You too will spend lots of time and little money!

Location: **170 Hwy. 7, Unit 8 (just west of Hwy. 10 or Main St. and 2 miles north of Queen St.), Brampton.**
Hours: M. to W. 9 - 6, Thu. & F. 10 - 8, Sat. 9 - 6
Telephone: (905) 456-8413

REPEAT PERFORMANCE
This shop raises funds for the Bayview Community Hospice. The Hospice provides compassionate end of life care, in the home, to people who are dying with cancer, ALS, AIDS and other terminal illnesses. A large selection of quality women's clothing and accessories arrives daily. Your purchases and donations of goods make this possible.

Location: **583 Mount Pleasant Rd. (south of Eglinton), Toronto.**
Hours: M. to Thu. 10 - 6, F. 10 - 8, Sat. 10 - 6
Last Sunday of every month 12 - 5 (Big sale day)
Telephone: (416) 483-5508

THE REPEAT RIDER
They offer gently used riding gear, seconds and horsey gift items.

Location: **1777 Avenue Rd. (south of Wilson Ave.), North York.**
Hours: M. to W. & F. 10 - 6, Thu. 10 - 7, Sat. 10 - 5
Telephone: (416) 256-5899

REPEATS
A large selection of upscale designer ladie's clothing & accessories.

Location: **3313 Yonge St. (north of Lawrence Ave.), Toronto.**
Hours: M. to W., F. & Sat. 10 - 6, Thu. 10 - 8
Telephone: (416) 481-2325

ES - METROPOLITAN TORONTO
AT FOR HUMANITY

...are used to build homes for hard-working people who might not otherwise be able to afford a home of their own. The concept of the ReStores is ...divert reusable materials from land fill sites - for builders and renovators the incentive is saving on dumping fees as well as paying peanuts for the donated materials. Some locations will also take working appliances which can provide real savings when compared to new prices. Some locations also take VISA,
Interac and of course all take cash. Volunteers are always welcome.

Location: 120 North Field Dr. East, (between Davenport Rd. and Bridge St.), Waterloo.
Hours: M. to W. 8:30 - 5, Thu. & F. 9 - 7, Sat. 9 - 3
Telephone: (519) 747-0664

Location: 128 Brock St., Unit 2, (west off Anne St. north of Essa Rd.), Barrie.
Hours: T. to Sat. 9 - 5:30
Telephone: (705) 735-2001

Location: 18 Coldwater Rd. (E. of Leslie St. between Hwy. 401 & York Mills Rd.), North York.
Hours: M. to F. 10 - 6, Thu.10 - 9, Sat. 10 - 5
Telephone: (416) 510-2223

Locations also in Ottawa, Thunder Bay, Windsor and London.

REUZE BUILDING CENTRE

Do you ever wonder where lavender sinks go when the previous owners remodel? ReUze accepts reusable building materials with a free pickup service (some restrictions) and sells everything from used windows and doors to kitchen sinks and toilets in its 10,000 square foot warehouse. No credit cards are accepted.

Location: 505 Ellesmere Road(between Warden & Birchmount)
Hours: M. to F. 10 - 6, Sat. 9 - 4
Telephone: (416) 750-4000

RUGGED REPLAYS

This is one of the few consignment stores in the Greater Toronto Area devoted exclusively to men, teens and boys. Brand name new and next to new clothing and accessories from jeans to tuxedos are offered in this well decorated, bright and airy store. Salesmen's samples and store close outs are cleared at below wholesale prices.

Location: **Burns St. Plaza, 19 Sawdon Dr., Units 1 & 2 (north on Thickson Rd. to Burns St., turn right to the first plaza on the left), Whitby.**
Hours: M. to W. 10 - 6, Thu. & F. 10 - 9, Sat. 10 - 5
Telephone: (905) 404-2063

SECOND DEBUT SHOPPE
Clothing for the entire family, accessories and small housewares.
Location: **221 McRae Dr., Leaside.**
Hours: T. & W. 10 - 5:30, Thu. 10 - 7:30, F. 10 - 5:30, Sat. 10 - 5
Telephone: (416) 425-4589

SECOND HAND ROSE
Fashions for the entire family, some vintage clothing.
Location: **3364 Yonge St. (south of Hwy. 401), Toronto.**
Hours: M. to Sat. 10 - 6
Telephone: (416) 481-0011

SECOND NATURE BOUTIQUE
Designer ladie's wear and accessories. Some menswear and distributor clearouts are available.
Location: **514 Mount Pleasant Rd. (at Millwood), Toronto.**
Hours: M. to Sat. 10 - 6
Telephone: (416) 481-4924

SHOPPE D'OR LIMITED
Resale ladie's designer clothing and accessories.
Location: **18 Cumberland St., Toronto.**
Hours: M. to Sat. 10 - 6
Telephone: (416) 923-2384

STILL GORGEOUS – WOMEN'S CONSIGNMENT SHOP
With a long list of well-dressed and well-heeled women supplying stock, Charlotte, the owner, has a flare for fashion and it shows with the nice displays of higher end designer wear. It's bound to be a zoo at the end of the month because their half-price sale starts January 30th.
Location: **13065 Hwy. 27, (north east corner at King Rd.), Nobleton.**
Hours: Normal ongoing hours are Tues., W. and Sat. 10-4, Thurs. 1-8, F. 10-8.
Telephone: (905) 859-0632.

Resale Goods

Resale Goods

SWEET REPEATS
This is a bright and airy store featuring a wide selection of new and nearly new children's clothing, furniture, equipment and accessories - sizes 0-12.
Location: 387 Jane St. (below Annette St.), Toronto.
Hours: T. to Sat. 10 - 6
Telephone: (416) 763-0009

TORONTO HOCKEY REPAIR LTD.
Not only do they repair equipment, but they sell new and used gear, and manufacture products as well. This location has three floors, offers a discount on new merchandise, and takes trade-ins.
Location: 1592 Bloor St. W. (just east of Keele St.) Toronto.
Hours: M. to F. 9 - 7, Sat. 9 - 5, Sun. 11 - 3
Telephone: (416) 533-1791

TORONTO PARENTS OF MULTIPLE BIRTHS ASSOCIATION - ANNUAL FALL/WINTER SALE
Friends with twins say this 1-day sale is a great way to shop for used children's clothing, toys, strollers, bedding & equipment. October Warehouse Sale.
Location: Cedarbrook Community Centre, 91 Eastpark Blvd. (south of Lawrence Ave, off Markham Rd.), Scarborough.
Telephone: (416) 760-3944

TWICE IS NICE
Several of our readers frequent this resale store for bargains on ladie's and children's clothing & accessories. There is also a large section with used toys for sale. Two sales a year offer 50% off so please call for details.
Location: 235 Lakeshore Rd. E. (east of Hwy. 10), Port Credit.
Hours: T. to Sat. 10 - 5
Telephone: (905) 274-5569

TWICE THE FUN - CHILDREN'S RESALE SHOP
This store offers quality used clothing, plus toys and accessories, at good prices. Bassinette rentals are available.
Location: Upper Canada Place, 460 Brant St. (west side and north of James St.), Burlington.
Hours: M. to W.& Sat. 9 - 5:30, Thu. & F. 9 - 8 (call for Summer hours)
Telephone: (905) 639-9105

TWINS PLUS ASSOCIATION OF BRAMPTON - RECYCLING BABY WEAR & GEAR
Expect to find everything in pairs as this non-profit support group holds its bi-annual sale of used baby & children's clothes, toys, books & equipment like double strollers, car seats & high chairs. Sizes are up to size 8. Cash or cheques with I.D. April and October Warehouse Sales.
Location: Locations vary, call for details.
Telephone: (905) 790-1451

WARDROBE EXCHANGE
They offer a wide assortment of ladie's fashions as well as children's clothing at reasonable prices.
Location: 856 Brock St. N. (north of Hwy. 2), Whitby.
Hours: M. to W. & F. 10 - 5:30, Thu. 10 -7, Sat 10 - 5
Telephone: (905) 666-9225

WASTEWISE - RECYCLING CENTRE/FLEA MARKET
In the Halton Hills area there's a community resource centre called Wastewise. It provides education on waste reduction & acts as a depot for recyclable materials & discarded items which it repairs & resells. Drop by Wastewise before discarding the item, & see if Wastewise can save it! Bargain hunters often pick up things for the cottage at very reasonable prices. Furniture, light fixtures, toys, clothing, sinks, toilets, hardware & more. Please drop items off only when they're open.
Location: 36 Armstrong Ave., Georgetown.
Hours: M. to W., F. & Sat. 9 - 5, Thu. 9 - 8
Telephone: (905) 873-8122

WHAT IN SAM HILL
Linda's Mother found this wonderful store that sells both new and used items - the day we were in they had just received 11 truckloads of collectibles, antiques, furniture, books, stained glass, hardware, artwork, tools and more. Lots of neat stuff, and perfect for browsing on a rainy day at the cottage.
Location: 101 Main Street, Unit 2 (Hwy 35 to Minden, turn left towards business section), Minden.
Hours: M to Sat 10 - 5
Sun noon to 3
Telephone: 1-705-286-2100

Resale Goods

miscellaneous

A Little Bit Of Everything

BACK DOOR STORE
This large warehouse is chock a block full of all kinds of items that have been brought in by an importer who clears out excess and discontinued inventory through occasional sales. The sales carry lots of small giftware items such as figurines, Christmas decor items, musical items, candles and keepsakes. No children or cheques.
Location: 25 Connell Court, Unit 1 (south of the Q.E.W west off Kipling Ave.), Toronto.
Hours: Call for Sale dates and hours.
Telephone: (416) 521-7299

BUSY BEE MACHINE TOOLS 💰
This once-a-year sale offers savings on demos, ends of lines, samples and more. Selling direct through its four locations and catalogue, Busy Bee has a wide assortment of woodworking equipment. May Garage Sale.
Location: 170 Brockport Dr. (north west corner at Belfield Rd. and Hwy. 27), Rexdale.
Telephone: (416) 665-8008

CANADA SALVAGE COMPANY
This company is an insurance salvor, and as such, sells a wide variety of products that change often. Goods are generally not damaged, but check items carefully. No credit cards. Cash or cheque with I.D are accepted.
Location: 505 The Queensway E., Unit 5 (one block west of Cawthra Rd. at Tedlo St.), Mississauga.
Hours: M. to F. 9 - 5
Telephone: (905) 897-7800

CENTURY SERVICES 💰
Century Services specialize in bankruptcy, liquidation and warehouse sales. You'll find a variety of discounts on family wear, shoes, toys, cosmetics, furniture, stationery, sporting goods and more.
Location: Locations and hours vary so please call for details.
Telephone: (416) 495-8338

CITY OF TORONTO DEPT. OF PURCHASING AND SUPPLY
This semi-annual event earns money for the municipal government by finding new homes for office equipment and furnishings, vehicles, motorcycles, construction equipment, industrial & consumer goods and lawn and garden supplies no longer needed by the City of Toronto. Please call the hotline number below for sale dates. T.B.A. Warehouse Sale.

Location: **Metro Transportation Yard, 64 Murray Rd. (west of Dufferin St. and north off Wilson Ave.), Downsview.**
Telephone: (416) 392-1991 (HOT-LINE)

CONSOLIDATED SALVAGE - INSURANCE SALVORS
Their stock changes frequently so it's a good idea to return regularly. Cash only.

Location: **2446 Cawthra Rd. (north of Queensway), Mississauga.**
Hours: M. to F. 9 - 4:30
After labour day they will be open on Saturday's from 9 - 3
Telephone: (905) 276-4230

CLOSE-OUT KING
You may have noticed a large sign as you go south on Hwy 400 proclaiming the Grand Opening of this newest liquidation store - they have just opened 113,000 square feet devoted to toys, cosmetics, housewares, giftware and lots more at close-out prices. You'll never really know what's in stock, as merchandise arrives daily and sells quickly. Great spot for picking up some real bargains.

Location: **137 Chrislea Street (Hwy 7 and Hwy 400), Woodbridge.**
Hours: M to Fri 9-9, Sat and Sun 9-6
Telephone: (416) 679-1264
Other Ontario locations include: Brampton, Rexdale, Rexdale Mall, North York, York, Toronto and Niagara Falls. Check local listing for address and hours.

CRAZY DAVE'S - LIQUIDATION OUTLET
The inventory consists of ends of lines, overruns and bankrupt companies' general products. Includes acrylic patio glassware, lawn and garden hand tools and accessories, shoes, compact discs and cassettes and even perfume and cosmetics. A really eclectic collection of goods but all priced to clear. Their stock changes monthly, so it's a good idea to call first.

Location: **Varies according to sales.**
Hours: Call for location and hours.
Telephone: (905) 692-8233

A Little Bit Of Everything

CROWN ASSETS - DISTRIBUTION CENTRE
One of our readers tipped us off to this government retail store, serving as a depot for items Canada Post is unable to deliver. CD's, books, tapes, cosmetics & sundry articles that haven't made it to their final destinations, end up here. Prices are low, but goods can look pretty beat up and tired. Public sales of vehicles & equipment are held once a month also.

Location: 6205 Kestrel Rd. (north of Hwy 401 in the Britannia & Tomken Rds. area), Mississauga.
Hours: T. & Thu. 10 - 3
Telephone: (416) 973-6300

DANBURY SALES
This company hosts a variety of warehouse and bankruptcy sales from electronics to cosmetics.
Location: 25 Civic Rd., (south of Eglinton Ave. E., east off Warden Ave. and just north of the huge water tower), Scarborough.
Hours: M. to F. 10 - 8, Sat. 10 - 5, Sun. 12 - 5
Telephone: (416) 630-5241

Our Special Kind of Service Brings Results

Auctioneers • Liquidators • Appraisers • Consultants

Danbury Sales
Our Special Kind of Service Brings Results

4122 Bathurst St., North York, Ont. M3H 3P2
Call (416) 630-5241 or 1-800-263-1469
Fax: (416) 630-6260
Visit us on the Web at: www.danburysales.com
email: info@danburysales.com

EMPIRE AUCTIONS
Once a month Empire Auctions offers, with no minimum and no reserve, a wide selection of furniture, estate and modern jewelry, collectibles and hand-woven Persian rugs. You'll find prices far below retail. Sales every four weeks – call for dates.
Location: 165 Tycos Dr. (south of Lawrence Ave. and west off Dufferin St.), Toronto.
Telephone: (416) 784-4261

HADASSAH-WIZO BAZAAR
Shoppers can delight in a cornucopia of bargains on everything from used clothing to stacks of books and lots for the home, all here at the biggest bazaar on this continent! There is an admission fee of $4 for adults and $2 for seniors and children ages 5 to 12. Make this a must-attend event. The October Warehouse sale is always the last Wed in October unless it is Halloween.
Location: Automotive Building, Exhibition Place, Toronto.
Telephone: (416) 630-8373

HERITAGE PET & GARDEN COUNTER - DIVISION OF B-W FEED AND SEED
An interesting shop for pet lovers and gardeners because feed and seed are always fresher. There are good buys on Purina and dry feeds, especially in bulk.
Location: 88 Huron Street, New Hamburg.
Hours: M. to W. 8:30 - 6, Thu. & F. 8:30 - 9, Sat. 8:30 - 5
Telephone: (519) 662-3684

KABOOM FIREWORKS
Kaboom is the choice for fireworks, a company that opens an outlet store just before long weekends & also operates trailer superstores at many area locations. Prices are competitive, with a large selection of items.
Location: Outlet store at 202 Laird Dr. (south of Eglinton Ave.), Toronto.
Telephone: (416) 467-9111

LIQUIDATION SALES BY IMPORTERS CLEARANCE CENTRE
This is one warehouse sale that covers it all - from product by Black and Decker to golf items, to loads of small electronics from Sony/ Panasonic and even racks and racks of ladieswear with fashions by Liz Claiborne Group, Anne Klein, and Vittadini. November Warehouse Sale.
Location: Call for location.
Telephone: (905) 470-7708

LOBLAWS/SUPERCENTRE PHARMACIES/ - INDEPENDENT GROCERS
Loblaws is not allowed to publicize its prescription dispensing fees but thank goodness a reader told us so WE can! There are several area Loblaws or Supercentres with some of the lowest prices on prescriptions in the province. The big secret? They dispense for only $5.99 and many of the remaining Loblaws pharmacies dispense at a good price - $8.49. The following stores have the $5.99 fee. With over 87 stores in Ontario, please call the location nearest you.
Location: 11 Redway Rd. (at Millwood Rd.), Toronto.
Telephone: (416) 425-8433
Location: 1450 Lawrence Ave. E., Scarborough.
Telephone: (416) 755-9201
Location: 17 Leslie St. (at Lakeshore), Toronto.
Telephone: (416) 968-7283
Location: 1880 Eglinton Ave. E., Scarborough.
Telephone: (416) 750-4494
Location: 245 Dixon Rd., Rexdale.
Telephone: (416) 614-9175

ERN AND SON - BARGAIN WAREHOUSE

For close to 30 years, they clear out surplus and salvage merchandise at discounts - everything from soup to nuts (literally!!). Inventory ... toys, baby equipment, tools, kitchen supplies, as well as non-perishable food items.

Location: 2420 Finch Ave. West, Units 21-22 (west of Weston Rd., behind Sunoco Station), Toronto
Hours: Thu.& F. 9 - 3, Sat. 9 - 12
Telephone: (416) 740-1696

METRO EAST TRADE CENTRE

Featuring a number of retailers gathered under one roof for convenient discount shopping. Great prices from Holt Renfrew, Corning, Cambridge Towel, Royal Doulton, Moulinex and several others. Expect to find clearances on footwear from Bata and Athletes World, with great names like Nike, Reebok, Converse and others. Sales throughout the year include Tip Top, Cambridge Towel, Procter and Gamble, Black & Decker, Liz Claiborne and Jones Apparel Group. Brand names may vary from sale to sale but they are always well known names. Warehouse sales happen periodically - call for info or to add your name to their mailing list. Parking and admission free. Wheelchair accessible.

Location: 1899 Brock Road, Pickering
Hours: M. to F. 9-5. Call for weekend and warehouse sale hours.
Telephone: For Warehouse information and dates call (905) 427-0744.

MEAFORD FACTORY OUTLET

From crackers to couches, rugs to wrenches, candles to BBQs and small appliances too, the selection is eclectic, interesting and extremely well-priced with 70,000 square feet of mainly brand name merchandise and up to 110,000 square feet in the future. The building was once a factory for Amerock that produced hinges and handles and is now on its way to becoming a bargain shoppers Mecca.

Location: 278 Cook St., (at the west end of town, off Sykes St.), Meaford,
Hours: Monday to Wednesday 10-6, Thursday and Friday 10-9, Saturday 10-6 and Sunday 11-5.
Telephone: (519) 538-4443.

SEARS CLEARANCE CENTRES & OUTLET STORES

Off season and clearance merchandise from the regular retail stores and catalogue operations are cleared through these outlets. There are several locations throughout Ontario.

Location: 939 Lawrence Ave. East, (at Lawrence Ave.) Don Mills
Telephone: (416) 383-0169
Location: 2200 Islington Ave., Rexdale.

Hours: M. to F. 10 - 9, Sat. 9 - 6, Sun. 11 - 5
Telephone: (416) 401-4545
Location: 253 Queen St. E., Brampton.
Hours: M. to F. 10 - 9, Sat. 9:30 - 6, Sun. 12 - 5
Telephone: (905) 796-6450
Location: 5000 Highway 7, E., Markham.
Hours: M. to F. 10 - 9, Sat. 9:30 - 6, Sun. 12 - 5
Telephone: (905) 278-6400
Location: Dixie Outlet Mall, Mississauga

THE SHOPPING CHANNEL CLEARANCE OUTLET

Now you can shop the Shopping Channel (tSc) in person at their first OffAir Outlet store. This new 15,000 square foot store is stocked with their most popular televised and clearance products. Discount levels increase each month the products remain in the store. Doorcrasher specials include products from Jerome Alexander, Joan Rivers, the Art Gallery of Ontario and more.

Location: 100A Orfus Road (west off Dufferin Street, south of the 401), Toronto.
Hours: Sun. to W., 10-6, Thurs. and F. 10-9, Sat. 10-6.
Telephone: 416-783-3961 or visit their web site at www.tSc.ca

VICTORY FIREWORKS

A dazzling selection of quality fireworks is available through this outlet year-round, and they always increase their hours around holiday weekends. Federally authorized products are available, with discounts of 25% off suggested retail prices. They provide free delivery on orders over $150 in the Toronto area and on orders over $300 anywhere in Canada.

Location: 19 Harlech Crt. (south of Hwy. 7, between Woodbine and Bayview Ave.), Thornhill
Hours: Call for store hours.
Telephone: (905) 771-0169.

YOU'RE THE GROOMER

This is one of the more interesting spots we've visited in a long time! If you and your pooch are looking for a new approach to grooming, you'll love this salon for dogs. Either have the knowledgeable staff groom your dog, or do it yourself for real savings over regular grooming prices. With raised tubs, hair dryers and grooming tools, you'll wonder why you ever tried doing this at home. Prices for do-it-yourself grooming are based on the size of your dog, with a maximum cost of $28.

Location: 8100 Yonge St., Unit 7 (south of Hwy. 7), Thornhill.
Hours: T. W. & F. 9 - 6, Thu. 9 - 9, Sat. 9 - 5
Telephone: (905) 886-8353

A Little Bit Of Everything

miscellaneous

Malls

CANADA ONE FACTORY OUTLET
Now that the second phase is completed at this outlet mall, they have a number of new stores, as well as many that are about to open over the next several months. Featuring fabulous houseware items, Villeroy & Boch is now open, as well as Black and Decker. Jay Set Fashion Outlet which sells popular lines of women's clothing has now been added to the mall, as well as Oromart Jewellery and Samsonite. Very shortly this month both the Phantom Outlet for hosiery will open, as well as the Cambridge Mill Outlet specializing in textiles for the bathroom, bedroom and kitchen. The upcoming line-up of stores will include MEXX, which carries a full range of clothing and accessories for women, men and children, Nine West, Esprit, The Body Shop and Escada.......all well known names in the retail sector and opening over the next several months. Of course existing stores like Tommy Hilfiger and Polo Jeans continue to sell their high profile brand name apparel, and other brand names include Guess, Nike and many more. You'll just need to plan a shopping expedition over the next couple of months to check them all out for yourself! . Wheelchair accessible.

Location: 7500 Lundy's Lane, Niagara Falls. Take the QEW to Niagara Falls, exit at Lundy's Lane. Turn left at Montrose Road, and then left at Lundy's Lane.
Hours: M to Fri 9-9, Saturday 9-6, Sunday 12-5.
Longer hours in the summer.
Telephone: 1-905-356-8989

See advertisement on inside front cover

I am not a perfectionist.
My parents were, though.

FACTORY OUTLET COMPLEX
This industrial-style complex with four outlets is situated toward the south end of Hamilton and close to the Q.E.W. Included here is Len's Mill Store, a large factory outlet that provides bargains on everything from work wear to fabrics, craft supplies to clothing for the entire family. The Arrow Shirt store has a wide selection of first and second quality men's clothing as well as some women's wear.

Location: 41 Brockley Dr.(Centennial Pkwy., South from the Q.E.W., Brockley is East of the Pkwy. off Barton St. E.) Hamilton.

Len's Mill:
Hours: M. to Sat. 10. - 5, Thu. & F. to 9, Sun. 12:30 - 4:30
Telephone: (905) 560-5367

Arrow:
Hours: M. to Sat. 9 - 5, F. to 9, Sun. noon - 4
Telephone: (905) 578-0055

COOKSTOWN MANUFACTURER'S OUTLET MALL
We've mentioned this mall before as a good discount mall containing a number of well known names such as Nike, Jones New York, Villeroy & Boch, Levi's, Olsen and many more. Now they've added even more names to the list with the recent addition of a Reebok Factory Store, a Hanes Outlet, the Umbro Company Store and the Kodiak Outlet Store. Reebok carries their well-known line of shoes and athletic clothing, the Hanes outlet stocks pantyhose, athletic wear and bathing suits, while the Umbro store carries their athletic clothing (well known to soccer fans), and the Kodiak store carries camping gear, outdoor goods, boots, shoes and workwear. All in all, a good reason to visit the mall again!

Location: About 35 minutes north of Metro. Take Highway 400 to Highway 89 and look for the water tower (southeast corner), Cookstown.

Hours: M. to F. 10 - 9, Sat., Sun. & holidays 9 - 6, except Christmas, New Year's Day.
Telephone: (705) 458-1371

Bricks & Blocks (Lego) Outlet
Accessory Express
Animale Outlet
Apparel Depot - Liz Clairborne Outlet
The Baby's Room Warehouse
The Bag Factory
Beardmore Leathers Factory Outlet
Black & Decker Factory Store
Bridges Home Decor
Cadbury Factory Store -
  www.cadbury.chocolate.ca/

Cambridge Towel & Bedding Outlet
Card & Paper Place
Corning Revere Factory Store
Cosmetics N'More for Less
Dansk Factory Store
Einstein's Laminated Art
Greg Normal Outlet
Hanes Outlet
Herbert's Outlet Post
Jack Rabbit's Clothing Co.
Jones Factory Finale

Malls

Malls

Kodiak Factory Outlet
Levi's Outlet
Mattel Factory Outlet
New York Clothing Company
Nike Factory Store
Nine West Shoe Studio
TheNorth Face Outlet
Olde Tyme Kettle Kitchen
Olsen Collection Outlet
Oromart The Jewellery Outlet
Paderno Cookware Factory Store
Philips Factory Store
Reebok Factory Direct
Rockport Factory Direct
Rogers AT&T Wireless Express
Royal Doulton Outlet
Samsonite Company Store
Shoe City
The Silver Dollar
The Sock Factory
The Time Factory - By Timex
Umbro Factory Outlet
Villeroy & Bock Factory Store
Warnaco Factory Outlet
Wonderbra Playtex Warners Plus
Food Services - Coffee Time
Harvey's/Swiss Chalet
Pizza Mondo
The Sandwich Outlet
Teriaki Wok

See advertisement on page A5

DIXIE OUTLET MALL

One of Canada's biggest and best - one stop shopping destinations. It has over 120 brand name stores, (including 13 shoe stores) at prices 30-70% off the regular retail price.

There is a wide array of new outlet stores including such names as Laura Secord, Au Coton and The Next Step Shoes and a new and improved Black and Decker. Of course there are original stores as well, including Northern Reflections, the Bata Outlet, Phantom, Footlocker, Radio Shack, Sunglass Hut and many more. Techno geeks are bound to find that great deal they have been looking for from Sony Televisions, Pioneer hi-fi Stereo, Bell mobility or Compaq Computers. Whether your needs are back to school basics or fashions for the entire family or tools for the home handyman, your budget will stretch further at Dixie Outlet Mall.

Location: 1250 South Service Rd., (QEW to /Dixie Rd. exit), Mississauga.

Hours: M. to F. 10 - 9, Sat. 9:30 - 6, Sun. 12 - 6
Telephone: (905) 278-7492

See advertisement on page A7

**Age doesn't always bring wisdom.
Sometimes age comes alone.**

HEARTLAND TOWN CENTRE
Bounded by Mavis and McLaughlan Rds. and Britania Rd. W. and Matheson Blvd., Besides the usual 'big box' stores you will find the following outlets:
Location: 5935 Mavis Rd.(Mavis & Brittania), Mississauga.
Hours:
Cotton Ginny Outlet Store:
It has lots of cotton casuals for women as well as some clothing under the Tabi International label and Plus Intimates for lingerie and sleepwear too.
Telephone: (905) 648-9868.
Roots Canada:
The name has become a Canadian icon for well constructed, easy to wear clothing and footwear for the entire family. This location is smaller than their Orfus Rd. outlet location but with similar stock, helpful staff and less than retail pricing.
Telephone: (905) 501-1200.
Danier:
It's always a great spot for well made and beautifully designed leather garments and accessories for men and women.
Telephone: (905) 501-1333.
Harry Rosen Menswear Outlet Store:
This is a name known to well dressed men; they have just moved from Markham and opened in this new location with savings on a wide assortment of men's wear.
Telephone: (905) 890-3100.

OTTAWA STREET
Dozens of stores & outlets, many focusing on textile bargains, are worth investigating, especially if you sew. We visited several fabric stores & others selling everything from candles & wrap to bath sets, silverware & even rubber dinosaur stamps at excellent prices. There are craft supplies & yarns - it's a treasure trove, but be prepared to spend time hunting for bargains.
Location: Ottawa St. (between Kenilworth and Gage Aves. Go south off Barton St. E.), Hamilton.

If a parsley farmer is sued, can they garnish his wages?

Malls

SOUTHWORKS OUTLET MALL
Wander through this converted 150 year old foundry...you will be stepping back into history as you walk around more than 140,000 square feet of magnificent old limestone buildings. Browse the stores where Brand Names like Corning, Jones New York, Florsheim Shoes, Cambridge Towel, Black & Decker, Far West, Kodiak, Muskoka Lakes and Paderno Cookware are marked way under regular mall prices. Southworks Antiques has 30,000 square feet of antiques and collectibles to make your shopping visit a great experience. Have Fun! Find Bargins!

Location: 64 Grand Ave. S., Cambridge;
Tel: 519-740-0380

The Shops at Southworks:
A Touch of Nature 622-9452 – Animale Women's Fashions 622-7888 – Black & Decker 624-8824 – Bookworks of Cambridge 623-7531 – The Café Grand 740-0110 – Cambridge Towel & Bedding 622-5542 - Cambridge Custom Brew 624-0791 – Corning Factory Store 624-9911 – Cosmetics N'More for Less (Revlon) 620-2625 - Down Under Wear 624-1552 - Endlines 740-0438 – Florsheim Shoes 621-7211 – The Flower Market 740-1802 – The Golf Ball Store 624-1331 – Island Beach Co. – JACKS Coffee Co. 624-1922 – Jack Rabbits Clothing Co. 622-6111 – Jones Factory Finale 740-3777 – Just because 624-0860 – Lakeland Trading Co. 623-5819 – Oromart Jewellery Outlet 624-8340 – Paderno Cookware Factory Store 623-8652 – Shoes 22 740-8093 - The Sock Factory 623-3069 – Southworks Antiques 740-0110 – Travellers Warehouse Ltd. 622-5232 (all phone numbers are in 519 area)

See advertisement on page A1

ST. JACOBS FACTORY OUTLET MALL
Many of you who like planning a day outing will want to plan a visit to this outlet mall - especially now that Phase Three is complete and the Cambridge Towel & Bedding Mill Outlet store has now opened with 10,000 square feet of savings on accessories for bedroom, bath and kitchen.

Three recent new stores are Cadbury Factory Store, Kodiak Outlet and Red Coral Classic and three additional stores for summer 2000 are Corning Revere Factory Outlet, Mattel Toys and Wicks and Wax.

Many of the existing stores have been newly renovated, and you'll find savings every day at brand name stores that include Levi's Outlet, Reebok, Jones New York, Florsheim Shoes, Tootsies Factory Shoe Market, Paderno Cookware, Royal Doulton, Villeroy and Boch, Storytime Book Outlet, Travellers Warehouse, Warner's Intimate Apparel. Cotton Wave, Country Blue, Country Gentleman Barber, Country Linens and More, Einstein's Laminated Art, Farm

Pantry, Jack Rabbit's Children's Clothing, Liz Clairborne, Mcgrillicuddy's, Olde Tyme Kettle Kitchen, Oromart, Pam Pam Leather, Scooter's Café, Sock Factory, and Spotlight Kidswear. LEGO lovers will want to see Countryside Toy Outlet's LEGO exhibit depicting scenes from ancient Egypt using more than half a million LEGO bricks.

Location: From Hwy 401 take Hwy 8 west to Kitchener Waterloo, then ramp to Hwy 86 Waterloo, to Road 15, left to Farmer's Market Road
Hours: Open daily including most holidays. M. to F. 9:30 - 9, Sat. 8:30 - 6, Sun. 12-5. For more info call 1-800-265-3353 or visit www.stjacobs.com.

See advertisement on page A24

THORNHILL SQUARE - SHOPPING CENTRE

Stores at this location include Phantom Outlet, (905) 889-2135, for brand-name hosiery, tights, socks, swimsuits and exercise wear, Cotton Ginny, (905) 889-7005, for casual cotton ladie's wear, and Dreams Downy Duvet, (905) 707-0887, for down duvets, pillows and linens. Also included is The Shoe Company (905) 886-3997, Winners (905) 731-3201 and their newest addition, Books for Less (905) 763-1543.

Location: John St. at Bayview Ave. (between Steeles Ave. & Hwy. 7), Thornhill.
Hours: Mall hours M. to F. 10 - 9, Sat. 9:30 - 6, Sun. 12 - 5
Telephone: (905) 886-2595

WARDEN POWER CENTRE

Lot's of new looks and new stores at this outlet centre means its probably time to drop in and see what's new for yourself. New to the Centre is Liz Claiborne and Thyme Maternity. The Liz Claiborne store offers a wide selection of clothing lines that include Liz Golf, Liz and Company, Liz Sport, Liz Claiborne and more in a full range of sizes. Items are at least 30% off, with some as high as 50-70%. Thyme Maternity knows that pregnant women want to look stylish and trendy but still be comfortable at a great price - which they do at prices that are up to 50% off regular retail.

Laura Shoppes is now a permanent store carrying a full line of professional women's wear, Warner's has moved to larger premises with a wider variety of women's lingerie, and Laura Secord has newly renovated their store and new even carries ice cream. Black and Decker have also moved into new space and offer a wide range of small appliances and outdoor items at 20% off regular retail. All items come with a 30 day guarantee.

Location: Warden Avenue, just north of St. Clair Ave., Toronto.
Hours: M to Fri 10-9, Sat 9:30 - 6, Sun 12-5
Telephone: (416) 752-8366

See advertisement on back cover

miscellaneous

Duty Free

PEACE BRIDGE DUTY FREE
Most of us don't even realize what terrific bargains there can be at a duty free shop - and this one is the largest in the North America. It's not just a shop - they also have a travel service center, a food court and a business centre. Merchandise areas include men's and women's clothing from top designers at an average savings of 25%, fragrances and cosmetics, sunglasses and watches (which average 30% less than retail), china and crystal, and of course alcohol. Any questions on allowances can be directed to the helpful staff who are well versed with the regulations. Next time you travel into the United States don't forget to take advantage of your right to shop duty free.

Location: **Last exit before the Peace Bridge as you head towards Buffalo at the intersection of the QEW and Central Avenue. Wheelchair accessible.**
Hours: Open 365 days/year, 24 hours/day.
Telephone: 1 - 800 - 361-1302.

WORLD DUTY FREE AMERICAS
If your summer travel plans includes a trip to the US, you really should drop into one of these duty free shops before returning to Canada. Choose from a wide selection of top brand names at prices that, even with our exchange, adds up to large savings. Save up to 50% on premium spirits, wine and beer, as well as tobacco. Designer fragrances, watches and crystal are also available. Other services include currency exchange, restrooms and free coffee - of course you must stay within the allowable government guidelines when returning to Canada, but their staff can help if you have any questions. **The three locations closest to Toronto are the following:**
Peace Bridge Plaza (I-90 to I-190, exit at Peace Bridge Plaza, **Buffalo, NY** 716-886-5000. Open 7 days/week, 24 hours a day.
Rainbow Bridge Plaza, Niagara Falls, NY 716-284-9736. Open 7 days/week, 8:00 a.m. - 9:00 p.m. (11:00 p.m. during the summer)

warehouse sales

Monthly Calendar

These dates were available at time of publication. For those not listed, or TBA (to be announced at later date), call for information and visit the weekly Shoestring Shopping Guide column in The Toronto Star.

January

warehouse sale

ANNA THE FASHION OUTLET	33
BARB'S FASHION OUTLET	33
BARRYMORE FURNITURE MANUFACTURER	96
CANADIAN HICKORY FARMS	80
CHERRY'S DESIGNER OUTLET	34
HAUSER FURNITURE	99
IMAGES THAT SUIT	36
LINA'S BOUTIQUE	58
SHAW-PEZZO & ASSOCIATES	103

February

warehouse sale

BIG TIME	158
ROOTS	17
TOMMY AND LEFEBVRE	70

March

warehouse sale

D&G TOGS INC.	6
DURHAM REGION PARENTS OF MULTIPLE BIRTHS	161

April

warehouse sale

BATHURST SALES	71
DAREE IMPORTS AND SALES INC.	74 & 147
GIFT-PAK	74 & 147
GREENHAWK HARNESS AND EQUESTRIAN SUPPLIES	66
MILLENIUM	24
O'BORN PRODUCTS	61
PHANTOM INDUSTRIES	43
SUNBEAM FACTORY OUTLETS	119
SWEET EXPRESSION	148

May

warehouse sale

ACCESSORY CONCEPT INC.	59
B.Y. GROUP	63
BATH N' BEDTIME	124
BATH N' BEDTIME DECOR	124
BUSY BEE MACHINE TOOLS	172
D. & G. TOGS INC.	6
DANBY	97
DICKIE DEE ICE CREAM W. H. SALE	82
DOWNTOWN DUVET	126
JORDI INTERNATIONAL FABRICS	129
MIKASA	113
MINNOW BOOKS	136
SHARC SALES	18
STEPTOE AND WIFE ANTIQUES	103

June

warehouse sale

BELVEDERE	72
D&G TOGS	6
DESIGNER'S WALK GARAGE SALE	97
HENRY	140
PAPER PEDDLERS	137
PRECIDIO INC.	116
ROYAL SHIRT COMPANY	24
THE BOOK SOURCE	133

July

warehouse sale

BARB'S FASHION OUTLET	33
FASHION ACCESSORIES W.H. OUTLET	59
GRANNY TAUGHT US HOW	112
IMAGES THAT SUIT	36
SHAW-PEZZO & ASSOCIATES	103
TOMMY AND LEFEBVRE	70

August

warehouse sale

BARTOLINI	106
BIG TIME	158
BOMBAY OUTLET STORE	96
GARBO GROUP	60

September

warehouse sale

BELVEDERE	72
D. & G. TOGS INC.	6
DISCOUNT INTERIOR DESIGNERS	98
DURHAM REGION PARENTS OF MULTIPLE BIRTHS	161
FABRICS FOR THE GREAT OUTDOORS	128
PRECIDIO INC.	116

October

warehouse sale

AURORA COLLECTIBLE FINE CHINA AND CRYSTAL	106
CANADIAN SKI PATROL SKI SWAP	64
COLLINGWOOD SKI CLUB SKI SWAP	65 & 160
DICKIE DEE ICE CREAM W.H. SALE	82
FREEMAN FORMALWEAR	22
GREENHAWK HARNESS AND EQUESTRIAN SUPPLIES	66
HADASSAH-WIZO BAZAAR	174
JOBSON	112
JORDI INTERNATIONAL FABRICS	129
PAVAN CYCLES INC.	68
ROYAL SPECIALTY SALES	145
TRINITY COLLEGE BOOK SALE	138
TUXEDO ROYALE	58
WILTON OUTLET SALE	123

November

warehouse sale

AC LIQUIDATION	71
B.Y. GROUP	63
BANFF DESIGNS	63
BATH N' BEDTIME	124
BATH N' BEDTIME DECOR STORE	124
CLEARANCE WAREHOUSE	73
D.&G. TOGS INC.	6
DANSK FACTORY OUTLET	110
DAREE IMPORTS AND SALES INC.	74 & 147
EVERGREEN PACKAGING	140
FASHION ACCESSORIES W.H. OUTLET	59
GARBO GROUP	60
GANZ	140
GIFT-PAK	74
GRANNY TAUGHT US HOW	112
HERITAGE INTERIORS	99
LIQUIDATION SALES BY IMPORTERS	175
MATTEL TOY CLUB	141
MIKASA	113
MILLENIUM	24
MUSKOKA LAKES W.H. SALE	14
O'BORN PRODUCTS	61
PAPER PEDDLARS	137
PHANTOM INDUSTRIES	43
ROYAL DOULTON	118

SWEET EXPRESSIONS 148
TILLEY OF CANADA 63
WILLIAM ASHLEY 123
RANS MATERNITY 42

December

warehouse sale

ACCESSORY CONCEPTS INC. 59
BATHURST SALES .71
C.W. & ASSOCIATES 108
COLONIAL JEWELLERY 59
D&G TOGS 6
DOWNTOWN DUVET 126
GARY GURMUKH SALES LTD. 10
GIFT-PAK/DAREE IMPORTS AND
  SALES LIMITED . . . . .74 & 147
HENRY LIMITED 140
MAGNOTTA WINERY 86
PLEASANT PHEASANT 61
QZINA 89
ROYAL SHIRT COMPANY 24
STUDIO SPECIALTIES 145
THE CASUAL WAY CLEARANCE SALE 35
THE UMBRA FACTORY SALE 121
WILLOW TREE COLLECTIBLES 123

To Be Announced

T.B.A. warehouse sale

ALDERBROOK INDUSTRIES 105
BASKITS 146
BEA SHAWN BRIDAL FASHIONS 57
BENIX AND CO. W.H. OUTLET 139
BLOW OUTS DESIGNER
  CLEARANCE OUTLET (LATE SUMMER/AFTER
  CHRISTMAS) 5
BLUE BAYOU FACTORY OUTLET 34
BOMBAY WAREHOUSE 107
BROOKERS 34
CANADIAN HOBBYCRAFT
  MANUFACTURER'S OUTLET 139
CENTURY SERVICES 172

CITY OF TORONTO DEPARTMENT OF
  PURCHASING AND SUPPLY 173
CSA 65
EBC GIFTS 110
GEAR FOR SPORT 65
GIFTS THAT MAKE A DIFFERENCE 111
GRAND REGAL .111
HARCOURT - BRACE 135
IN-LINE & ICE SKATE LIQUIDATION 66
KOBE FABRICS OUTLET 129
LADIES DESIGNER FASHIONS 40
LISA COSMETICS .75
LIZ CLAIRBORN/DKNY JEANS 40
LYNN FASHION FACTORY CLEARANCE 42
METRO EAST TRADE CENTRE 176
MIRAGE 113
MR. B 76
NORMA DESIGN 16
PARKHURST WAREHOUSE
  (SEMI-ANNUAL SALE) 42
PLAYBACK ELECTRONICS (4 X YEARLY) 155
PETITE PALETTE MANUFACTURER'S
  WAREHOUSE SALE 30
PIONEER STAR (CANADA) LTD. 116
PROCTOR & GAMBLE 77
REVLON 77
ROMANTIC NIGHT BY LILLIANNE
  FACTORY OUTLET (YEAR END) 40
SPINRITE FACTORY OUTLET 138
TALBOTS 44
THE BODY SHOP WAREHOUSE SALE 73
THE BUTCHER SHOPPE (MONTHLY SALE) 79
TONI+ 44
VARIMPO-CANHOME 122
VENDABLES 122

Don't forget to call for information and sale dates.

T.B.A. TO BE ANNOUNCED - DATES NOT AVAILABLE AT PRESS TIME

THIS SYMBOL INDICATES WAREHOUSE SALES

index

A.G. LIQUIDATION	71
ACADIA CANDLE OUTLET STORE	105
ACCESSORY CONCEPTS INC.	59
ACTION INVENTORY COSMETIC SALE	71
ADVANCE FURNITURE LTD.	95
ALDERBROOK INDUSTRIES	105
ALDO - CLEARANCE OUTLET	46
ALIRON MARKETING	139
AMADEUS - FINE CAKES LTD.	78
ANDERSON'S FINE FURNITURE	95
ANNA THE FASHION OUTLET	33
ARCH INDUSTRIES	158
ARORA	105
ARROW SHIRTS - FACTORY CLEARANCE STORES	21
ART IN IRON - FACTORY OUTLET SHOWROOM	95
ATHLETIC SPORTS SHOW - EXERCISE AND BODYWEAR	5
AU COTON - LIQUIDATION CENTRES	33
AUNT SARAH'S - CANDY FACTORY OUTLET	78
AURORA COLLECTIBLE FINE CHINA & CRYSTAL	106
B.Y. GROUP - FACTORY OUTLET	63
BABY PLUS AND BUNKS 'N' BEDS	26
BACK AGAIN	158
BACK DOOR STORE	172
BACKERHAUS VEIT	78
BAGS OF FUN	139
BAKER'S HOUSE	79
BANFF DESIGNS	63
BARB'S FASHION OUTLET	33
BARDEAUS FAMILY FASHIONS AND SPORTING GOODS CENTRE	5
BARRYMORE - FURNITURE MANUFACTURER	96
BARTOLINI	106
BARTOLINI DESIGN STUDIO	96
BASKITS WAREHOUSE SALE	146
BATA SHOE OUTLET/ ATHLETES WORLD OUTLET	46
BATH 'N BEDTIME DÉCOR STORE	74 & 147
BATHURST SALES	71
BEA SHAWN BRIDAL FASHIONS	57
BEAMSCOPE - WAREHOUSE OUTLET	153
BEAN SPROUT	158
BEAUTY CLUB	72
BEAUTY INDUSTRIES - MILL OUTLET	26
BEAUTY SUPPLY OUTLETS	72
BELVEDERE INTERNATIONAL FACTORY OUTLET SALE	72
BENIX AND CO. - WAREHOUSE OUTLET STORE	107
BEST SHOE	47
BIG CHIEF CANOE COMPANY	64
BIG TIME	158
BILLY BEE HONEY PRODUCTS LTD.	79
BLACK & DECKER CANADA INC.	107
BLOW OUTS - DESIGNER'S CLEARANCE OUTLET	5
BLUE BAYOU FACTORY OUTLET	34
BLUE SURF OF CANADA - SWIMSUIT FACTORY OUTLET	34
BOCCI SHOES - OUTLET STORE	47
BOLTS HOME FASHION OUTLET	124
BOMBAY WAREHOUSE SALE	107
BONCHEFF GREENHOUSES	79
BONNIE STUART SHOES - OUTLET STORE	47
BRAEMAR/BRAEMAR PETITES - CLEARANCE STORES	34
BROOKER'S	34
BROWN'S SPORTS	64
BRUZER FACTORY STORE	64
BUSINESS DEPOT / STAPLES BUSINESS DEPOT	151
BUSY BEE MACHINE TOOLS	172
C.W. & ASSOCIATES	108
CADBURY OUTLET STORE	80
CAMBRIDGE TOWEL MILL OUTLET	124
CAMCO TENT SALE	97
CAMP CONNECTION GENERAL STORE	6
CAMPBELL'S SOUP FACTORY OUTLET	80
CANADA ONE FACTORY OUTLET	178
CANADA SALVAGE COMPANY	172
CANADIAN HICKORY FARMS	80
CANADIAN HOBBYCRAFT - MANUFACTURER'S OUTLET	139
CANADIAN SKI PATROL SKI SWAP	64
CANALITE HOME FASHION	125
CANDLES BY MONTANNA	108
CANDY OUTLET	80
CANLY SHOES	47
CARDINAL MEAT FACTORY OUTLET	81
CASH CONVERTERS	159
CAULFEILD OUTLET STORE	6

Entry	Page
CAYNE'S SUPER HOUSEWARES	108
CENTURY SERVICES	172
CHERRY'S DESIGNER OUTLET	34
CHIC REPEATS	159
CHOCKY'S	6
CHU SHING TEXTILES	125
CILENTO WINES	81
CITIZEN ELECTRONICS	153
CITY OF TORONTO DEPT. OF PURCHASING AND SUPPLY	173
CJ - TEA IMPORTERS	81
CLARKSBURGERS	7
CLEARANCE WAREHOUSE	73
CLOSE-OUT KING	173
CLOTHES FRIENDS - FASHION BOUTIQUE	160
CLUB MONACO - OUTLET STORES	7
COLLINGWOOD SKI CLUB SKI SWAP	65 & 160
COLONIAL JEWELLERY	59
COLOURS EXCHANGE	160
CONCORD CANDLE CORP. - FACTORY OUTLET	108
CONSOLIDATED BOTTLE COMPANY	109
CONSOLIDATED SALVAGE - INSURANCE SALVORS	173
CONTENTS CONNECTION	161
COOKSTOWN MANUFACTURER'S OUTLET MALL	179
CORNING - OUTLET STORE SALE	109
COSMETIC WAREHOUSE	73
COSMETICS 'N' MORE	73
COTTON GINNY – POWER CENTRES OUTLETS	36
COUNTRY FLOORS	109
CRAFT TREE	133
CRAFTER'S CORNER	134
CRAWFORD AND CO. - BOYS' CLOTHING	26
CRAZY DAVE'S - LIQUIDATION OUTLET	173
CREATIVE BAG	140
CROWN ASSETS - DISTRIBUTION CENTRE	174
CSA CANADA WAREHOUSE SALE	65
D & G TOGS INC.	7
DACK'S SHOES	48
DAN HOWARD'S MATERNITY - FACTORY OUTLETS	27
DANBURY SALES	174
DANBY APPLIANCES	97
DANIER LEATHER - FACTORY OUTLET	8
DANSK FACTORY OUTLET	110
DAREE IMPORT AND SALES LTD.	74
DAVID ROBERTS FOOD CORPORATION	81
DAY-TIMER OF CANADA	152
DEAR-BORN BABY EXPRESS	27
DEBLINS LINENS SUPERSTORE	125
DEL'S PASTRY LTD.	82
DEMPSTER'S/ENTENMANN'S BAKERY OUTLET	82
DESIGNER FABRIC OUTLET	126
DESIGNER FRAGRANCES - OFF-PRICES PERFUMES	74
DESIGNERS WALK GARAGE SALE	97
DIAPER FACTORY OUTLET	27
DIAPERS ETC. - FACTORY OUTLET	28
DICKIE DEE ICE CREAM WAREHOUSE SALE	82
DIMPFLMEIER BAKERY OUTLET	82
DISCOUNT CHILDREN'S	28
DISCOUNT INTERIOR DESIGN WAREHOUSE	98
DIXIE OUTLET MALL	180
DONINI'S CHOCOLATE OUTLET - FACTORY OUTLET	83
DOVER FLOUR MILLS	83
DOWN UNDER - WAREHOUSE OUTLET	126
DOWNTOWN DUVETS & LINENS	126
DRAPERY AND UPHOLSTERY OUTLET	128
DREAMS DOWNEY DUVETS - FACTORY OUTLET	127
DRESSMAKERS SUPPLY	127
DURHAM REGION PARENTS OF MULTIPLE BIRTHS ASSOC.	161
EASTERN TEXTILES	127
EBC GIFTS & COLLECTIBLES - WAREHOUSE SALE	110
EDDIE BAUER	8
EGLI'S MEAT MARKET	83
EGLINTON WHOLESALE PAINT & HARDWARE	110
ELIZABETH STUART DISCOUNT BRIDAL - ONGOING OUTLET	57
EMMANUEL BITINI FASHION OUTLET	36
EMPIRE AUCTIONS	174
ENCORE	161
ENDS - CLEARANCE OUTLETS	8
EUROPE BOUND	65
EUROPEAN CHEESECAKE FACTORY LTD.	83
EUROPEAN HOTEL & RESTAURANT IMPORTS LTD.	111
EUROPEAN QUALITY MEATS & SAUSAGES	84
EVERGREEN PACKAGING INC. OUTLET SALE	140
EXCELLENCE IN ART - WHOLESALE OUTLET	98
EXECUTIVE FURNITURE RENTALS	98
F.I.N.D.S.	37
FABRIC CLEARANCE CENTRE	128
FABRICS FOR THE GREAT OUTDOORS	128
FACTORY OUTLET COMPLEX	179
FACTORY OUTLET SALES	76
FACTORY SHOE	49
FAIRLAND	28
FANTASTIC FLEA MARKET	162
FASHION ACCESSORIES - WAREHOUSE OUTLET	50
FEMINE LA FLARE INC. - IMPORTER'S OUTLET	36
FINE DESIGN FABRICS -	128
FISH DISTRIBUTORS	92
FLOWER DEPOT	146
FLOWERS & GIFTS BY WANDA	57
FOOD DEPOT INTERNATIONAL	84
FOOTWEAR FACTORY OUTLET	49

FORSYTHE FACTORY STORES	21
FREDA'S	37
FREEMAN FORMALWEAR - WAREHOUSE SALE	21
FUTURE BAKERY - FACTORY OUTLET	84
G H JOHNSON TRADING	99
G. BRANDT MEAT PACKERS	84
GANZ WAREHOUSE SALE	140
GARBO GROUP	60
GARY GURMUKH SALES LTD.	10
GEAR FOR SPORTS CANADA - WAREHOUSE SALE	65
GEORGE BOND SPORTS	66
GERTEX factory outlet	49
GIFT-PAK	74
GIFT-PAK/DAREE IMPORTS AND SALES LTD.	72 & 147
GIFTS THAT MAKE A DIFFERENCE	111
GOODMAN'S CHINA	111
GOODWILL STORE	162
GORDON CONTRACT	50
GRAND REGAL INTERNATIONAL LTD. - WAREHOUSE SALE	111
GRANDE CHEESE COMPANY - FACTORY OUTLETS	65
GRANNY TAUGHT US HOW	112
GRATRIX GARDEN LILIES	147
GREENHAWK HARNESS & EQUESTRIAN SUPPLIES	66
GREG NORMAN OUTLET	23
GROCERY WAREHOUSE - CLEARANCE CENTRE	65
HADASSAH-WIZO BAZAAR	174
HALTON LINEN COMPANY	128
HAMPSTEAD HOUSE BOOKS - OFF-PRICE OUTLET	135
HAND ME DOWNS	162
HAPPY HARRY'S	163
HARCOURT BRACE - EDUCATIONAL BOOK WAREHOUSE SALE	135
HARPUR'S CLOTHING COMPANY LTD. - FACTORY OUTLET	10
HARRY ROSEN MENSWEAR OUTLET STORE	23
HARRY ROSEN MENSWEAR OUTLET STORE:	23
HATHAWAY FACTORY STORE	23
HAUSER FURNITURE - FACTORY DIRECT	99
HEARTLAND TOWN CENTRE	181
HENRY LIMITED	140
HERITAGE CASTING AND IRONWORKS - FACTORY OUTLET	99
HERITAGE INTERIORS	99
HERITAGE PET & GARDEN COUNTER -DIVISION OF B-W FEED AND SEED	175
HERSHEY CANADA INC.	65
HILL STREET BLUES	11
HI-TEC FACTORY DIRECT	10
HOLT RENFREW'S - LAST CALL	37
HONOR'S PASTRIES	86
IANA CHILDREN"S CLOTHING OUTLET	29
IBM HOME COMPUTING STORE	154
IBM WAREHOUSE OUTLET	154
IDEAL PAINTS - WAREHOUSE OUTLET	112
IDOMO	100
IMAGES THAT SUIT	37
INESRA - I'LL NEVER EVER SHOP RETAIL AGAIN	163
INGEBORG'S SHOES - WAREHOUSE OUTLET	50
IN-LINE & ICE SKATE LIQUIDATION	66
INTERNATIONAL - WAREHOUSE SUPERSTORES	11
INTERNATIONAL KIDS - IMPORTERS OUTLETS	29
INTICRAFTS - IMPORTERS' STORES	135
IRWIN TOY - FACTORY OUTLET	140
IT'S WORTH REPEATING	163
J. MICHAEL FASHION OUTLET STORE	38
JACK AND PETER'S PLACE	11
JACK FRASER - MENSWEAR OUTLET STORE	23
JACK RABBITS CLOTHING COMPANY	29
JAYSET - MANUFACTURER'S CLEARANCE STORES	38
JES HANDBAG DESIGN	60
JOBSON AND SONS LTD.	112
JOE SINGER SHOES LTD. - DISCOUNTED LADIE'S FOOTWEAR	50
JONES FACTORY FINALE	39
JORDI INTERNATIONAL FABRICS - WAREHOUSE SALE	129
JOTANI SPORTSWEAR - CATALOGUE OUTLET SALE	67
JUST DEALS	11
KABOOM FIREWORKS	175
KAD-OH! - CLOTHING OUTLET	12
KAUFMAN FOOTwear - FACTORY OUTLET	50
KETTLE CREEK OUTLET STORE	12
KID'S COSY COTTONS - FACTORY OUTLET	30
KIDS KONSIGNMENT	164
KOBE FABRICS OUTLET	129
KRUG'S MEAT MARKET	86
L'ELEGANTE	164
LA CACHE - CLEARANCE STORE	160
LA FORÊT	39
LABELS	12
LADIES DESIGNER FASHIONS	40
LADY ANGELA GIFTS AND BOMBONIERE	57
LADY ROSEDALE - WAREHOUSE OUTLET	60
LANCE LORENTS	40
LE CHATEAU - FASHION OUTLET	40
LE FIRME	13
LE FIRME	40
LEDA'S ATTIC - FURNITURE MANUFACTURER'S OUTLET	100
LEISURELAND	100
LEN'S MILL STORE	13
LEVI'S OUTLET`	14
LEVY'S DISCOUNT DESIGNER ORIGINALS -	

Entry	Page
LADIES, MEN'S & CHILDRENS FASHIONS	40
LIB & IDO'S ROSE EMPORIUM	147
LINA'S BOUTIQUE	58
LIQUIDATION SALES BY IMPORTERS CLEARANCE CENTRE	175
LISA COSMETICS / FRAGRANCES LTD. - WAREHOUSE SALE	75
LITE KING	100
LITEMOR	156
LITTLE SHOE PALACE	51
LIZ CLAIBORNE/DKNY JEANS	41
LIZZY-B UNIFORM SALES	41
LOBLAWS/SUPERCENTRE PHARMACIES/ -INDEPENDENT GROCERS	175
LOOTBAG EXPRESS	141
LORNE'S FASHIONS - FACTORY OUTLET	41
LYNN FASHIONS - FACTORY CLEARANCE	42
LYNRICH ARTS	136
M.S. HALPERN AND SON - BARGAIN WAREHOUSE	176
MADAWASKA DOORS INC.	112
MAGGI-B LIMITED	60
MAGNOTTA WINERY	86
MALABAR	136
MALABAR	14
MAPLE LODGE FARMS LTD.	87
MAPLE ORCHARD FARMS & MARBLE DEPOT	101
MARILYN'S	42
MARKA CANADA - CLEARANCE OUTLET	141
MARKHAM WAREHOUSE OUTLET - NUTRITIONAL PRODUCTS	87
MARKY'S WAREHOUSE OUTLET - OFF-PRICE STORE	14
MARY MAXIM CLEARANCE SALE	136
MASSAGE THERAPY CLINIC - CENTENNIAL COLLEGE	75
MATTEL TOY CLUB	141
McGREGOR SOCKS FACTORY OUTLETS	15
McGREGOR SOCKS FACTORY OUTLETS	51
MCINTOSH & WATTS	113
MEAFORD FACTORY OUTLET	176
MEI	155
METRO EAST TRADE CENTRE	176
MIKASA	113
MIKO TOY WAREHOUSE	141
MILLENIUM	24
MILLWORKS FACTORY STORE	15
MINNOW BOOKS	136
MIRAGE - FACTORY WAREHOUSE SALE	113
MISSISSAUGA BEDDING SUPERSTORE	130
MODERN WATCH CANADA	61
MONARCH PAINTS LIMITED	114
MOORES MENSWEAR	24
MORETTE'S FURNITURE	101
MOSSMAN'S APPLIANCE PARTS LTD. – PARTS	102
MOUNT 'N SEAL	114
MR. B'S	76
MR. BILLIARD	67
MUSKOKA FURNITURE OUTLET	102
MUSKOKA LAKES WAREHOUSE SALE	15
NABISCO/CHRISTIE FACTORY OUTLET STORES	88
NATIONAL BOOK SERVICE SALE	136
NATIONAL CHEESE COMPANY LTD.	88
NATIONAL SPORTS EQUIPMENT REPAIR	164
NATIONAL SPORTS EQUIPMENT REPAIR	67
NEO-IMAGE CANDELIGHT LTD.	114
NEW YORK CLOTHING COMPANY	16
NEWSON'S BIKE AND SKATE EXCHANGE	67
NOAH'S ARK INDOOR PLAYLAND	142
NORAMA DESIGN INC.	16
NORAMPAC - BOX OUTLET	142
NORMA PETERSON	42
NORTH FACE	67
NORTHERN REFLECTIONS AND GETAWAY	16
NOVITA FASHIONS	16
O'BORN PRODUCTS	61
OAK GROVE CHEESE FACTORY - OUTLET STORE	88
OF THINGS PAST - CONSIGNMENT FURNITURE SHOWROOM	164
OFF THE CUFF	165
OLD COLONY CANDLE FACTORY OUTLET	115
ON COURT SPORTS LTD.	68
ON THE FRINGE	17
ONCE UPON A CHILD	165
ONEIDA FACTORY OUTLET	115
ONTARIO PAINT AND WALLPAPER	114
OTTAWA STREET	181
PACKAGING WORLD	142
PADERNO FACTORY STORE	115
PAINT, WALLPAPER AND FABRIC SOURCE	115
PAPER PEDDLERS WAREHOUSE SALE	137
PARKHURST - WAREHOUSE SALE	42
PARNETT TEXTILES	17
PARTY CITY STORES	143
PARTY PACKAGERS	143
PASTA INTERNATIONAL	88
PASTA QUISTINI INC.	89
PASTACO	89
PATONS CLEARANCE CENTRE	137
PATRICIAN LINENS	131
PAVAN CYCLES INC.	68
PAYLESS SHOESOURCE	52
PEACE BRIDGE DUTY FREE	184
PERFECT FLAME CANDLE	116
PERFUME GALORE	76
PETITE PALETTE	30
PETITES PLEASE	165
PFALZGRAF CANADA INC.	89
PHANTOM INDUSTRIES - FACTORY OUTLET STORES	43
PHASE 2 CLOTHING INC. - RESALE CLOTHING	165
PICADILLY FASHIONS - LADIESWEAR FACTORY OUTLET	43
PIONEER STAR (CANADA) LTD	165

Entry	Page
PLAY 'N' WEAR	166
PLAY IT AGAIN SPORTS - SECOND-HAND SPORTING GOODS	166
PLAYBACK ELECTRONICS	155
PLEASANT PHEASANT	61
PLUMLOCO CLOTHING COMPANY	30
PORTOLANO FACTORY OUTLET STORE	61
POSTERS INTERNATIONAL	116
PRECIDIO INC WAREHOUSE SALE	116
PREMIER CANDLE CORP.	117
PROCTER & GAMBLE	77
PROVIDENCE RETAIL OUTLET	167
PSH - THE POTTERYSUPPLY HOUSE	137
QHP/TRESSES - QUALITY HAIR PRODUCTS OUTLET	77
QZINA WAREHOUSE SALE	89
RAN'S MATERNITY WAREHOUSE SALE	43
RECYCLING BABY WEAR & GEAR	203
REEBOK - WAREHOUSE OUTLET	52
REGAL GREETINGS AND GIFTS	144
REINHARDT FOODS - FACTORY OUTLET	90
RENEE'S GOURMET	90
RENNIE - THE SHIRT STORE - FACTORY OUTLETS	24
REPEAT PERFORMANCE	167
REPEATS	167
REPLAY ELECTRONICS	156
RESTORES - METROPOLITAN TORONTO HABITAT FOR HUMANITY	168
REUZE BUILDING CENTRE	168
REVLON	77
RHODES INC. - FACTORY OUTLET	53
RICH HILL CANDLES AND GIFTS - FACTORY OUTLET	118
RIDOLFI SHIRTMAKER INC. - FACTORY SHOWROOM	24
RIZZCO TOY AND GIFT SALE	144
ROCOCO DESIGNERS OUTLET	44
ROMANTIC NIGHT BY LILIANNE - FACTORY OUTLET	44
ROOTS CANADA LTD. - CLEARANCE CENTRES	17
ROSES ONLY	148
ROYAL DOULTON - WAREHOUSE SALE	118
ROYAL SHIRT COMPANY LTD	25
ROYAL SPECIALTY SALES	145
RUGGED REPLAYS	168
RUNNING FREE	53
SAMKO SALES - TOY AND GIFT WAREHOUSE OUTLET	145
SAMPLE SHOP	18
SAMUEL HARRIS 1994 LTD.	119
SANDYLION STICKER DESIGNS	145
SARA LEE - BAKERY OUTLET	90
SATIN PARTY SHOES	58
SCRATCH AND DENT WAREHOUSE SALE	97
SEAFOOD DEPOT	91
SEARS CLEARANCE CENTRES & OUTLET STORES	176
SEARS CLEARANCE CENTRES	102
SECOND DEBUT SHOPPE	169
SECOND HAND ROSE	169
SECOND NATURE BOUTIQUE	169
SESCOLITE - LIGHTING CLEARANCE CENTRE	103
SHARC SALES - WAREHOUSE CLEARANCE	18
SHAW-PEZZO & ASSOCIATES INC.	103
SHOE HEAVEN WAREHOUSE OUTLET	55
SHOE MACHINE - FACTORY OUTLET	55
SHOPPE D'OR LIMITED	169
SI VOUS PLAY	69
SIENA FOODS/COLIO WINES - OUTLET STORE	91
SIGMA GIFTS	119
SILENT SPORTS - BICYCLING/ WINDSURFING	69
SIMON'S SMOKEHOUSE - FACTORY OUTLET	91
SNOWBOARDING/ CROSS COUNTRY SKIING OUTLET	70
SNUG AS A BUG	31
SNUGABYE FACTORY OUTLET	31
SOUTHWORKS OUTLET MALL	182
SPARE PARTS CLOTHING OUTLET	18
SPINRITE FACTORY OUTLET	138
SPORTING GOODS LIQUIDATION	70
SPORTS WORLD RENT AND SALES	70
SPORTSWAP	70
SPOTLITE CASUAL WEAR	31
ST. JACOBS FACTORY OUTLET MALL	182
ST. MARCO IMPORTING	18
STEPTOE & WIFE ANTIQUES LTD. - ANNUAL SALE	103
STILL GORGEOUS – WOMEN'S CONSIGNMENT SHOP	169
STUDIO SPECIALTIES	145
SUMMERHILL HARDWARE/ELTE CARPETS	103
SUNBEAM FACTORY OUTLETS	119
SUPER SELLERS	44
SUREWAY TRADING - SILK WHOLESALERS	131
SUSSMAN'S - MEN'S AND LADIE'S WEAR	19
SWEET EXPRESSIONS	148
SWEET REPEATS	170
SWISS OUTLET	119
TALBOTS WAREHOUSE SALE	44
TANDY LEATHER COMPANY - OUTLET STORES	138
TEDDY BEAR DIAPER SERVICE - FACTORY OUTLET	31
TEN THOUSAND VILLAGES - IMPORTER'S STORE	120
TERRACE GALLERY AND ART & FRAME - LIQUIDATION SALE	120
TERRACOTTA HOUSE AND SALTILLO IMPORTS	104
T-FAL ELECTRICAL APPLIANCES	120
THE BODY SHOP OUTLET	73
THE BOMBAY COMPANY OUTLET STORE	96

THE BOOK DEPOT INC.	133
THE BOOK SOURCE	133
THE BUTCHER SHOPPE	79
THE CASUAL WAY CLEARANCE SALE	35
THE CHOCOLATE FACTORY	87
THE CLASSY ATTIC	160
THE COAT CLUB	35
THE COMEBACK	160
THE CRAFTERS MARKETPLACES	134
THE DOOR FACTORY	110
THE ELECTRONICS OUTLET	153
THE ELEGANT GARAGE SALE	161
THE FABRIC SOLUTION	127
THE FACTORY STORE	10
THE FASHION GO ROUND	162
THE FRUGAL SCOT	162
THE GRACIOUS LIVING CENTRE	98
THE LACE PLACE	130
THE LINGERIE HOUSE	41
THE NEXT STEP - CLEARANCE STORE	51
THE PANTYHOSE SHOP – BELLISSIMO	17
THE PICTURE PICTURE CO.	117
THE REPEAT RIDER	167
THE RUBBERY	118
THE SALAD KING	90
THE SHOE CLUB	53
THE SHOE COMPANY	54
THE SHOPPING CHANNEL CLEARANCE OUTLET	177
THE STOCKROOM	19
THE SUIT EXCHANGE	25
THE UMBRA FACTORY SALE	121
THE URBAN MODE	104
THE VICTORIAN SHOPPE	120
THE WAREHOUSE- CLOTHING CLEARANCE CENTRE	21
THORNHILL SQUARE - SHOPPING CENTRE	183
TIGER BRAND KNITTING - FACTORY OUTLET	19
TILLEY OF CANADA	62
TIMBERLAND - OUTLET STORE	25
TIMEX - CLEARANCE OUTLET	62
TOM'S PLACE	20
TOMEK's NATURAL PRESERVES	91
TOMMY AND LEFEBVRE - WAREHOUSE SALE	70
TONI+WAREHOUSE	44
TOOTSIES FAMILY SHOE MARKET	56
TORONTO HOCKEY REPAIR LTD.	170
TORONTO PARENTS OF MULTIPLE BIRTHS ASSOCIATION - ANNUAL FALL/WINTER SALE	170
TRE MARI BAKERY - FACTORY OUTLET	92
TRINITY COLLEGE BOOK SALE	138
TUXEDO ROYALE	58
TWICE IS NICE	170
TWICE THE FUN - CHILDREN'S RESALE SHOP	170
TWINS PLUS ASSOCIATION OF BRAMPTON -	171
UB WORLD FASHION OUTLET	20
UNIVERSITY CLASS - FACTORY OUTLET	20
UPGRADE FACTORY	156
-UPPER CANADA SOAP & CANDLE MAKERS	
UPPER CANADA SOAP & CANDLE MAKERS - FACTORY OUTLET	121
URBAN BEHAVIOUR	21
VALERIE SMYTH BRIDAL FASHIONS	58
VANHORN SEAFOOD WHOLESALE -	92
VANI METAL ART - FACTORY OUTLET	104
VARESE SHOES - OUTLET CENTRE	56
VARIMPO-CANHOME- WAREHOUSE SALE	122
VENATOR ELECTRONICS - CLEARANCE CENTRE	122
VENDABLES - WAREHOUSE SALE	122
VICTORY FIREWORKS	177
VIDAL SASSOON SALON	77
VILLAGE WEDDING BELLES	58
VIVAH	62
VOORTMAN COOKIES	92
WARDEN POWER CENTRE	183
WARDROBE EXCHANGE	171
WARNER'S - FACTORY OUTLET STORE	45
WASTEWISE - RECYCLING CENTRE/FLEA MARKET	171
WEEBODIES FACTORY STORE	32
WEEKEND WARRIOR - MANUFACTURER'S CLEARANCE OUTLET	21
WESTON BAKERY OUTLET - FACTORY OUTLET STORE	93
WESTPOINT STEVENS FACTORY OUTLET	131
WHAT A BASKET	148
WHAT IN SAM HILL	171
WHOLESALE FLORISTS	149
WILD FLOWER FARM	149
WILLIAM ASHLEY	123
WILLIES MERCANTILE	93
WILLOW TREE COLLECTIBLES	123
WILTON OUTLET STORE	123
WINNERS - OFF-PRICE FAMILY WEAR	21
WORLD DUTY FREE AMERICAS	184
WORLD OF GIFTS	123
YOU'RE THE GROOMER	177
ZACKS – FASHION OUTLET	45

NEVER GO SHOPPING WITHOUT IT

"The Shoestring Shopping Guide"

Available through your favorite bookseller, on newsstands and through many featured retailers. If it is not in stock, have your retailer call our distributor, Hushion House at 416-285-6100 or 1-800-819-8614.

We also offer a mail order service. Just complete and mail the following form with your cheque or money order.

NB: The Shoestring Shopping Guide makes an excellent Christmas gift. We will waive shipping costs and include a free bonus copy for all orders over five books.

Please send me _____ copies of The Shoestring Shopping Guide©
at $10.95 each. $_____

Postage and Handling: $2.00 for one book,
$1.00 for each additional books 2-5
(Shipping costs waived for orders over 5 books) $_____

Subtotal $_____

Canadian residents add 7% GST $_____

Total Amount Enclosed $_____

Name_____

Address_____

City_____ Postal Code_____

Province_____ Phone_____

Please make cheques and money orders payable to:
The Shoestring Shopping Guide©!
P.O. Box 575, Brantford, Ontario, N3T 5N9
ALLOW ONE WEEK FOR DELIVERY

A Note from Cathie.......

This year's Shoestring Shopping Guide has been expanded to 232 pages, including a 32 page colour (A-1 to A-32) section highlighting a number of our advertisers.

We have also added a "NOTES" section to assist you in recording your shopping experiences throughout the year as you visit many of the 600 businesses and warehouse sales featured in The Guide.

We hope you will find this a useful place to make those notes and observations that so often go astray when you need to refer to them at a a later date.

Notes

Notes

Notes

Notes

Notes